Keeping Up the Good Fight

KEEPING UP THE
Good Fight

From the Emergency to the Present Day

PRABIR PURKAYASTHA

MONTHLY REVIEW PRESS
New York

Copyright © 2024 by Monthly Review Press
All Rights Reserved

Originally published in India by LeftWord Books © LeftWord Books 2023.
U.S. edition published by Monthly Review Press 2024.

Library of Congress Cataloging-in-Publication Data
available from the publisher

ISBN: 978-1-68590-074-8 paper
ISBN: 978-1-68590-075-5 cloth

MONTHLY REVIEW PRESS, NEW YORK
monthlyreview.org

5 4 3 2 1

In memory of Ashoka

Contents

Foreword by Lalita Ramdas	11
1. Does Every Generation Have to Face an Emergency?	17
2. Learning to Fight: A Personal Journey	45
3. To Delhi and a Turning Point	84
4. A University Under Emergency	100
5. Life in Jail	127
6. The Last Chapter of Mrs Gandhi's Emergency	156
7. Living Politics	176
Acknowledgements	209
Annexure 1: From the Shah Commission Report	210
Annexure 2: MISA Detentions During the Emergency: Prabir Purkayastha	220

'Men make their own history.'
Karl Marx

'They cannot make history who forget history.'
B.R. Ambedkar

Foreword
Lalita Ramdas

Keeping Up the Good Fight. Since I am often called a *'ladaku'*, how can I pass up the chance to say a few words for a book with such a provocative title?

THE PERSONAL IS POLITICAL —
THE POLITICAL IS ALSO THE PERSONAL

This feminist credo has been a seminal part of my own work, beliefs and activism — and this is the connecting current that runs through the entire work. So let me begin with what hit me as I started reading this fascinating personal and political testimony. Prabir has woven a personal narrative that is inseparable from the growth of his own political consciousness — and that too in a style and language which is easy, unpretentious, and keeps you asking for more.

It is essentially to the compelling warp and weft of both these elements that I would draw the attention of the uninitiated reader, who might find that she has wandered unsuspectingly into a complex maze of ideas, challenges and contradictions. These descriptions of seemingly mundane events of a middle class Bengali bhadralok family do not really prepare you for the challenges and depths of the political awakening which Prabir undergoes. It was both fascinating and educative to read about the diverse influences during his transition from being a student and dealing with frequent changes of location, to a growing sensitivity to major national and international events — such as the Vietnam war and the declaration of Emergency in India.

So, what does Prabir Purkayastha's journey tell us? What is the significance of this seemingly modest memoir which, to my mind, covers some of the most significant 'happenings' in India and the region in the past 50 years?

For many of us who have lived through these eventful decades between the late sixties and today, Prabir has provided a fascinating road map and connected the dots between apparently disconnected flashpoints. Even for someone like me, who, from 1978 onwards, had been actively involved with the women's movement and other struggles for human rights, the question he raises at the outset is significant: Does every generation have to face an emergency?

In a masterly yet understated fashion, he starts his narrative on the morning of September 25, 1975, on the lawns of Jawaharlal Nehru University (JNU), when a burly man in plainclothes stepped out of a black Ambassador car and, in Prabir's words, 'proceeded to kidnap me in broad daylight'. This was the beginning of one year in jail under the MISA, or the Maintenance of Internal Security Act.

Prabir then proceeds to make a neat segue to another morning, more recent, February 9, 2021, when a group of men from the ED (Enforcement Directorate) arrived at his home and the office of his news portal NewsClick, to conduct what would turn out to be a very long raid. And the scrutiny continues as I write.

One of the fascinating aspects of *Keeping Up the Good Fight* is the way Prabir takes the reader back and forth from the declared Emergency of 1975 to the undeclared one in our times today. And by recounting the small details as part of his 'annual ritual' of looking at whether or not democracy is in suspension, he leaves us in no doubt that the threat to democracy is perhaps greater today than ever before.

It is this deep and abiding concern about the assault on the constitution and the foundation of our democracy, that Prabir repeatedly demonstrates through the recounting of his personal journey, and its periodic intersections with some of the most significant events in our own times, whether political, economic or social.

MEDIA THEN AND NOW

I found especially compelling the sections where the author reflects on the state of 'the media then and now' — including a mention of those who refused to 'crawl' in the earlier Emergency.

As a 'techno professional', Prabir has consciously chosen to use media and technology to tell the most important stories of our times, especially through a visual medium. And given his deeply held convictions about equality and justice for all, it is the 'educator' in him that has influenced his unorthodox trajectory of using media as a powerful tool to attract those who might not, otherwise, hear many of these stories on any other forum. The writing of the book itself speaks to this compelling drive to inform and educate.

WHEN LAWS DISABLE JUSTICE

The other important area of scrutiny is, of course, that of the law and the judiciary. Prabir flags this key area early in the book in a section he rightly terms *When Laws Disable Justice*, and points out that the use of draconian laws is a strong common point between then and now.

Having spent a year as the guest of the Government of India under the notorious MISA, Prabir is best qualified to dilate on how law and justice can be made handmaidens of coercive regimes. It is fascinating to read his almost tongue-in-cheek accounts of life in jail — the friendships made, the human frailties, and a veritable 'who's who' of so many familiar names. There was a strong personal interest for me since two of my closest friends, Primila Lewis and Srilata Swaminathan, were among those who were in jail in 1975.

Of course many of these laws were part of our colonial legacy of Preventive Detention Laws. But the book emphasises that while Emergency 1 had MISA, the undeclared Emergency 2 has the draconian UAPA, or the Unlawful Activities (Prevention) Act, 1967, amended to include so called 'special measures' such as shifting the burden of proof onto the accused, and bail being made the exception.

We are left in no doubt that the combination of 'lawfare through agencies, stormtroopers on the ground', and the lethal addition of ideology in our present times, has led to the 'hollowing out' of state structures. We are also reminded that the big difference between then and now is 'the sustained and multifarious attacks on our secular ethos, on culture, on education, on science and reason.'

BACK TO THE PERSONAL

Let me conclude on a personal note. I met Prabir in the dark days following the assassination of Prime Minister Indira Gandhi. The state sponsored pogrom against the Sikhs led me to new but unavoidable roles. I was out on the streets, defying curfew, taking part in protest and peace marches which led to a deep 24x7 engagement with thousands of brutalised and terrified victims, and close confrontation with the instruments of the state. Perhaps this is where I cut my political teeth, so to speak.

Prabir was a highly cerebral, committed party member and involved with several high-level committees. I was a service wife catapulted into activism, venturing into totally unfamiliar worlds! But the chemistry was instant despite the yawning gulf in our individual trajectories. There is an intellectual integrity about Prabir which I deeply respected, and this has not changed.

Prabir and I have been comrades and colleagues, working together — be it literacy campaigns, the anti-nuclear movement, peace in our neighbourhood, or anti-communalism. We have also remained friends. And through me, Prabir and my husband Ramu, a former Navy Chief [Admiral Ramdas], met and developed a

Foreword

mutual respect for each other. The admiral actually read the manuscript before I did, and could not put it down. He explained why:

> I was deeply struck by the simple way he told the story of his life, and his passions and his politics, with no pretentiousness, no high-sounding theorising or sermonising. Here was a decent, ordinary human being telling us the story of his life, his growing social and political consciousness — an honest account of what drove him to do all that he has done. More than anything else, it is Prabir's open-mindedness and the lack of a dogmatic approach, that stand out as hallmarks of a unique and committed human being.

Salute to the quintessential story teller — there are important learnings on every page of Prabir's book, lessons for our time, and lessons for each of us who is a citizen, a pragmatist and a dreamer at the same time. I recall Lao Tzu's immortal words: 'Go to the people. Live with them. Learn from them. Love them.' It is people's power which will ultimately prevail, and restore peace and justice. Bravo Prabir, and Keep Up the Good Fight!

Detained for year on mistaken identity

NEW DELHI, February 17.

PICKED up by the police due to mistaken identity, a Ph.D. student of Jawaharlal Nehru University languished in jail under MISA for exactly a year during the emergency, the Shah commission was told today.

The authorities knew very well that the arrested person was not the one they wanted, yet nobody dared to release him because the instructions apparently came from the then prime minister's house. The student, Mr. Pravir Purkayastha, was arrested half an hour after the striking students of the JNU prevented Mrs. Maneka Gandhi, wife of Mr. Sanjay Gandhi, from entering the class rooms of the university where she was studying at that time.

Mr. P. S. Bhinder, the then DIG, it came out during the examination of witnesses, was the key figure in the arrest and detention of the student. Police officers told the commission that Mr. Bhinder came to the university campus straight from the prime minister's house and arrested the student despite the protest of Mr. Purkayastha that he was not Mr. Devi Prasad Tripathi, the president of the students' union, whom Mr. Bhinder was looking for.

Detention order under MISA against the student was served only after a great deal of hesitation by the ADM after consulting his superiors, including the then Lt.-Governor of Delhi, Mr. Krishan Chand.

The matter was taken up by the university authorities, Mr. Samar Mukherjee, CPM leader in the Lok Sabha, and also by the home ministry. According to the case history, Mr. Krishan Chand was unwilling to release the student until a year after the detention.

The main witness, Mr. Krishan Chand, admitted that his decision in the case was greatly influenced by what Mr. P. S. Bhinder had told him. He, however, could not recollect much of the details of the case. He came to know about the mistaken identity only much later. Mr. Bhinder had told him that the prime minister's house had sufficient information against the student and he believed the DIG.

Mr. Krishan Chand also claimed that he was not given details of the case at the time either by Mr. Bhinder or others.

Mr. Justice Shah at one stage asked the witness: "Why are you trying to hedge?"

On another occasion, Mr. Justice Shah wondered whether he was getting confused by Mr. Krishan Chand's replies or the witness. "I think I am getting confused, sir", Mr. Krishan Chand said amidst laughter.

Mr. Purkayastha, the first to be

Continued on Page 14, Column 5

Report in the *Times of India*, February 18, 1978.

1. Does Every Generation Have to Face an Emergency?

September 25, 1975. It was not the usual campus morning at Jawaharlal Nehru University (JNU). A strike called by the Students Federation of India (SFI) to protest the expulsion of Ashoklata Jain — an elected councillor of the students union — was in its second day and the campus was tense.

It was also three months since Prime Minister Indira Gandhi had declared a state of Emergency.

I was on the lawns of the School of Languages that morning, with a few friends from the SFI, when a black Ambassador stopped near us and a burly man got out. He came up to me and asked if I was D.P. Tripathi — then president of the students union. I replied that I was not, but my questioner was a cop, DIG-Range P.S. Bhinder, and he didn't believe me. He and his men, all in plainclothes, swiftly proceeded to kidnap me in broad daylight. I would end up in jail, kept there for a year under the Maintenance of Internal Security Act (MISA).

Fast forward by five decades. The government led by the Bharatiya Janata Party (BJP) and Prime Minister Narendra Modi have been in power since 2014. They won a second term in 2019. The India we knew, that we thought of as home, was being changed by the day, in myriad ways.

February 9, 2021. Morning again. I was at home. I had just finished breakfast and was reading the newspapers when the doorbell rang. It was a group of men, one of them with an official-looking paper in hand. They were from the Enforcement Directorate, he announced. The ED was here to conduct a raid. Their target was NewsClick, the digital web platform I had set up in 2009, and which had grown over the years in terms of both its work and its viewership.

The raid continued through almost five days or 113 hours, and was one of the longest raids of a private residence. The record, as I would come to learn, is held by a raid lasting nearly ten days. It had taken place at the Jaigarh Fort of Rajmata Gayatri Devi — a place covering three square kilometres, somewhat larger than my second-floor flat. But no, the ED was not busy searching my flat all the time they were there; they could have easily finished within a few hours. Except that they had a 'high-tech' problem: how were they to download my voluminous data from Google? Since Google throttles the speed of downloads beyond a certain limit, the downloading becomes excruciatingly slow after a few hours. My poor digital housekeeping had created a problem for the ED and, of course, for me. Hosting the ED, or any agency of the state, for almost five days is going beyond the call of hospitality, to put it mildly!

My earlier 'emergency encounter' was in the context of the students' resistance in JNU. D.P. Tripathi, Ashoklata (usually called Ashoka), Sitaram (Yechury) and others were among the key figures in that resistance. My encounter in the current 'emergency' took place in rather different circumstances. NewsClick, a relatively small outfit, was somehow perceived to be a 'problem'. Perhaps the problem was not so much NewsClick as the range of movements it covers. Just prior to the government's unwelcome attention, NewsClick had covered the farmers' movement quite thoroughly, coverage that drew significant viewership, and not just in India.

But then again, NewsClick was not, and is not, unique in its coverage. Many other digital platforms, and even certain mainstream media, have covered assaults on people, livelihood and reason, as well as the public protests that take place in response. Like us, some of these media organisations are very much under the Government's scanner.

I do not want to go into the various cases that NewsClick and I continue to face; or the campaign unleashed against us by a hounding variety of media. The legal matters are in the courts and we will fight the cases there. I have no desire to become the news. Nor does NewsClick; its job is to cover the news. It will continue to do what it has done from the time it was set up: follow people's movements on the ground and amplify the voices of those who are rarely heard in our society.

For many years now, I have taken part in an annual ritual in the month of June — of looking back to when democracy was last in a state of suspension. The Emergency was declared on June 25, 1975, and remained in effect till March 21, 1977. The intervening 21 months made up a grim period in India's post-independence history. There were widespread arrests and 'preventive detention' of the opposition, from political leaders to students. Protest and dissent were crushed, the media was censored, and there was fear in the air, a sense of persecution and paranoia. In short, fundamental rights were curtailed to the extent that they seemed, in these months, absent. This development was all the more shocking because till the Emergency, India was proud of the fact that it was a democracy — the reigning cliché of the time, world's largest democracy, remains much in use — and was also proud of the fact that it had become a democracy immediately after independence in 1947. It was as if, in one stroke, dissent, free speech and all the other characteristics of a democracy could be struck down by the administrative machinery of the state.

It was not, of course, a matter of one swift stroke. A range of issues came together to create an authoritarian government for 21 months.

Looking back again, what do I see first? Not the more distant past, but the fairly recent one. When young people today ask me what the 1975 Emergency was like and how it could happen, there is a more urgent counter-question I ask myself; urgent because it is what we live with in the present. Are we in the midst of an emergency by another name, an emergency like the old one in some ways, but also with its own unique features? This question holds me here, firmly in the present, even when I am asked to look back to 1975. If I am to go back in time, I would go back just a little, under ten years.

From then to now, an atmosphere of hatred and fear has gradually built up in the country. In the initial years, perhaps this did not seem qualitatively 'new'. But it would intensify, with two sets of actions that ran on parallel tracks: one, the increasing use of the state's machinery against activists, newspersons and minorities; and second, the increasing aggression of the Hindutva forces towards inter-faith marriages (or relationships), and vigilantism in the name of cow protection. The violence on both counts has today become normalised. We are no longer shocked by such attacks or even such killings; our senses have been dulled by the regular, constant repetition of this violence.

How did it all begin, the hatred-driven hounding and trolling, the assaults, the detention, the spurts of violence, and above all, the fear? Perhaps the first *visible* attack was against secular intellectuals using reason to fight communal and obscurantist politics. Narendra Dabholkar, a rationalist and writer, was assassinated in Pune on August 20, 2013. His movement, the Andhashraddha Nirmoolan Samiti, and the people's science movement to which I belong, have worked together for many years to fight against superstition and fraud by 'babas', self-proclaimed religious leaders. His murder was a shock to us all, as we could not believe that Dabholkar, who did not oppose religion but only its misuse, could even be a target.

On February 16, 2015, the veteran trade unionist, communist leader and rationalist thinker, Govind Pansare, was shot outside his house. He died on February 20. On August 30 the same year,

Does Every Generation Have to Face an Emergency?

Professor M.M. Kalburgi, a writer and scholar, was shot and killed at point-blank range in Dharwad. Kalburgi had highlighted the anti-caste core of the twelfth-century reformer Basavanna and the movement he founded. The assassination of public figures for their cultural and political views is unusual in India. Unfortunately, mass violence and state terror are not.

The assassinations created shockwaves all over India. While we held public meetings and issued statements and asked the state to take quick action, Indian writers took their protests to a different level. They began returning their awards to the Sahitya Akademi; they demanded that the state take quick action to find the murderers. It began with a few writers returning their awards. Then, the well-known literary figure Nayantara Sahgal returned her award on October 6, 2015. (She had also criticised the 1975 Emergency despite being Indira Gandhi's cousin.) In addition to condemning Kalburgi's assassination, Sahgal described the September 2015 mob lynching of Mohammed Akhlaq (on the suspicion that he was storing beef at home) as the 'final straw'. She defined this moment in our recent history as the 'unmaking of India', and returned her award 'in memory of the Indians who have been murdered, in support of all Indians who uphold the right to dissent, and of all dissenters who now live in fear and uncertainty.'

What followed was an avalanche of sorts. Writers from all parts of the country, writing in different languages, some of them household names, some of them new voices, participated in this spontaneous campaign. (Which came to be called, rather mockingly, *award wapsi* by the establishment.) The writers also put together a statement signed by perhaps the widest range of writers — geographically, linguistically, and in terms of their beliefs — except perhaps compared to the 1940s when the newly-founded Indian People's Theatre Association (IPTA) was in its prime. But that had been against the British rulers at the time of the Bengal Famine. This was in independent India, and in protest against the specific path the country was now travelling.

Some of us wanted to respond to the writers' protest through support from the community of scientists. We wanted scientists to issue a statement protesting the assassinations of rationalists and scholars, and the mob lynchings that were taking place under the pretext of opposition to cow slaughter. I thought I should ask Professor P.M. Bhargava to sign such a statement. As one of India's leading scientists, and also as one of the signatories to P.N. Haksar's statement on scientific temper in 1981, Bhargava's name would carry weight in the scientific community.[1] I found that he too was thinking about what the scientific community should do at that point. He agreed a statement was urgently required, though that, he said, was not enough. The statement, released on October 28, 2015, raised concerns from scientists on 'the ways in which science and reason are being eroded in the country.' Thus, a parallel effort by scientists took place, and the statement from them also got a very good response. Both statements appeared at the same time. But what made an enormous impact, on par with Nayantara Sahgal's gesture, was Professor Bhargava renouncing his Padma Bhushan to protest 'the government's attack on rationalism, reasoning and science'. Academics, scholars, filmmakers and a range of artists added their voices to this protest.

Their protests did not change the pace of investigations into the assassinations of the rationalists, but they did have an impact on the people. As a member of the activist community, it was clear to me that the political scene was changing and we needed to change in response. Yes, the political space was shrinking in many ways, with mass violence and the public trolling of secular opinions and voices. The state machinery and the ruling BJP were encouraging the rise of vigilantism in the name of cow protection. Hindu women choosing inter-religious marriage were depicted

---

[1] The full text of the 1981 statement and the list of signatories is to be found here:
https://www.eklavya.in/pdfs/resources/A_Statement_On_Scientific_Temper.pdf

Does Every Generation Have to Face an Emergency?

as victims of 'love jihad'. Minorities were accused of 'promoting conversion'. Public spaces were becoming increasingly hostile to minorities, especially when used by them for worship.

The secular activists realised that we had to work at a much broader level than before. We worked together on programs for the public, such as a series of talks and discussions on the 'Idea of India'. Seema Mustafa, Shabnam Hashmi, Harsh Mander and I worked on some of these programs together. Though Harsh is a Gandhian in both belief and action, and I am a Marxist, we have always agreed that talking is never enough. We need some form of solidarity actions as well, even if they are symbolic. Harsh is extremely brave on a personal level. He began his journey of what he calls bandhutva by expressing solidarity with the victims of communal violence in the name of the cow. During his marches of peace and outreach to these victims and their families, he was often confronted by threatening mobs, but he never gave up. It says a great deal about our times that even people like him are in the cross-hairs of the Government. He, his organisation, and family, are all targets of various arms of the state, with, again, the ED in the lead.

The assassination of journalist and activist Gauri Lankesh was another tragic milestone in the onward march of hatred across the country. She was shot by three assailants just outside her house on September 5, 2017. The chain of assassinations that began with Dabholkar had now claimed its fourth victim, a testament to police incompetence — if not inaction — in tracing the perpetrators of the earlier three assassinations.

Gauri Lankesh's murder shocked the country, and large numbers of people expressed their grief and solidarity in marches and public meetings. When the Karnataka police cracked the case, a clear link emerged between her assassination and members of the Sanathan Sanstha.[2] Also, the Special Investigation Team

---

[2] Founded in 1999 by a man described on its website as the 'Vishnu-like Paratpar Guru (Dr)' Jayant Balaji Athavale, the Sanatan Sanstha is

recovered a diary from suspects that had a hit-list of those who stood against hardline Hindutva; the list included eminent writers such as Girish Karnad. The chain of evidence also uncovered links among the assassinations of Dabholkar, Pansare and Kalburgi.

I was among the people — from every section of society, I believe — who were shocked in 2014 when, despite the 2002 Gujarat riots, we got a Modi-led government at the Centre; and again, in 2019, when Amit Shah became the home minister. Of course, the BJP had won elections in Gujarat in spite of the riots. Again, many of us thought that even if the BJP won in Uttar Pradesh (UP), Adityanath, with his incendiary statements and strong-arm reputation as the head of the Gorakhnath Math in Gorakhpur, would not be selected as chief minister. But that is exactly what happened in 2017. Henceforth, UP would plot a course in which the law itself would be weaponised against the minorities and all those critical of the Government — whether through arrests, punitive fines, or by levelling houses under the flimsy pretext of their non-compliance with various municipal or city laws. Even prominent civil society figures were not spared.

This marked the beginning of a new phase in BJP politics: Bulldozer Raj. But it did not end there. Soon after, 'encounter killings', always a part of Indian policing, became more commonplace.[3] Some, including the chief minister of UP, openly talked of 'summary justice' to deal with those accused of

---

headquartered in Goa. In January 2023, the Sanstha joined hands with other Hindu extremist outfits in Maharashtra to launch a movement against 'love-land jihad'.

[3] According to a Factchecker.in report published by *The Scroll* on July 28, 2022, India registered 813 'encounter killings' in the period 2016–22, or one in every three days. In only one instance had the National Human Rights Commission recommended disciplinary action against the official involved. https://scroll.in/article/1029119/data-check-in-last-six-years-india-has-registered-a-case-of-encounter-killing-every-three-days

Does Every Generation Have to Face an Emergency?

violating the law, with the police virtually acting as judge, jury and executioners.[4] This was different from the mob lynchings in the name of cow protection. The purpose of the demolitions and the encounter killings was to show that protests — indeed anything or anyone viewed as opposition — now faced not only the risk of being jailed, but also of losing property, and, possibly, life. The 'bulldozer' and 'thokai' (killing) became the symbols of the new UP *sarkar*.

But the story of our recent past (and one that continues to unfold) is not just about repression; the story is incomplete without the resistance we have witnessed, written about, and been part of. The Shaheen Bagh protests come to my mind immediately.

The controversial Citizenship Amendment Act (CAA), 2019,

---

[4] Questioned before a studio audience about suspects dying in police custody, Adityanath grinned and responded, 'People can always meet with accidents' — a wisecrack that drew laughter and applause at a show called 'UP Panchayat' hosted by *India Today* and posted to their Facebook page on August 6, 2021.
https://www.facebook.com/IndiaToday/
videos/821210558766684/?extid=SEO----
Killings in state custody reached a new level of collaboration between the police, mass media, vigilante actors and the larger public on April 15, 2023, when two convicted criminals (and former legislators), Atiq Ahmed and his brother Ashraf (aka Khalid Azim), were shot dead on live television by a man posing as a journalist, who was swiftly joined by two others. Atiq and Ashraf were being led in handcuffs by the police at Prayagraj when the three shooters emptied the barrels of their pistols into them. Four days earlier, Atiq had been convicted in a kidnapping case and was transferred by road from Gujarat to UP. That journey was also telecast live by a gleeful media; 'scoops' along the way included videos and discussions of him urinating. He had twice approached the Supreme Court in March, saying that he feared for his life if transferred to UP, but was turned down each time: 'The state machinery will take care of you,' said the Court.
https://reutersinstitute.politics.ox.ac.uk/news/indian-tv-channels-show-live-shooting-convicted-criminals-what-does-it-say-about-medium
Atiq's son, Asad, along with an associate named Ghulam, was shot dead in Jhansi by the UP STF, two days before the father, in an execution applauded by Adityanath.
https://www.thehindu.com/news/national/other-states/up-stf-kills-gangster-atiq-ahmeds-son-another-accused-in-encounter/article66732424.ece

was passed in Parliament on December 11, 2019. For the first time, we saw citizenship defined in terms of religion. Next, the National Registry of Citizens (NRC) would register citizens and non-citizens on the basis of documents in their possession. Assam was the only state that had tried to create a registry of citizens, based on proof provided by people that they or their parents/forebears had been residents of India.

About 19 lakh residents of Assam were excluded from the final NRC published on August 31, 2019, out of which the Foreigners' Tribunal has declared 1.43 lakh as foreigners — who are now in limbo. There is little chance that Bangladesh or Myanmar would accept the Tribunal's judgement that these people are de facto illegal immigrants who arrived from there.

In August 2019, the Assam NRC Report was already out. Given the brutality of that process, the intent of the CAA and the decision to create an NRC for the country had an ominous ring. This led to protests in Shaheen Bagh in South East Delhi, a sit-in by women that blocked a major road. What began as a local protest snowballed, leading to many such protests springing up in Delhi (and other cities and states). The issue was not just to do with Muslims. Most people in India do not have papers to prove they (or their forebears) were in India before 1971. For most of those who are poor, the only proof would be their name on the voters' list. But how does a migrant worker or his family access such proof? Of course, for the Muslims in other states of India, the Assam Registry showed that the bias of the Tribunal could mean being declared a non-citizen. Coupled with the CAA, which had created a path for South Asian refugees other than Muslims to claim Indian citizenship, the process looked like it was intended to isolate and, possibly, disenfranchise a large number of Muslims.

The protests ended tragically in the capital, with large-scale violence breaking out, and communal riots in northeast Delhi. Various reports by civil society groups have highlighted the links between the violence and the incendiary speeches of BJP leaders such as Kapil Mishra, police collusion, and the completely partisan behaviour of the state machinery during the riots.[5]

The state machinery was also unleashed against university students in Jamia Millia Islamia — this police action must be among the worst we have seen in the country. It signalled the beginning of a new regime of executive impunity, not bound by the norms of police entry into educational institutions. The aftermath included a series of cases against students, women activists and other social activists, with the enlarged version of the draconian UAPA (or Unlawful Activities Prevention Act) slapped against a number of them.

In all of these events, NewsClick, like many other news organisations, carried out its task of coverage — reporting, speaking to the leaders of people's movements and those participating in the marches and other civic protests, and so both disseminating news as well as providing a platform to broadcast people's voices. What I had in mind when I first set up NewsClick was a low-budget news and views organisation that would run text and videos. I believe that we, as progressives, need to include, if not focus on, a new video generation brought up on a diet of Facebook and YouTube. Print no longer commands the status it held in our eyes. If we do not keep up, they would be lost to a different kind of politics.

What did this 'different politics' mean in terms of our actual day-to-day work? It meant that NewsClick would cover movements, farmers, workers, Dalits, women, forest dwellers, and

---

[5] *Uncertain Justice: A Citizens Committee Report on the North East Delhi Violence 2020*, Justice Madan B. Lokur, Justice A.P. Shah, Justice R.S. Sodhi, Justice Anjana Prakash, G.K. Pillai, IAS (Retd.), Constitutional Conduct Group (CCG), October 2020.
chromeextension://efaidnbmnnnibpcajpcglclefindmkaj/https://constitutionalconduct.files.wordpress.com/2022/10/uncertain-justice-citizens-committee-report-on-north-east-delhi-violence-2020.pdf

other 'excluded' sections, the ones whose voices are not usually heard in mainstream or big media. I always find it disturbing that when the workers march in the city, news reports are too often about the traffic jams they caused, rather than their demands.

One important example of such coverage — of people's movements — was the Kisan movement. We sent a small team to cover the Kisan Sabha's march in Sikar, Rajasthan, in September 2017. Once the Kisan Sabha declared a bandh, no news team could get into the town or leave. So, our team stayed in Sikar and reported on what had become big enough to attract considerable attention. Our team sent dispatches with 'live visuals', including that of the march through the city. We followed this up with the Kisan Long March from Nashik to Mumbai in 2018. When the march began, we were among the few news organisations that turned up, and one of the very few that accompanied the march. But as the kisans continued on their journey, more news organisations began to cover the march. By the time the kisans entered Mumbai, the march was front page news.

In keeping with our policy of covering movements, NewsClick foregrounded the Kisan Morcha's protests over the three farm laws that the BJP government introduced in Parliament and adopted virtually without a debate, in September 2020. The farmers saw this as an attack on their livelihood. Already, farming was becoming increasingly unprofitable, and the three farm laws would open agriculture for big capital to take over the supply chain from farms to supermarkets. Already, the Ambanis and Adani were planning to enter the market for agriculture, from seeds and fertilisers to reaching food to the market. This trio of laws sounded the death knell for farmers and, quite possibly, India's food autonomy. The farmers mobilised in large numbers to come to Delhi and protest against what they rightly perceived to be anti-farmer laws. Their year-long struggle forced the government to withdraw the three farm laws in November 2021.

Struggles and victories like these keep people's movements

Does Every Generation Have to Face an Emergency?

and the will of the people alive. And my colleagues and I at NewsClick have always agreed that our work is firmly located in such histories-in-the-making. Is this why NewsClick, despite its modest size, came under the government's radar? NewsClick and the other media organisations are by no means alone in facing such tactics to silence them, or punish them for doing their job. Our cases number just a few among the thousands we have seen — and continue to see — building up against media houses, political opponents, and civil society activists. Teesta Setalvad is a case in point.

So, once again, we return to the nagging question: Have we seen this before, during Mrs Gandhi's Emergency? And what is different about what we are living through now?

The conventional story of the 1975 Emergency is that of heroes and villains, with a number of cowards who did not quite measure up to history. In this morality play, there does not appear to be much space for real-life ordinary people, who are generally neither heroic nor villainous. From a distance, it appears that they approved of the Emergency when it was on; then rejected it summarily when they found an opportunity — the 1977 elections called by Mrs Gandhi. In retrospect, it is clearer than ever that these 'ordinary' people were the real protagonists of the rejection. This is why I would say that the real significance of the Emergency lies in the confidence the Indian people gained in 1977: the people could teach their leaders a lesson if they strayed beyond the permissible.

The current leaders have once again fallen into the trap of believing their own propaganda, just as Mrs Gandhi and the Congress did during the Emergency.

Undoubtedly, the 1975 Emergency was an acid test for many sections. The media, the bureaucracy and a number of political parties and personalities were found wanting. The highest judiciary in the country, the Supreme Court, failed to show even the courage the High Courts did, sanctioning the formal butchery of our fundamental rights to life, liberty and free speech.

But for many others, the Emergency was also a time to assert their beliefs. Some resisted quietly, out of the public eye. Others expressed their opposition more visibly. For the generation born after the freedom struggle, this was arguably the first big political test. While the people, the Indian citizenry in general, passed this test, the same cannot be said of some of the more elite sections and bourgeois institutions.

The Indian people are quite often mistaken to be passive. They do not rise up in revolt periodically against the terrible burden of oppression that they carry; this is a criticism commonly levelled against them. Yet, this mass of 'passive' people routed Mrs Gandhi in 1977 and asserted the primacy of Indian democracy. This forced Mrs Gandhi to apologise to the people for the Emergency. Some have argued that if the verdict of 1977 was so unambiguous, how is it that the same people voted her back to power in 1980? The answer lies in the confidence that the people had acquired in 1977. They had taught Mrs Gandhi a lesson they were sure she was not going to forget. And to their credit, they were proved right — Mrs Gandhi did not re-impose an authoritarian regime.

But to get back to the question of then and now: To begin with, it appears that an 'emergency' — as a general description of repression — is a destructive situation that develops if the political dispensation of the time erodes people's fundamental rights in numerous ways. This is one way to frame the similarities between then and now. But with each point of 'similarity', there are differences as well. Some are rather stark, such as that of the ideology driving the attack on citizens' rights in the present. Some of the differences are, perhaps, more nuanced — in, for example, the ways in which authoritarianism is expressed.

Let me, as a 'midnight's child', consider the situation in India today, not just keeping in mind the 1975 Emergency to compare two aberrant periods, but also keeping in mind the larger context of 75 years of the secular, diverse, democratic, constitution-guided republic of India.

THE MEDIA THEN AND NOW

Among the most enduring memories of the Emergency (other than enforced vasectomies) are those of a scared, docile press. The administration had powers to muzzle the media — what the press wrote had to be submitted to censors. Everyone recalls L.K. Advani's chastising remark to the press after the Emergency: 'You were asked only to bend, but you crawled.' But we also have to remember and salute honourable exceptions that didn't bow down, or carry government propaganda. *The Indian Express* managed to operate within the new constraints. Its blank editorial was a powerful symbol of protest against the attack on the role of the fourth estate. Smaller organisations also resisted the bully censor; for instance, the journal *Seminar* run by Romesh Thapar. Of course, what they could do was necessarily limited.

How does the Indian media scene today compare with those times? Media then meant mainly the print medium — the 'press'. We have a number of platforms today, and it's certainly much harder to control them all.[6] The media is much more heterogeneous; and the agenda for media has been set differently. Earlier, print media set what made news. The headline of the day would determine what the news was. Now that we have 24x7 news channels on television, the news has changed. Watching prime-time news 'debates' can give us a preview of the news cycle.

Social media has completely changed the landscape of what

---

[6] Not for lack of trying, though. The Digital Personal Data Protection Act 2023 may impede journalists' access to government records sought under the right to information, and compel them to reveal their sources, as well as enabling the government to censor news stories.
https://scroll.in/article/1054094/a-censorship-tool-in-disguise-how-the-data-protection-bill-will-hurt-journalists

was earlier considered news or commentary, and so also with the influence and reach of media. Social media even sets the news now — what issues will be discussed and commented upon by both journalists and readers. This is, obviously, much more difficult to control. Which is why, despite the best efforts of the BJP and Modi acolytes, you do hear other voices. Of course, the government and its cohorts are anxious to control the large number of individuals using social media; to do this, they have to come up with measures different from what sufficed during the earlier Emergency.

In other words, a technological change has taken place which makes the task of muzzling the press rather different from what it used to be. If you want to muzzle a million or more people, you cannot use the Emergency instrument, which was direct censorship. What are the new censors — official and unofficial — to do? They make an example of a few to create a chilling effect. They make people afraid; self-censorship becomes the norm. They make use of continuous harassment, by filing FIRs all over the country; what used to be called lawfare in other jurisdictions. Remember the case of the artist M.F. Husain? Cases were filed against him practically everywhere. Criminal proceedings were initiated against him for allegedly hurting public sentiment with his paintings. Groups such as the Vishwa Hindu Parishad (VHP) and the Bajrang Dal issued threats against the 90-year-old painter. Finally, unable to take it anymore, Husain left the country and lived in self-exile till his death.

The more recent examples are in some senses even more alarming. Any perceived criticism of the government or the Hindu supremacist project makes the journalist vulnerable to trolling, physical attacks, prosecution under the Information Technology Act and IT Rules of 2021, or detention under draconian counter-terrorism and sedition laws. Independent news organisations are definitely on the hit list, especially of government agencies such as the ED and Income Tax department. Critical journalists have been charged for tweets, and social media users for sharing posts

Does Every Generation Have to Face an Emergency?

on Facebook. Students have been booked for sedition, for allegedly cheering for Pakistan in a cricket match. Advertisers have been threatened with boycotts for using words or symbols perceived as Muslim, and bullied into withdrawing advertisements that represent a syncretic culture. The list of restrictions and attacks on media freedom is long and varied, and grows every day.

As always, the muzzling of the media is one part of the narrative, whether we are talking about the bad old days of the Emergency or the arguably still worse days of today's unnamed Emergency. At every turn, I think it is essential to see with clear eyes the terrible details of repression, but also the brave resistance offered by people. We see this courage around us, in the present and the very recent past. Take the media, for instance. There are many critical voices on the news platforms today, and not just digital platforms. We read, see and hear criticism even in mainstream news. We saw, for instance, how newspapers, even those who were pro-government earlier in Gujarat and Uttar Pradesh, exposed undeclared COVID-19 deaths. Of course, they paid a price for this transgression later, with income tax raids on their premises spread across the country.

Another phenomenon is a kind of double role some of the mainstream newspapers seem to play. They provide a platform for government 'news' as well as some manicured real news, the proportion waxing and waning, perhaps depending on how much readers will accept before they stop reading the paper altogether. This is true of television as well, as the prime-time news spots have been replaced by gladiatorial contests, with the anchors playing ringmasters goading the opposition or critical voices. Despite this, some critical strands continue to find their way even into the mainstream media. Although even here, certain developments are carefully ignored. I am referring, of course, to news and commentary on people's struggles and popular movements. If we look at the 'national' or 'mainstream' media spaces today, where is the working class? Where are the unions? The farmers? The industry beat is essentially about the industrialists; you hear the voices of the management, and you discuss the finances of the company. The shift away from people working in the industry and towards its owners is stark. So is the growth of what used to be called the society page or page 3 — fashion and lifestyle — as celebrity news spreads across the entire paper, sometimes reaching even the front page. Development journalist P. Sainath, founder of the People's Archive of Rural India (PARI), has pointed out if there are 40 media persons covering fashion shows in Mumbai, there may be just the one journalist covering rural Maharashtra and the deaths of agricultural workers and small farmers.

People's movements, so critical in any impetus to change, are often innocent of social media and unused to the ways media is used by the current generation. I remember my grandmother's generation saying that if something was in print, it must be true. In a similar vein, older people today seem to think anything on WhatsApp must be true. The younger lot may well be a little more discerning. At any rate, it will take a while for us, whether old or young, to acquire social media literacy. Unfortunately, the various organs of the BJP and RSS have had a head start in the manipulation of social media, reinforced by the money power they wield.

How do we increase social media literacy and how do we increase social media capabilities in the movements? That's a tremendous challenge, but when you have the numbers, it will happen. This is what we saw in the case of the farmers' protests: they found their own voices; they found their own media. Yes, they had access to sympathetic news platforms, including NewsClick. But their content, their take on the movement, was their own, whether it was the broadcast of their marches, their music or their first-person reports, all expressed in a multitude of voices, often with humour. And all this was often directly communicated on platforms they set up, whether on YouTube or Facebook, or with their four-page bi-weekly, *Trolley Times*. This is only one example. Unlike the earlier Emergency, where cutting the electricity supply to the newspapers stopped the printing presses, now, in the digital age, shutting down all forms of media, including social media, is much more difficult.

WHEN LAWS DISABLE JUSTICE

The use of draconian laws is a common point between then and now. The earlier Emergency made use of a range of coercive instruments from the curbing of press freedom, to the Defence of India Act of 1915, to MISA or the Maintenance of Internal Security Act. An entire legal structure was used to muzzle the voices of people. Protests were not allowed; mass movements were viewed as dangerous. The mindset was that all authority would be given to the administration, and they would do everything for you. It was a kind of distorted 'mai-baap sarkar' model.

MISA, passed by the Parliament in 1971, gave the administration, including the law enforcement agencies, some very broad powers. It allowed for indefinite preventive detention. It allowed wiretapping. Property could be searched without warrants and seized. In the name of 'threats to national security' the law allowed the use of coercive methods to achieve what can only be described as undemocratic and unconstitutional ends. Moreover, the law was amended several times during the Emergency to crush political dissent.

Like so many of the undemocratic laws citizens in independent India have suffered from, the MISA is a part of the colonial legacy. It is a direct descendant of the preventive detention laws under the British. And if Emergency 1.0 had its MISA, Emergency 2.0 — what we are now living through — has the UAPA. The BJP government amended the Unlawful Activities (Prevention) Act, 1967, through a bill introduced in the Lok Sabha in 2019. The resulting Unlawful Activities (Prevention) Amendment Act, 2019, provides 'special measures' to deal with terrorism, including shifting the burden of proof onto the accused, and making bail the exception, not the rule. The draconian nature of UAPA has been amply proved by the Bhima Koregaon case in which as many as 16 citizens, numbering activists and teachers and writers among them, have been arrested and held without a trial. One of these 16 political prisoners, octogenarian Stan Swamy, an activist for Adivasi rights, died in detention. Five out of the 15 — Sudha Bharadwaj, Varavara Rao, Anand Teltumbde, Arun Ferreira and Vernon Gonsalves — have bail, while Gautam Navlakha is under house arrest with a makeshift arrangement in Mumbai. The others continue to languish in jail. And the Bhima Koregaon case is only the most well-known example of what UAPA does.

There have been many objections, and from many quarters, to the amended UAPA. In addition to organisations, individuals can now be labelled terrorists. The amendment violates the principle of innocent till proven guilty, and also the International Covenant on Civil and Political Rights (1967), which sees this principle as a universal human right. The amended act can only be used 'to repress rather than combat terrorism since the amendment provides that designation of an individual as a terrorist would not lead to any conviction or penalties'. Also, 'no objective criterion has been laid for categorisation, and the government has been provided with "unfettered powers" to declare an individual as a terrorist.'[7]

Will the courts intervene on the use — i.e., the misuse — of laws to undermine fundamental rights? In 1976, during the Emergency, the ADM Jabalpur judgement on habeas corpus was a blot in Indian judicial history. A constitutional bench of the Supreme Court comprising five judges, with one honourable dissenting exception, ruled that detention could not be challenged in court since Emergency had been proclaimed and Article 21

---

[7] See Deepali Bhandari and Deeksha Pokhriyal:
https://www.jurist.org/commentary/2020/06/bhandari-pokhriyal-uapa-free-speech/

Does Every Generation Have to Face an Emergency? 37

(which protects life and personal liberty), had been suspended.[8] The MISA was finally repealed in 1977 when Indira Gandhi lost the general elections, and the Janata party came to power. The ADM Jabalpur judgement was not overturned till 2017, and we can only hope that it has, at last, been buried.

The UAPA has also been challenged in the courts as unconstitutional. The challenge in November 2021 was in response to the law being used to book lawyers and journalists for their social media posts on communal violence in Tripura. The petitioners, represented by Prashant Bhushan, point out that the definition of 'unlawful activity' is vague. They also argued that 'the "wide net" the law casts on freedom of speech and expression; its tendency to bring within its fold mere criticism of government policies or actions that have no effect on public order or the security, sovereignty and integrity of India; and its indiscriminate use against those critical of the government produces a "chilling effect" on the freedom of speech and expression.'[9]

In the current repressive period, in which judicial action needs, more than ever, to provide a check on the government, it is imperative for people's opinions to be expressed in various forms, and so act as a corrective.

LAWFARE AND HARASSMENT THROUGH AGENCIES

Another point of comparison between then and now is the use of government agencies to harass or intimidate critics, whether individuals or organisations, as well as opposition parties and political figures. Every day, we hear about hounding and harassment through police cases and investigative agencies such as the ED, the Economic Offences Wing (EOW) or the NIA (National

---

[8] H.R. Khanna was the lone dissenter of the five-judge bench that included M. Hameedullah Beg, P.N. Bhagwati, Y.V. Chandrachud and Chief Justice A.N. Ray.

[9] See: https://www.livelaw.in/pdf_upload/uapa-tripure-writ-petition-403894.pdf

Investigation Agency). FIRs are filed by a huge number of people, and the police are then told, 'Look at these FIRs, but not at those.' At one level, there is much more widespread resistance now, but there is also a more pervasive attack, and I think that's one clear distinction between the Emergency then and the 'emergency' now.

Control by the state blends seamlessly with the intimidation unleashed by the ground-level stormtroopers. During the earlier Emergency, the Chhatra Parishad, the Youth Congress, created what we later referred to as the Sanjay Gandhi Goon Brigade. However, it was not an organised movement; the Emergency did not have an organised force supporting the government on the streets. Restrictions were imposed from above, through the administrative machinery. The ground-level stormtroopers on the rampage now are different, and their reach too is more wide-ranging — from censorship with bullets, of scholars and rationalists, to gau rakshaks trolling on social media. They make up a kind of organised complement to state power, and the gau rakshaks and vahinis and senas the BJP or the RSS have at their command quite often act as an adjunct to the state. Or as the spear point of the attack. They are involved in actual physical violence, including lynching, in the name of protecting cows. There is also the terrible violence of language in social discourse, and in social media by the Troll Brigade. The IT cell of the major political party in India today is at the helm of the new media onslaught, an organised force with huge resources.

AND THEN, IDEOLOGY . . .

The major difference between then and now is at the fundamental level of ideology. The Congress ideology did not view certain sections of the people as outsiders, to be treated either as second-class citizens or excluded from citizens' rights.

Since 2014, there has been a dramatic increase in what we can only call hate crimes. Muslims have been the target in a significant

Does Every Generation Have to Face an Emergency? 39

number of these crimes; Dalits, Adivasis and women form part of the list as well, as do secular activists. Was it the same situation during the Emergency? Yes, there was oppression; but it was secular oppression. Yes, there was the Turkman Gate incident during the Emergency, when Muslims (and other residents of the area) were attacked. This incident illustrates a particular toxic combination of the Emergency agenda: family planning in the form of vasectomy, and demolition of poor areas to prettify the city. (Family planning expressed the fear of the middle classes that the poor were breeding too much, a favourite bugbear in the West, which saw the population growth of countries like India as a threat to their control over the globe's resources.) But overall, the Emergency government was not trying to exclude minorities. Ideologically, the Congress was not following the Savarkar thesis which plays out today both formally and informally: Minorities can remain in the country but only as second-class citizens.

That was not what the Congress ideology was. Nor what the national movement had built; certainly, the Congress could not publicly espouse such an ideology. The Congress could and did say that the Emergency was a necessary interim period of 'discipline' — or, as Vinoba Bhave put it, 'a festival of discipline' (*apaatkal ka anushaasan parv*). The Emergency was described as a short-period fix; whether this was the only intent or not, it was not translated into a structure within the state.

We are seeing something different today. The structure of the state is apparently the same, but it is being hollowed out. There is an organised force that has risen to complement state power. This organised force takes on any resistance that comes from the people, and there is a compact between the state and this kind of intimidation politics. It's important to remember that these forces do not comprise fringe elements; they are a significant political force in the country, they are 'mainstream'. They help to build a kind of destructive and sectarian politics. The object is to exclude people on the basis of their community, to the extent of eroding the citizenship rights of some Indians. The Congress did not have all these exclusionary politics in its genetic composition; the RSS has them in its genes. That's the crucial difference.

The other difference between then and now is the sustained and multifarious attacks we see today on our secular ethos, on culture, on education, science and reason. This is, of course, part of the ideology-driven project of building a Hindu Rashtra which will have little to do with the inclusive, secular nation with a scientific outlook envisioned by so many of our freedom fighters. The Hindutva brigade failed the national movement. They did not fight for independence. So their vision for India is to take it onto a different trajectory from the attempt in 1947 which had, by and large, consensus among the people. Their battle was and has been against the Muslims. To put it another way, possibly a more precise way, it was, and is, for Hindu supremacy. The India they are fighting for will have one religion and one people, *Hindi-Hindu-Hindu Rashtra*; this means large numbers of Indians will become second-class citizens. In many ways, the Hindu supremacists are still fighting their battle in the past, whether it is by renaming streets and cities, pulling down monuments, or finding mandirs everywhere. The battle they are engaged in looks backwards; they have nothing to offer for the future.

How do we resist this new powerful Emergency without a name? I think we need a much larger coming together of people. This is why the farmers' movement has been so important. In Western Uttar Pradesh, for example, the Muslim and Jat farmers came together through the movement. To understand how significant this is, we have to recall that in September 2013 riots broke out between Muslims and Jats in the Muzaffarnagar district. Several members of the BJP were accused of instigating the riots; and the BJP won the subsequent general and assembly elections from the region. The fracturing between the two communities that took place during the Muzaffarnagar riots was, to some extent, healed by the farmers' movement.

Movements build this kind of unity. This is why the rightwing considers movements based on class issues dangerous: they make it impossible to build on caste and community divisions, which is what the BJP does. Is it any surprise that movements — from farmers' movements and workers' movements to anti-caste movements and students' movements — become ideological threats to the RSS and the BJP?

During the Congress Emergency, the jailers were quite aware that some of the people they were holding in prison could well become the rulers someday. That was a clear motive to treat these prisoners differently. Mrs Gandhi's government also accepted the fact that these prisoners were not 'ordinary' people they had to 'break'. Their plan of action was to take control of the media and its messaging, and to marginalise opponents.

The methods, and in fact the overall plan to silence people, seems quite different today. The driving question seems to be, *How do we break the people who are standing up to us?* The aim is to remould the state *without* these dissident voices; and ensure that nobody is able to stand up to the government or the rightwing forces in all their various avatars. This may explain some of the terrible pettiness we have seen in the current regime's handling of political prisoners. The most obvious example is that of Stan Swamy, the 83-year-old activist who worked with Adivasis and who was jailed for alleged involvement in the Bhima Koregaon case. Here was a frail old man who suffered from various medical conditions including Parkinson's. He had to apply for a sipper and straw because of the tremors in his hands. The NIA 'sought time' to consider his request; a special court turned down the request. The activist had to make a fresh application for the sipper cup as well as winter clothes. Such banal acts of cruelty, such dehumanising acts, seem to carry a message: We can do anything we want to you, and no one can stop us. As long as the courts do not give political prisoners the protection they should, the message may well continue to hold true.

Our hope is that as these flagrant violations of rights become more visible, more questions will also grow audible. One positive development is that the courts seem to be taking up more of these cases. Perhaps the ice is cracking a little? We will have to see.

A personal digression is in order here. In 2015, I responded to an invitation by Prime Minister Narendra Modi to an event organised for the felicitation of those who had fought the Emergency. I found it ironic: the present government, busy creating a different kind of Emergency, felicitating those who had fought the 1975 Emergency. The irony grew deeper and uglier because some people from the RSS and the Sangh Parivar were in jail during Mrs Gandhi's Emergency. Had they learnt nothing from the experience? Or had they learnt too much and too well?

This was my RSVP:

> I have received an invitation to be present at the 'Loktantra Prahara Abhinandan' on October 11, 2015, when some of those who fought the Emergency are, apparently, to be felicitated in 'the august presence' of Prime Minister Narendra Modi.
>
> I assume I have been asked to be part of the audience in His August Presence because I was in jail for a year during Indira Gandhi's Emergency.
>
> The Emergency created a culture of subservience to power. Political thuggery, backed by the repressive organs of the state, ruled the people's lives. Those of us who fought the Emergency know well what an authoritarian government is like. We know how important free speech is. And we know, most of all, the necessity of resisting a culture of authoritarianism. When we

came out of jail, and when the Emergency was lifted, all of us hoped the republic would not have to face such dark days again.

We hoped in vain.

Having lived through an earlier emergency, what can I share with my young colleagues, friends and comrades? Whether I look back to the 1975 Emergency or at the one today, I do not want to look at it from the point of view of a victim. Victimhood robs us of participation in the creation of history; it reduces us to mere objects of history. Instead, I would like to assume the vantage point of people as *makers* of history. Yes, the government of the day wields powers that seem to overwhelm individuals and organisations. But it is people, and their actions, that finally determine history; not as we please and when we please, but in ways that neither the people nor their rulers anticipate. Mrs Gandhi's Emergency was eventually laid to rest in the 1977 elections in a way that even the opposition parties had not anticipated. A hesitant opposition, unaware of the people's sentiments about the Emergency, was swept into power, just as a shocked Congress was swept out. If the state was the principal actor onstage during the Emergency, the people took over the stage in its dismissal.

Don't take people's silence for assent: This was the crucial lesson of the Emergency for our generation. Mrs Gandhi knew that she needed the affirmation of the people through an election that was truly free. The current dispensation believes that the facade of freedom, combined with control over media, including social media, is enough. Yes, it may be possible to do this for a short time, maybe in a few states, often by creating warlike conditions with a neighbour, and, throughout, appealing to people to close ranks behind the great leader. But not for long, not across the country. As Shelley's immortal line says: 'Ye are many, they are few'!

To mark our fight against the 1975 Emergency under the aegis of a government that is introducing a different, and an even more dangerous emergency, would be a travesty. Instead, we need to recreate the resistance that led to the defeat of the Emergency. We need to defeat the forces who are, as Nayantara Sahgal has said, threatening to 'unmake the nation'.

2. Learning to Fight: A Personal Journey

There is one thing that holds together past and present for me — my commitment to responding to the world around me politically, and as part of a collective, in my case, the Communist Party.

How is an activist born? When young comrades today ask me how I got politicised, I feel the need to explain those times to them — not just the Bengal and the world of the fifties and sixties, but also my specific family background.

I come from a typical middle-class Bengali family. Of course, the word 'typical' hides specific details that may have influenced my choices. My father was in the Customs and Central Excise Department, a part of the Indian Revenue Service. I still remember how important the Budget was in our household, because it had direct implications for excise and customs duties. My father's job was transferable and we would have to move every few years. This meant, each time, a new school, new teachers and new friends. My mother was a good and efficient 'administrator', and would set up a new home every two to three years.

I was a sickly child. I had child asthma, and repeated throat and chest infections. My brother stayed at first with my grandmother, later in a hostel, and still later with an aunt, all in Calcutta (as it was then). He remained in a Bengali medium school — the Scottish Church Collegiate School. I could not stay at any school for long; in fact, I had two and a half years of homeschooling in Anantapur, Andhra Pradesh. This changed my medium of instruction from Bengali to English, though I kept my thick Bengali accent. (I doubt anyone understood my English except my mother.) Much worse, homeschooling meant no school friends and mostly adult company. But it also meant discovering friends in books. I used to

Parents, Amulya De Purkayastha and Samjukta.

cycle a few kilometres to the district library in Anantapur to read fiction, what we called storybooks, and I went through books at a speed that surprised the librarian. One good thing about this kind of reading was that it was unsupervised. I read pretty much everything I could lay my hands on, including fairly adult literature that I understood very little of.

All in all, it was a lonely childhood. I had my mother's company, and she was willing to discuss all kinds of things with me. (Sometimes, her conversation was coloured by her partition-bitterness. Her family was from the Comilla District in East Bengal, now Cumilla in Bangladesh.) My father did not think discussion with children was important or necessary, but he had a whole range of books from Bertrand Russell to Shakespeare. I recall reading Russell's essay 'Why I Am Not a Christian'. I could read Bengali quite well, having been in Bengali medium schools earlier, and I read the Bengali translations (the long versions, not just the abridged ones) of the Mahabharata and Ramayana. I remember being struck by the 'adult' bits in the epics.

Learning to Fight

My brother was fortunate in being a healthy child — his education was uninterrupted, and he had steady friends — but he had to stay away from the family except for the summer and Puja holidays. When he came home during the holidays, we would do things together, or fight over who should get more of the food we liked, or argue with my mother about larger issues. One recurring discussion was on love marriage versus arranged marriage. (Unfortunately, this does not sound archaic today, with inter-faith marriages under attack by the BJP and inter-caste marriages by the khap panchayats.)

We were much closer to the maternal side of the family as they were in Calcutta. My father's two brothers were in Assam, one sister in Delhi and one in Asansol — all of them 'service families' with no interest in politics. Both sides of the family were Congress voters, strongly nationalist, and also committed to retaining their Bengali-hood despite our wanderings from Jalpaiguri to Calcutta (twice), Anantapur, Allahabad and Poona. These were the four places where I studied, in and out of school. And, of course, schooling was supplemented with drilling in the works of Rabindranath, Bankim Chandra and Sarat Chandra at a fairly early age.

My maternal grandmother was the matriarch of the family. My grandfather played a marginal role in family issues; I guess the division of the Home Office and External Affairs of the nation-state was the role model for families as well. The External Affairs may be glamorous, but the Home Office calls the shots for its citizens. My grandmother ruled over the daughters — even after their marriages — and her opinion was important in all family matters.

There was a history here that I did not fully understand till later. My grandfather was active in the independence movement in Comilla. Though he was a part of the Indian National Congress, he was also sympathetic to the strand of the independence movement that believed in armed struggle. My grandfather's activities with the Indian National Congress led to his internment in Cox's Bazar for five years. It couldn't have been easy for my grandmother and her four children, because they had to stay with her family as dependants. Not surprisingly, the family as a unit was held together by my grandmother; my grandfather remained a distant figure to the children. Tragically for him, my grandmother prevailed on him to stay away from the 1942 struggle so he could provide for the family.

For his time, he was well-read, had gone to college and even written a book on the First World War. But he had few marketable skills. He set up a cloth business, which did not last too long. Meanwhile, it kept him out of a critical period of Congress history, including the 1942 Quit India movement. He was also out of the Congress organisation post-independence. My cousins, my brother, and I remember him as a part of a retired group in Belghoria, a suburb of Calcutta, where he had bought a small plot of land and built a little house we would visit on weekends. It had no electricity or running water, but we children did not notice these things. Belghoria and the grandparents made us feel free, away from our parents' control.

My grandfather never talked about his life, or the opportunities he had missed by joining the independence movement only to withdraw from it. Both choices must have cost him dearly. He taught us to play chess and cards, which, perhaps, was the only way he could pass time. All the four grandchildren in Calcutta were taught chess and bridge — he did not like games of chance. We became his chess partners, and would make up the fourth in bridge with adults.

Did he influence my politics? Not in any direct sense. But we children had an example before us — of a person who had given up a normal life, with no expectations of reward. We saw what it was to have a larger vision of society, to have politics. We also saw what it can do to families. While my grandfather never passed on his politics to us, he taught us two games in which thinking and strategy are important. Chess would later stand me in good stead

Learning to Fight

in jail, helping me to make friends and pass time. At one point, though, people stopped playing with me — maybe my grandfather had taught me too well!

I returned to the formal school system when my father was posted to Calcutta, and I joined Class VII at the St Thomas' Boys School in Kidderpore, in the middle of the school term. As a midterm outsider not used to a peer group, my ability to make friends was limited. And fortunately, the teachers also did not take much notice of a gangly kid with glasses. I was always a backbencher because of my height, and this helped me avoid the teachers' attention. I could continue my exploration of the exciting world of books: adventure stories, detective fiction and historical romances.

My father was then transferred to Allahabad, where I joined St Joseph's School (now called St Joseph's College), again in the middle of term. I could cycle to school, but what was more important, to second-hand bookshops that were also lender's libraries. For a small fee and a deposit, you could borrow several books. In school I continued to sit as far back as I could, away from the teacher, and read storybooks in class. I couldn't remain anonymous indefinitely, though. I finally got noticed for doing reasonably well in the exams.

The school in Allahabad had good teachers in English, mathematics and the sciences. Our science teacher was quite brilliant. Much later, when I was doing my Master's, his son was with me in the Allahabad Engineering College. Only then did I learn that my teacher was a communist and, although good science qualifications were rare, his political past had ensured that he could only get a school teaching job.

Of the many schools I went to, it was St Joseph's that developed my basic skills in writing, maths and science, and also fostered a lifelong interest in history and politics. I learned, maybe because of being a loner, to think independently. I didn't always see the need to agree with the teacher. When our history teacher spoke of the enlightenment the British had brought us, and the merits of Christianity as compared to Hinduism, my nationalist genes and rational beliefs were immediately challenged. I stood up and got into an argument with the teacher, who was quite unused to being challenged by his students. I also recall a Moral Science class in which a teacher attempted to prove the existence of god and to argue that ethics can come only from religion. More than Russell, I suspect this teacher was responsible for my lifelong atheism.

In 1961, when I was in Class IX, the Indian Army marched into Goa in response to a brutal crackdown by the Portuguese authorities on the Goan freedom movement to join India. The US, UK and France tried to pass a resolution in the Security Council against India, but it was vetoed by the Soviet Union. The Catholic Church, which ran the school I was in, and the padres, many of whom taught us, were bitterly against the Indian intervention. They argued that it was violence and that Goa belonged to the Portuguese. British colonialism might have gone officially, but it remained in the mindset of the church and the books we read as part of our Senior Cambridge curriculum. As I left St Joseph's, I remember Father A.G. Rego, our English and Moral Science teacher, telling me that it was a pity I would miss his lectures on communism the next year. He would show students how bad communism was, he said. Maybe it was a loss — had I heard him, I might have become a communist much sooner.

From St Joseph's Allahabad, I moved to Bishop's School Poona, again in the middle of term. I was quite shocked at the sharp difference in teaching, and quickly decided I had little to learn from my teachers. My English teacher was partial to big words and complicated syntax, the kind of style my English teacher in St Joseph's had railed against. The teacher who taught us physics and chemistry dictated notes from the textbook, and expected us to write them down dutifully. When I refused, telling him I already

Learning to Fight

had the book, he threw me out of his class. Relieved, I made my way to the school library. The teacher hated me, but he gave up at some point. He let me sit peacefully in class, reading novels. The only teacher I liked was the geography teacher, who shared with us his love of maps, and taught us that we cannot understand history, politics or economics without them. From a subject I hated, geography became a subject I loved. This love has lasted to this day, and I lecture my NewsClick colleagues regularly on why we need maps to understand and explain geopolitics. I owe this love of maps to Mr Bloud, my geography teacher in Bishop's School Poona.

I finally found friends — both in Allahabad and Poona. In Poona, I also discovered that I was not completely hopeless at sports, and could play a middling game of badminton and table tennis. But football, hockey and cricket remained lost causes. Sadly, I had to give up any hope of emulating the heroes of the adventure books I was reading. Much later, I would feel vindicated. A great number of these 'adventure books' recounted the stories of the colonising barbarians from Western Europe, who brought slavery, genocide and plunder to Africa, the Americas and Asia. These stories wore the guise of adventure, whether it was cowboys protecting settlers against 'savage' Red Indians, or the 'civilised' Europeans bringing Christianity to a 'heathen' Africa. It was at this later time that I came across Desmond Tutu's famous words: 'When the missionaries came to Africa, they had the Bible, and we had the land. They said, "Let us close our eyes and pray." When we opened them, we had the Bible, and they had the land.' A few years after school, I learned, too, of the genocide of the indigenous people in the United States, from Dee Brown's *Bury My Heart at Wounded Knee* (1970). Since then, my learning has involved a lifetime of unlearning what I had unconsciously imbibed through adventure stories, detective fiction and what passed for children's literature in my times.

I guess politics enters a life in many ways, even before we are conscious of it. Now, in retrospect, I can ask myself: When did I consciously 'enter' politics?

Only when I joined college did I finally get to stay in one place for more than a year or two. In 1965, I joined the Bengal Engineering College, one of the oldest engineering institutes in the country, and stayed put for the next five years. (At that time, B.E. was a five-year course after Class 11.) I now had friends with whom I shared hostel, classes, and, of course, keeping with the stereotype of good Bengalis, passionate discussion on every topic under the sun, from politics to football. I loved sports, and like the lead character in Jerome K. Jerome's book *Three Men in a Boat* (who loved work and could watch it for hours), I watched sports rather than play. To be precise — since it was still the age of radio — I listened to football or cricket commentary for hours.

But sport was not the only thing that brought us young people together. This was a period of major social ferment. The sixties witnessed the food movement in Bengal, student struggles, and the protest against the rise in bus and tram fare. In the world beyond our shores, the Vietnam war was being fought. All this became a part of our discussion, helping to form our political consciousness.

Each of the ideas of struggle or change I encountered had its counterpart in the world of books. I read about socialism in George Bernard Shaw's works as I saw the students' struggle unfold in Bengal. Again, the Paris upsurge was not just a local phenomenon but had a worldwide impact. So did the civil rights movement in the US and the global (as well as Indian) anti-war movement focussed on Vietnam. If I think of what led to my becoming politicised, consciously political, I can trace it back to all of these three currents — the personal, the social and the political.

In BE College, rules about attendance were not really enforced as long as we submitted all our tutorial papers. I took advantage of this and did not attend college most of the time. I submitted my tutorials, spent a mere month preparing for the final exams, and

Learning to Fight

passed them — obviously with pretty mediocre results. I guess it was a wonder that I passed at all.

So, apart from not attending class or studying, what was I doing? I would get into flaming arguments with my friends on the left as well as the right. I loved to argue, and for a long time, I thought of myself as a contrarian. But I was also trying to find out for myself what politics was, and what the churning I saw around me was all about.

Books continued to exert a powerful influence, Bernard Shaw's books, for example. Shaw's *Arms and the Man* was the English text in my second year, and I fell in love with his writing. I loved his wit, his debunking of the 'heroic' and the 'romantic', and his humanism. Shaw made me understand why I did not enjoy the more romantic Bengali books, and why I preferred Rabindranath's *Gora* to his *Shesher Kobita*, and Sarat Chandra to Bankim Chandra. My father had government quarters in Belvedere Estate, which also housed the National Library. I still remember a summer vacation spent sitting there, devouring the two fat volumes of Shaw's collected prefaces and plays.

My friends and I were still navigating politics in an undecided way. We were certainly not rightwing, but we didn't really know where we were going. Because I loved Shaw, for a while I thought I was a Shavian socialist. But I was not very sure of that either.

There was much happening in the background, of course. In 1967, the Congress dismissed the United Front coalition government of West Bengal — in which the left was the driving force. Calcutta's streets exploded. Then, the Vietnam war brought students to the streets everywhere, including Calcutta, where they demonstrated before the USIS building. The war was in the papers every day. In my usual way, I headed to the National Library where I came across the wonderful books of the Australian journalist, Wilfred Burchett, who had spent a lot of time in South East Asia.[1]

---

[1] Burchett (1911–83) was the first news reporter to write about the dropping of the atomic bomb on Hiroshima. His report titled 'Atomic Plague' was

Books like his gave me a clearer understanding of what the Vietnam war was about, and how imperialism and colonialism were very much a part of the present.

My friends also played a role in my transition to politics at this time. Some of my friends were already close to the CPI(M) and the Students Federation, at that time the Bengal Provincial Students Federation (BPSF). The Federation had split in two — one section was with the CPI(M), and the other with the CPI. The key person for me was Ashim Ganguly, a close friend, and he was the first among us to identify himself with the CPI(M). (He was killed by Naxalites near his house in December 1970 during the internecine battle that divided the left in Bengal.)

There was no BPSF unit in my college which, till then, had been largely apolitical. Even though the student movement in Calcutta and West Bengal was strong, the engineering colleges remained more or less apolitical. Some of the students who were politicised before us had set up leftist study groups in the campus. But they had a low opinion of students in engineering colleges: we were careerists who could not be politicised. Ashim Ganguly thought differently — he didn't see why engineering students could not be politicised.

Apart from the general ferment, which affected all of us, this was a period of industrial recession; engineers were not getting jobs. Earlier, the middle class had considered two professions safe — medicine or engineering — with lifelong earnings or job guarantees. This would change during the mid-sixties, and it made our generation more willing to take to politics.

---

the first to break the Western media's silence about the effect of the atomic bomb, and drew a worldwide response.
https://assets.cambridge.org/97805217/18264/excerpt/9780521718264_excerpt.pdf from *Rebel Journalism, The Writings of Wilfred Burchett.*

Learning to Fight

Ashim influenced our entire group. His conviction attracted us; unlike the rest of us, he seemed to know what he wanted to do. Most of my close friends were attracted, over a period of time, to the CPI(M), but I was still unsure. Once again, books helped me cover the final lap. At the Annual College Reunion in December 1969 — this was a big event every year — I found a bookstall of Marxist literature. I bought the *Selected Works of Marx and Engels*, from Progress Publishers and sold unbelievably cheap.

I was bowled over, excited by the language and clarity of Marx: I still remember this. *The Communist Manifesto*, one of the first pieces I read, was one long gooseflesh moment. Here was the answer to all the things I was thinking about. It was not rhetoric; it was not bleeding-heart liberal romanticism. There was passion and power in the writing, but it explained its themes within a logical framework. It was the framing of the problem, the *intellectual* framing of the problem, that drew me first to Shaw and, in this instance, to Marx's writing. The transition was almost immediate.

This was also the time of the Naxalite movement, especially among the students. There was a great deal of romanticisation of the Naxalites, more so in Bengal. Bengal has a history of romanticising the armed struggle or, as it was called then, terrorist movement. Individual heroism appealed to the middle-class Bengali mind. And it drew the middle-class youth and students towards Naxalism. But I was never attracted to the theory of revolutionary violence. I decided from the beginning that if you want a revolution, if you are talking of revolutionary politics, you need mass politics. I was completely convinced that only mass politics can change society. Yes, force is an instrument of change, especially when people are compelled by the violence of the ruling classes to resort to force. This is what happened in many colonies — the French, Belgians, and even the British, didn't leave till people took up arms against them.

When Marx writes about the role of force in history, he does not necessarily refer to violence. He is talking about the coercive power of the state, and the coercive power of the oppressed classes when faced with violence. Force is the larger coercive power, whether of the state or of the masses — of which the direct physical manifestation is only one form. That is the concept of force as an instrument of change that Marx refers to when he speaks of its role in history. A very simplistic understanding of force, equating it with violence, is shared by many on the left who believe in armed struggle as the only revolutionary path. I am sceptical of individual violence calling itself revolutionary or a transformative use of force. I have always believed that a Marxist should be concerned with mass movements rather than with individual heroes.

Interestingly, this issue of the romantic revolutionary versus mass politics has an earlier history in Bengal. In Sarat Chandra's *Pather Dabi* (published in 1926 after being serialised), Sabyasachi, the key character (and almost a superhero), believes in armed struggle but not mass politics. He asks the poet to write for the middle class he belongs to, and not for peasants and workers. Sabyasachi phrases this in terms of authenticity: the song of the plough (*langal* in Bangla) can only be written by the peasants. This may appear to be Sarat Chandra's poetic attempt to explain the authenticity of language or creativity. But it takes on a different meaning when we consider it as a critique of the communist poet Nazrul Islam, who had just set up the literary magazine *Langal*.

Sarat Chandra's sympathies were with the armed struggle against the British, but he clearly believed in the middle-class hero as the driver of history. He thought of the middle class as the vanguard, and he was as contemptuous of worker-peasant struggles as he was of the non-violent, Gandhian mass struggles.[2]

---

[2] It is interesting that Sarat Chandra parallels Tolstoy on this. In *Resurrection* Tolstoy described the populists (Narodniki) with warm sympathy, but Kondratyev, the worker who reads Marx, is treated with ironic condescension. See Stefan Morawski, 'Lenin as a Literary Theorist', *Science and Society* 29.1 (Winter 1965): pp. 2–25.
https://monoskop.org/images/9/97/Morawski_Stefan_1965_Lenin_as_a_Literary_Theorist.pdf

Learning to Fight

The possibility of a mass struggle which could evolve into armed resistance was effaced, or missing, in Sarat Chandra's world. So was the agency of the oppressed classes.

I did not really grow up in Bengal; maybe this is one reason I was saved from being influenced by this kind of sentimental romanticism. Of course, we are discussing what happened almost a lifetime ago. I think I took my time to make the choice, but once I had made up my mind, I decided I was not going to agonise about it every day. You choose sides, not just a party. Graham Greene has a novel — *The Confidential Agent* (1939) — in which two Spanish professors meet in a pub in England during the Spanish Civil War. The professor who is on the Royalist/Franco side asks the other, the one with the left, 'Do you think your leaders are better than mine?' The left professor says, 'No, but I like the people they lead.' As far as I am concerned, the real question is about side of history you are on.

When did I actually make a commitment to the CPI(M)? My friends persuaded me to attend a CPI(M) meeting that took place in Bardhaman in 1970. This was after a series of clashes during the Kisan Sabha's land agitation in the sixties. The Kisan Sabha had issued a call to occupy surplus land and they had been attacked by landed interests. The rally and the meeting were held in a very charged atmosphere. It was a huge rally, and all the major state leaders were to speak: Jyoti Basu, the leader of the CPI(M) in the Assembly and also home minister in the second Ajoy Mukherjee ministry; Promode Dasgupta, the state secretary; and Hare Krishna Konar, the Kisan leader from Bardhaman, minister in charge of land revenue and reform, who had also become the general secretary of the All-India Kisan Sabha.

I remember I had a splitting headache that day, and couldn't really listen to the speeches. Then Hare Krishna Konar began to speak. He related class struggle on the ground in Bengal to the larger Marxist framework. Slowly, my headache disappeared. Comrade Konar explained that the movement had not only to abolish landlordism and give land to the tillers, but also change how people perceived themselves and their oppressors. All this he based on classical Marxist framing without lazy quote-mongering. For me, to hear the *Communist Manifesto* recreated in the backdrop of peasant struggles for land was a revelation.

I had already decided I was a Marxist before this rally, but I was not drawn to either the CPI or the Naxalites. I had recognised that the CPI(M) was the major Marxist current in the country, but had been unsure about whether I wanted to be in any party. I returned from Bardhaman completely convinced that if I was committed to mass politics, I should be in the CPI(M). Once I made that commitment, the question of where I wanted to be located politically was settled. It was settled for the rest of my life. This does not mean I do not re-examine my beliefs or the party's policies. But I have little patience with those who vacillate and worry about the 'right line' every time there is a political crisis. That is not a luxury we have. Of course, we do and should re-evaluate everything if there's a fundamental challenge. But otherwise, agonising at every instance can be debilitating. In the case of the middle class, it can use up their energy in fighting the movement rather than fighting the real enemy. Instead of engaging with the movement and helping it do better, they could end up becoming what I call left consultants: telling the left what they should do, rather than contesting the ideologues of the ruling classes.

My young friends ask me sometimes what sort of relationship we had with the Naxalites. The relationship between the CPI(M) and the Naxalite movement began with a basic political difference — about whether there was already a revolutionary situation in India in which people could take up arms and join the revolution if a vanguard gave the call. The tensions also have to be seen in the context of the Communist Party of China welcoming the Naxalbari

Learning to Fight

uprising as 'Spring Thunder Over India' (1967), and denouncing the CPI(M); and then, the bloody clash between the Soviet Union and China along the Ussuri River border in 1969. This clash led to the Communist Party of China deciding that the Soviet Union was not only revisionist, but also social-imperialist.

The differences turned to discord during my fifth year of college. The Naxalites in Bengal had by then formed the CPI(ML) under Charu Mazumdar. The students who were with the CPI(ML) decided to 'follow the cultural revolution model' and burn the books in the college library. We held a meeting, and marched against such an attack. Burning engineering books in the library had nothing to do with a cultural revolution and would only hurt students. It would not burn away what was called *apo sanskriti*, bad or decadent culture. This divided the college into two zones and triggered violence. An unfortunate period began when the two sides attacked each other, and we lost some very good comrades.

The Students Federation of India (SFI) had not yet been formed. The student movement close to the CPI(M) was still called BPSF. My friends and I had thought about setting up a students' organisation in the engineering institutions, as the students there were still relatively apolitical, and we thought they might not accept a left students' organisation. Unfortunately, the campus became polarised after the attack on the college library and the subsequent violence. We were identified as CPI(M), while the other side was the Charu Mazumdar-led CPI(ML).

Once we opposed the burning of the college library and identified with the CPI(M), we became class enemies — the Charu Mazumdar line of annihilation of class enemies ensured that we, too, got included in the list. The Naxalites put up posters against five people who were going to be killed, including me. Ashim Ganguly, the person who drew me to the party, was killed close to his house in December 1970. Another close friend was stabbed in both lungs very close to his hostel. He survived, but with seriously impaired lung function for the rest of his life.

Our campus — it was a large one — got divided into two areas: one side belonged to the CPI(M) supporters, the other to the Maoist supporters. This was a dark chapter in our history. In the long term, it damaged both sides, leaving psychological scars. We lost Ashim Ganguly; we marked his fiftieth martyrdom day on December 20, 2020. He wanted to work as a whole-timer in the party after college. Had that happened, he would certainly have been one of the leaders of the party today in Bengal.

Looking back, what makes this a tragedy for the left is that both sides were caught in a violent spiral while subscribing to the same goals. There were losses on both sides. We still carry an unfortunate legacy from this internecine battle of the left. While it is true that we were attacked, could we have handled it better? In retrospect, probably yes. But remember, like the Charu Mazumdar acolytes in college, we, too, were very young.

This division also ruptured the unity we had built among the workers on the campus, the other employees, and a section of progressive teachers and students. The rupture between the two left sections on the campus meant that the larger unity we had hoped to build now faced a new faultline. Interestingly, during the memorial meetings held at BE College on the fiftieth anniversary of Ashim Ganguly's death, the mess workers, as well as the left students, participated, cutting across all left identities. Hopefully, this is a sign that old divisions are healing at a time when new dangers loom before us.

The state of sharp hostilities lasted till about 1972. In 1971, the CPI(M) won half the parliamentary seats in Bengal. The Congress did not want the CPI(M)-led left alliance to win in the 1972 Assembly elections. The Bengal Assembly elections were rigged, and the Congress came back to power. It then smashed the Maoists physically. (Earlier, the Congress had been happy to see the left forces fight each other.) Post the 1972 elections, the government under Chief Minister Siddhartha Shankar Ray not only unleashed a reign of terror and smashed the Naxalite movement, it also attempted to do the same with the CPI(M). A large number of people had to leave their houses and their areas during this time — what Ashok Mitra called the hoodlum years. Priyaranjan Dasmunshi, leader of the Youth Congress, and Subroto Mukherjee, leader of the Chhatra Parishad, emerged as the key figures of the hoodlum years, and these two formations, the Youth Congress and the Chhatra Parishad, made up the strong-arm of the Congress, backed by the state government. Mamata Banerjee also emerged at that time, though she was, of course, a much younger figure. I recall a picture of her dancing on Jayaprakash Narayan's car when JP had come to Calcutta.[3] Her propensity for a certain kind of politics was evident even in the early years. This was the kind of politics the Congress introduced in Bengal for the next five years till it lost the 1977 elections. For those interested in the history of the Emergency, its declaration was drafted by Siddhartha Shankar Ray, the chief minister of West Bengal, who was also a lawyer. The unofficial emergency in Bengal under Siddhartha Shankar Ray was a good dress rehearsal for Mrs Gandhi's 1975 Emergency — and this included the role of Sanjay Gandhi's Youth Congress hoodlums.

To get back to the early days of my own political journey. As I said, the international scenario had played a major role in this process. Students all over the world were marching in the streets against the Vietnam war. I have mentioned how much I learnt from Wilfred Burchett's books on the US war against the Vietnamese people. The slogans we shouted as we marched still ring in my ears. One was 'Ho Ho Ho Chi Minh, We shall fight, We shall win!' Also 'Amar Naam, Tomar Naam, Vietnam, Vietnam!' Of course, we didn't have too many symbols of US imperialism in Calcutta, so

---

[3] https://www.bengaldaily.com/when-mamata-danced-to-mrs-gandhis-tune-on-the-top-of-jayaprakash-narayans-car/

we took our protest to the USIS, or the United States Information Service — not the most impressive outpost of imperialism.

When we talk about the international scenario then, the first thing that comes to mind is the intellectual ferment of the time — students in Paris occupying the campuses in 1968, and later the anti-war movement in the US and worldwide. In India, there was a struggle for land, and this is what fuelled the Naxalite movement. The movement had an immediate resonance among the tribal communities, since they were losing land even faster than the others.

We must also remember the different political formulations that existed among the youth in different countries. There was the Rote Armee Fraktion (Red Army Faction) in West Germany, called Baader-Meinhof by its critics and a hostile media; and the Red Brigade in Italy who kidnapped Prime Minister Aldo Moro. (We now know that the CIA played a significant role in abetting and funding agents provocateurs and rightwing violence to discredit the left.[4]) There was also a much broader development of different kinds of left movements, such as the Autonomia movement in

---

[4] General Gianadelio Maletti, a former head of military counter-intelligence during the 1970s, made a statement in court in March 2001 about the role of the CIA in promoting rightwing terrorism in Italy. One example is that of Gianfranco Bertoli, a supposed anarchist, hurling a bomb in Milan, killing 4 and injuring 45, in 1973.
https://www.theguardian.com/world/2001/mar/26/terrorism
Bertoli was part of a rightwing group and a long-standing Italian Defence Intelligence (SID) informant. He had informed his handlers in SID of what he planned to do. There is also the infamous Gladio project, in which the US agencies had people, caches of arms and ammunition all over Western Europe. The links still remain opaque, between Operation Gladio, the CIA-backed secret groups with arms caches in their countries, and such agents provocateurs working with the CIA and various intelligence agencies of Italy, Germany, France, etc. In the trial of the right-wing extremists, General Maletti stated, 'Among the larger West European countries, Italy has been dealt with as a sort of protectorate. I am ashamed to think that we are still subject to special supervision.'
https://www.theguardian.com/world/2001/mar/26/terrorism

Learning to Fight

Italy, the Weathermen, and the Black Panthers in the US.[5] Their imprint, so to speak, remained long after they were physically weakened or decimated. The exposure of Cointelpro,[6] the FBI's operation to plant informers and agents provocateurs to carry out 'executions' of Panther leaders, was exposed after a radical group[7] broke into the FBI's media office in Pennsylvania and took a set of secret documents which they posted to newspapers. Cointelpro, a program set up by FBI head J. Edgar Hoover, targeted not only communists and radical groups, but also peace and civil rights activists — such as Paul Robeson and Martin Luther King. The fallout from the FBI's break-in finally led to the exposure of Cointelpro. (In 2010, I interviewed Bernardine Dohrn, one of the leaders of the Weathermen, and her adopted son Chesa Boudin, for NewsClick.[8] Chesa's birth parents were also in the Weather Underground and serving life sentences.[9] He was till recently the district attorney of San Francisco.)

The Vietnam war was a defining moment for my generation. Everyone came together to respond to this brutal and visible symbol of US imperialism. The US had inherited the mantle of France, the ex-colonial power in Vietnam. The war was, in effect, a continuation of the colonial war. People in the West did not easily

---

[5] The name Weathermen is from a 16,000-word manifesto issued in 1969 by the Students for a Democratic Society (SDS), titled 'You Don't Need a Weatherman to Know Which Way the Wind Blows'.

[6] Ward Churchill and Jim Vander Wall, *The COINTELPRO Papers: Documents from the FBI's Secret Wars Against Domestic Dissent*, South End Press, originally 1990.

[7] Who had carried out this audacious break-in at the FBI office in 1971 became known only in 2015, with the release of the documentary film *1971* (now available on Netflix).
https://www.zinnedproject.org/news/tdih/cointelpro-exposed/
They included a cab driver, a daycare provider, two professors, a homemaker and three others.

[8] See the NewsClick video, Prof Bernardine Dohrn on Obama's Policies.
https://www.newsclick.in/articles/Bernardine%20Dohrn

[9] His mother, Kathy Boudin (d. 2022) was released on parole in 2003, but his father, David Gilbert, remained a prisoner till late 2021, when he was finally given parole.

understand why so many newly liberated countries supported a communist Vietnam despite their talk of non-alignment and irrespective of their relationship with the socialist bloc. For these countries, including India, it was not a fight between Russia plus China versus the US and the colonial powers, France and the UK. What we saw was the freedom struggle of the Vietnamese people, first against the French; and, after the French lost in Dien Bien Phu (1954), against the US. Even sections of the left in the West did not understand that non-alignment was not simply a question of saying 'A plague on both your houses', but was about decolonisation.

Vietnam was a powerful symbol of resistance. The completely unequal struggle of the Vietnamese people against the biggest military power in the world was truly inspiring. The Vietnamese peasantry was heroic, armed with just spades to dig tunnels, and, at best, AK-47s, against the air and firepower of the US. This was not the story of a few heroes, but of the Vietnamese peasantry and the support that the liberation struggle enjoyed among the people. Reading Wilfred Burchett on Vietnam made me understand the context of the liberation struggle there, and the much larger geopolitical picture of the world. It was also a strong antidote to the Eurocentric vision of sections of the international left who frame the history of the world as essentially a history of the West, one in which other countries and continents enter history only upon their encounter with the West.

I graduated from college in 1970 and worked at various jobs in and around Calcutta. I worked in Hind Motors, the factory where the Ambassador car was manufactured. The Ambassador, the Fiat Premier Padmini and the Standard Herald were pretty much the only three cars on the Indian roads those days. I was on the shop floor, the section that dealt with machining gears.

Though I did not learn any engineering there, I did get my

first lessons in the sociology of the shop floor. The first lesson was that I was not there because I knew something about either gears or their machining — the machines were quite sophisticated and there was no way an engineer fresh out of college was going to figure them out. Another engineer, who was the 'shift-in-charge', explained that our role was not engineering but managing. We were there to 'manage' the workers. The second lesson was that the workers knew much more about machining gears than we did or could, but this was not to be revealed or we would lose control. We had to pretend we knew it all. I guess it worked — when I asked a worker what he thought about our shift-in-charge, he said he must be knowledgeable even though he didn't say anything.

We also learnt about caste in practice on the shop floor. The machines and the drawings were in English, as the Ambassador was really an Oxford 14, manufactured by Morris Motors. Having bought the designs and the machines required for manufacture, Hindustan Motors reproduced the designs in its cars. This meant the workers had to read the drawings and understand the various knobs and buttons on the machines, all labelled in English. So, the 'skilled' workers on the shop floor were those who could read English, not those who had the necessary manual skills.

The terrible injustice of the caste system makes sure that those who create new artefacts and new knowledge, those who innovate using both hand and mind, are not considered skilled workers in our factories. Instead, workers and engineers who are educated (or have learnt by rote), are labelled as skilled workers because they can read drawings and instructions in English. Those who can develop new tools or machines have never been taught the theory behind the working of the machines. Those who learn this theory despise working with their hands. This is the tragedy of the Indian factory floor: those who work with their hands, those who are innovative, are 'unskilled workers' because of their literacy level. The skilled workers or engineers have learned theory but have no history of working with their hands.

What, then, does skilled labour do in an automated factory? Skilled labour can press the buttons and follow the instructions, because skills have been transferred to the machine. The workers are no longer required to have skills — that is the job of automation. Retrospectively I understand what Marx is saying in *Das Kapital*, when he talks about the development from manufacture to machino-facture, and the role of automation in the textile industry in England. My own short stint on the floor gave me an insight into the nature of the factory, the nature of work, and the relationship among the caste hierarchies that exist in India — how it manifests itself on the factory floor.

The other side of India's industrialisation was that manual skills, and design and engineering skills, were not required if all you did was reproduce the same car over and over again, with virtually no change. This is what Hindustan Motors under the Birlas did, from 1956 to 2014. This is one of the problems of monopoly, when self-reliance comes to be understood simply as import substitution. Import substitution can be the first step. But how do you become self-reliant without developing the technology to produce the next generation of equipment and goods? In this case, cars. Tata Motors[10] achieved this in the sphere of trucks and buses, as Bajaj Autos did for two-wheelers. That is why they still exist while Hindustan Motors (shortened to Hind Motors) does not.

I also learned a political lesson in Hind Motors. I was talking to a worker, who was, I think, from Tamil Nadu. He explained to me, 'You know, in my part of the country, they give you money and they ask you to vote for the party. Here, the CPI(M) asks for money and asks you to vote for the party.' He found this ethos most peculiar, as his experience had always been that politics meant trading votes for money.

---

[10] Earlier known as TELCO, it had an Engineering Research Centre, a Machine Tool and a Press Tool Division which allowed it to build the next generation of its trucks and later its cars. Something that Hindustan Motors could never do in its entire period of existence, beyond executing minor tweaks.

Learning to Fight

In 1971, while I was working for Hind Motors in Uttarpara, my father, who was in the Central Excise & Customs, was attacked in the Customs House and stabbed. A union close to the Naxalites was involved. I was staying near the Hind Motors factory as a tenant. My landlord was also in Hind Motors. On his way to office, he saw the news item about a senior customs officer being stabbed. The name Purkayastha was enough for him to conclude it had to be my father. He came back to the house, and without saying why told me we had to go to Calcutta to my parents. He told me why only when we were on our way there. Fortunately, my father's wound did not have any long-term effect.

By that time, I was quite fed up with a job where I was supposed to 'manage' people, with no development of knowledge or skills. I left Hind Motors to join a company in Howrah that made switch-gears. It was a small factory. Initially, I was in maintenance, and all at sea since I knew very little about the machines I was supposed to maintain. I had an assistant who was equally clueless. If anything went wrong, we would open up the machine, and if we could not spot anything obviously wrong, we would put it back together, hoping it would now work. Sometimes it did, and sometimes it didn't. If it didn't, we would open it up again to try and figure out what to do next.

Despite myself, I learnt some lessons as an engineer that have stayed with me. I remember a machine with a broken belt, for which I went to a market where belts were sold, but couldn't get a belt of the same size. I came back and told the chief engineer in charge of the factory that nothing could be done because a belt of the correct size was not available. He replied that he didn't need an engineer to tell him that. He needed an engineer who could work out what to do when only a belt of the wrong size was available. This was not something we were taught in college — that we are actually supposed to find ways to solve problems and not just go by the book.

I also learnt what experience is. In engineering, great value is placed on the number of years of experience you bring. It is assumed that if you have the experience, you have also learned something new, so the experience is equivalent to an additional acquisition of knowledge. Debunking this, one of our senior colleagues told us: 'The question is not whether you have ten years of experience as an engineer. The question is whether it is the same two years of experience five times over, or really ten years of experience.' Again, this is something that has stuck in my mind. Am I learning anything new, or only repeating what I already know?

But all this wisdom came later. At the time, I was fired. But I was quite happy to be fired. My father had been transferred to Kanpur after his stabbing and I was staying in a rented place after my parents left Calcutta. I stayed on another three months but found it hard to carry on without an income. I shifted to Kanpur for a while.

I came across the party in Kanpur, and got to know the textile workers' unions, and even helped form a union in a small manufacturing unit. I also came to know Subhashini Sahgal (now Ali), and a very charismatic trade union leader, Comrade Ram Asrey (Yadav), who was the district committee secretary of the CPI(M).[11]

This was my first brush with inner party issues. In Calcutta, we admired our leaders or spoke of them — Jyoti Basu, Hare Krishna Konar, Promode Dasgupta, Niren Ghosh, and many others — but we did not know them personally. Our Howrah district secretary was Naresh Dasgupta, who took our classes initially, and our local committee secretary was Dipak Dasgupta, who is now a member

---

[11] Subhashini Ali, 'What it Was Like to Be a Young Communist and Trade Unionist in 1971 Kanpur', *The Wire*, March 19, 2021.
https://thewire.in/history/what-it-was-like-to-be-a-young-communist-and-trade-unionist-in-1971-kanpur

of the state secretariat in Bengal. We knew Biman Basu, who had looked after the BE College unit as the leader of the BPSF. But our view of the party leadership was quite distant. There were many layers between the leadership of the party and those of us who had just joined the party and the movement.

In UP, the party was much smaller. Even though we were young, we interacted with the state leadership. That meant we got to see up-close both personal and ideological inner-party differences. From the outside, a part of this appeared as differences between B.T. Ranadive, president of the Centre of Indian Trade Unions (CITU), and P. Sundarayya, general secretary of the party. In his letter giving up the general secretaryship, Sundarayya referred to Kanpur and its party factionalism. He and Ranadive had differences about how the party should develop. They also differed on the role of the working class and the peasantry. Some of these differences were older, dating back to the fifties. Comrades Ranadive and Sundarayya had very different visions of the Indian revolution. They were both revolutionaries, but neither realised that several others in the party were not really looking at revolution the way they were, but were far more concerned with their position in the party. A section of the leadership in UP used the ideological differences of the leadership at the top to maintain bureaucratic control over the UP party at the expense of the mass leaders the party had in UP.

As somebody completely unaware of deeper divisions, I had a somewhat different take on the Kanpur situation. I saw a mass leader in Comrade Ram Asrey, an undisputed leader of the Kanpur workers. I also saw some lesser leaders trying to sideline him. Subhashini, not much older than me, was already a mass leader of the workers. Comrade Asrey died during a long strike of the Kanpur jute workers.[12] Still, inner party differences resulted in some disciplinary action against various associates of Comrade

---

[12] Ibid.

Asrey. I was virtually unknown to the UP leadership; even so, I too was subject to disciplinary action. It took me a while to get back into the good graces of the party. But I never considered myself out of the party. I was not going to break with the party or become a bitter ex-communist like some who found themselves at the wrong or receiving end of inner-party differences.

When I look back on my Kanpur days, I see how much I learnt. It is not enough to agree with somebody's politics; we have to also see what role he or she is playing in the larger movement. In other words, I go back to a central issue in my life, the key determinant to judge a person: Which side of the larger class struggle are they on? Though I have strong views on political issues, I have never had a problem working with people who may not agree with my politics. This would prove important later, particularly in the science movement or the free software movement, where the sections working together were even more heterogeneous than the UP party!

I made some good friends in Kanpur. Subhashini and I became close, partly because we read *Social Scientist* and similar literature and had many questions. I met Subhashini's parents — Captain Lakshmi Sahgal and Colonel Prem Sahgal, names out of the history books as far as I was concerned.[13] In Bengal, Captain Lakshmi and Colonel Prem Sahgal were names to conjure with, given their association with Netaji Subhas Chandra Bose. To meet the two legendary figures in person should have been an inspiring moment for me. But I was too overawed to make much of the meeting. Much later, when I met Captain Lakshmi in Delhi, she

---

[13] Lakshmi Sahgal (née Swaminathan; 1914–2012), a doctor by training, formed the Rani of Jhansi Regiment of the INA and was taken prisoner in Burma in 1945. In 1971, she joined the CPI(M) and represented the party in the Rajya Sabha. She practised medicine into her nineties and was also, in 2002, fielded jointly by the left parties as their candidate for the presidency of India. Prem Kumar Sahgal (1917–92) was commissioned into the Indian Army in 1939. Captured by the Japanese in Malaya in 1942, he joined Bose's INA. Following the surrender in Burma in 1945, he faced trial for treason; the charge was not upheld. In 1947, he married Captain Lakshmi Sahgal.

gently chided me for not coming to see her in so many years. That's how she was — accessible to all in the clinic she set up in Kanpur after her INA days.[14] Captain Lakshmi was an inspiration to us all in so many ways. (I often recalled her humility when I met those who seemed to think a short stint in jail during the 1975 Emergency gave them a halo for the rest of their lives.)

In Kanpur, I also came to know Daulat Ram, Devsena (Comrade Ram Asrey's daughter), both youth leaders then, and Arvind Kumar, who was already the general secretary of the workers union of Indian Explosives Limited (IEL), a fertiliser plant with Imperial Chemicals. Daulat Ram passed away in 2014 after a life of struggle. I also frequented the Kanpur Book Depot, run by Comrade Khaitan and Dhaniya Guru, the only place in the city where we could find leftist literature.

Apart from the Book Depot and the party office, the other place I frequented in Kanpur was the IIT campus. One of my brother's close friends, Ashok Mallik, taught there.[15] I found a small BE College group over there among the faculty. I also came to know a group of leftist students, particularly among the research scholars who had been influenced by Professor A.P. Shukla.[16] At the time, I was unaware of postmodernism, or its offshoot, the Ashis Nandy kind of nativist view of knowledge. I remember the discussions we had, not only on politics, but also the philosophy of science, with people like Jayanta Bandyopadhyay and R. Sadananda.[17] Sadananda later helped me join the Computer Science Department in JNU, after I got admission in the Science Policy Department there.

[14] Indian National Army formed by nationalists in 1942 under Subhas Chandra Bose.
[15] https://iitk.ac.in/dora/profile/Prof-A-K-Mallik
[16] Professor Shukla taught physics in IIT Kanpur. He was also active in labour movements and in the people's science movement.
[17] Jayanta Bandyopadhyay took his doctorate in engineering from IIT Kanpur. He was subsequently closely associated with research on science, environment and economy in the mountains. Dr Sadananda did his PhD in electrical engineering from IIT Kanpur.

Later on, some of the Kanpur group would join hands with persons like Dharampal, a Gandhian turned nativist, who argued that the caste system was not discriminatory and had held India together. It was only the British, according to Dharampal, who gave caste the hierarchic structure it has attained today. Both sets agreed on the need to replace 'Western science' with Indian science, and formed the Patriotic and People-oriented Science & Technology (PPST) group, with Dharampal as its founding president. Dharampal later went on to justify the demolition of the Babri Masjid.

Remembering my encounter with the Kanpur group brings to mind a recurring fundamental question I have had, especially when I was younger: Should I abandon science and technology and become a full-time activist? Or could I reconcile my passions somehow? I had yet to become passionate about technology; but I was already deeply interested in science. Discussions in the Kanpur group strengthened my interest in the philosophy and history of science. I was always interested in history, but till then saw science and history as two non-intersecting disciplines. Sadananda gave me a short introduction one evening to Gödel's theorems and Russell's paradox, and I realised that philosophy has to continuously address advances in other disciplines. The philosophy of science is intimately related to the history of science, despite the current fashion to purge it of its historical roots.

There was an amusing consequence of my ignorance of many things. I had always been interested in libraries, and spent a lot of time in the library when I visited IIT Kanpur. I found a book by Noam Chomsky to my delight — I knew of him as an important radical voice against the Vietnam war. I plodded through the book, waiting for the good parts, his radical politics. Finally, I realised the book was on linguistics, and learned that he was the world's foremost figure in the field. At any rate, I picked up a smattering of linguistics, having understood that what Chomsky

Learning to Fight

means by grammar is very different from the deathly boring rules of grammar we learnt from Nesfield.[18]

The other incident I remember was a conference that IIT Kanpur had organised on science and technology. This was an initiative of the radical students and a few of the faculty there. I had come from Allahabad with Alok Rai who was teaching at Allahabad University in the English department. Apart from philosophy, he and I also shared an interest in pulp fiction. He introduced me to the very superior pulp-spy thrillers of Len Deighton, who, unlike John Le Carré, deals with class in the UK and its role in the spy agencies. I spent a lot of time arguing with the Kanpur 'school' who considered the laws of science entirely subjective, and a part of our false consciousness. Alok, who was much more well-read and aware than I was, made me think of what ideology as false consciousness is; that false consciousness is not false in the trivial sense, but false by way of having a distorted or inverted relationship with reality.

Perhaps the highlight of my Kanpur group encounter was an attack by leftist students on Professor Amulya Reddy. The professor had made an appropriate-technology model — a model gobar gas unit. He explained how such plants would make a huge difference by providing energy, fertiliser, and by monetising gobar for the peasantry. I was not too taken with his appropriate-technology model. But a part of his response to the students' attack still resonates in my mind. He said, 'When I was doing basic research, I was attacked for not doing anything useful for the people. When I worked on improving the battery technology in my laboratory, I was told I am only helping capital with such advances. Now I am trying to help the people, and you tell me that this is reformism.[19] As an electrochemist, what should I do?

---

[18] John Nesfield's *English Grammar: Past and Present* (1898) was written for the market in colonial India, where he worked as an educator — at the Presidency College and the Benares College, among other places.

[19] I am told by my editors that the word 'reformist' is not so clear to readers today.

I am not going to make the revolution, so are you telling me that as a scientist/technologist, I have no role in social transformation through my work?' (I am quoting from memory, admittedly an old one.) That encapsulated for me the question I had been grappling with: Are politics and technology mutually exclusive? And is there a way of being involved with both?

The Kanpur interlude ended in 1973 when I joined the mechanical engineering department at Motilal Nehru Regional Engineering College, a part of Allahabad University, for my Master's.

Obviously, Kanpur and Allahabad were both very different in terms of student movements, compared to Bengal and Calcutta. I was not a complete outsider to Allahabad, having gone to school there. But that was very different from the engineering college environment. I had some advantages as a Master's student. In the highly hierarchical atmosphere of engineering colleges, I earned automatic respect as a 'senior'. But it was all very different, especially in two important ways. One was the social and political sophistication of the students. I do not mean it in the sense of political theory or the understanding of society, but the sheer skill with which people can hide their feelings, or how they can manipulate people without seeming to. I later understood this comes from generations of manipulative politics created by a hierarchic caste system, where numerically small 'upper' caste communities dominate by dividing and manipulating others.

The second way in which it was different was the sheer muscle power involved in student politics, with landed families sending

> In our time, it meant somebody who thought that incremental changes could lead to a fundamental change in society. Others who identified themselves as revolutionaries believed that the path to a fundamental change meant a sharp break with the current system. Violence and non-violence were the other elements in this discussion, but I believed, as I have stated earlier, that the role of force in society was not summed up by violent revolution but required a wider discussion on what coercive force is. So, reform versus revolution in my dictionary is not to be confused with a violent overthrow of the state but connects to fundamental changes in society.

Learning to Fight

their children for a BA degree before getting into some government service or the other, or coming back to the village to rule over their lands. In our times, the Thakurs dominated strong-arm student politics, with the Yadavs still way behind in contests for power. The Brahmins and Kayasthas were also present in student politics, but the Thakurs were the dominant force — they had the most muscle power. The Dalit students were still to emerge as a political force in the campuses, and even their hostel — Iswar Sharan Hostel — was, unlike other hostels, located some distance away from the university campus.

Frankly, this was my first close encounter with caste and politics. The only earlier encounters had been at home, where the caste hierarchy was implicit when arranged marriages were discussed, or when caste discrimination was made out to be a 'hygiene' issue, the seamless integration of the modern 'scientific outlook' with age-old caste oppression. We were still unaware that 'chhotolok' and 'bhadralok' was as much about caste as about being 'genteel' and distinct from the 'lower' classes. That evolution of understanding had yet to happen for me. But UP student politics served as my first encounter with social power and caste politics, shorn of any cover, with the muscle power of the dominant castes clearly visible.

The second culture shock for me was the extent of social division in the engineering college, in terms of region. The students from Western UP and Punjab (at that time including Haryana) made one group, and those from Eastern UP and Bihar another. This was not friendly rivalry. It was a physical battle about who would control the college; the battle would periodically erupt in violent fights that involved the use of firearms. Fortunately, the firing did not lead to deaths. I knew the political violence of student politics first-hand, and was not surprised by the violence so much as by its apparently shallow basis. Today, I guess I would ascribe it to language, culture and caste differences in North India. In UP and Bihar, Hindi seems to have subsumed older languages whose cultural identities persisted. Another factor was a difference in terms of caste and land holdings — in Punjab and Western UP, land was with the Jats, while in Eastern UP and Bihar it was with the Thakurs and the Bhumihars. Unlike other hostels in Allahabad, the Thakurs here had to contend with the physical nature of Jat politics. It was a contest in student politics between two sets of 'bahubalis' (or 'strongmen') who dominated their sides of the region.

Student politics in Allahabad University included various political streams: the left, the Congress, ABVP, and the socialists. There was a strong ABVP unit on the campus backed by members of the science faculty — including Murli Manohar Joshi, who was a professor in the physics department. The Naxalite movement had some influence as well, as did the SFI. Among the socialists, the Samajvadi Yuvajan Sabha (SYS) was a major force. The Congress had a diffuse political base and was mainly organised by recruiting the bahubalis into Youth Congress politics. They inculcated a direct patronage relationship, with Hemwati Nandan Bahuguna already their chief patron at the time.

Somewhat to my surprise, I found an SFI unit in the engineering college, built up by a Bengali student, A.K. Roy (no relation of the legendary trade union leader of Dhanbad). At one point he had been able to build a group that included both sides of the regional divide, but it collapsed soon after another of their gun battles in college. Though he had graduated, he still stayed on campus. He had a long unkempt beard and looked almost like a baba. Over time, I discovered that though the students held him in high esteem as someone idealistic and completely different from them, they also thought he had no clue about the 'real world'. Their real world comprised groups based on caste and regional alliances. I realised soon enough that the SFI members' primary loyalty was not to the SFI, but to their regional alliances. That, to them, meant survival.

I decided that instead of the engineering college, I would involve myself with the politics of Allahabad University. I found a set of friends from the university that included Ashish Bannerjee, a student in the English department.[20] His father was an old communist and quite happy to see his son turn to the left. We had a small group which discussed everything from philosophy to politics. Through Ashish, I came to know Alok Rai, who had then come back from the UK to teach in the English department at the university.[21] There was also Harish Pandey, the only SFI activist in the campus, as the earlier unit had disintegrated amid the factional politics of the party unit in Allahabad. The party unit was extremely weak; a major section had left the party in 1968–69 and joined the Naxalites. Many of them came back, but that was later, after I had left Allahabad. The only other known CPI(M) figure who was politically active in Allahabad was Hariram Pandey, who led a militant kisan struggle in Meja, a tehsil of the Allahabad district. But I did not know him, since my activities were more or less limited to the university and my college.

Meanwhile, a big issue came up in the engineering college which I had more or less abandoned, politically. The students got into a clash with a major goonda figure outside the campus. There were cases filed against the students but none against the politically well-connected goonda. The students were hindered by their regional divide, and their two sets of leaders. Neither set — those from Bihar-Eastern UP or the Western UP-Punjab section — was willing to be led by the other. The college needed to be united to fight politically, and at least get the cases of the students dropped, if not action taken against the goonda. But where were they to find a neutral leader?

Both sides decided I was acceptable as this college leader. I was Bengali; I was a senior because I was in the Master's course; and I was seen as neutral between the two factions. I also had a political

---

[20] Later member-secretary at Indian National Trust for Art and Cultural Heritage, 1998–2002.
[21] Alok Rai is a highly respected writer and translator, author of books such as *Orwell and the Politics of Despair* and *Hindi Nationalism*. He also taught in the University of Delhi.

identity so they knew I could be trusted to fight the state. Suddenly I became the convenor of the engineering college. I created a short-term unity, and an action committee; I led delegations and got the cases withdrawn. I even stood before the entire college and gave a bhashan, the first time I spoke publicly. I was not a public speaker in those days, and used to be quite petrified of public speaking. I could take Marxist classes entirely in 'shudh Hindi'. Of course, being a Bengali helped, as the Sanskrit-based technical words in Hindi are often more commonplace in Bengali, which had been Sanskritised earlier.[22] This was my trial by fire as a student leader. But being a student leader in Allahabad was not easy, as the average age of leaders in Allahabad University was 30–35 years!

At that time, there was a group of poets and bright young students on the way towards an engagement with politics. This group included Devi Prasad Tripathi (DPT), Dinesh Kumar Shukla, Krishna Pratap Singh, Ramji Rai, Vibhuti Narayan Rai, and a few others.[23] Gorakh Pandey had considerable influence over them —

---

[22] Alok Rai in his book *Hindi Nationalism* (Tracts for the Times) identifies the Bengali diaspora in UP and Bihar as a force for the Sankritisation of Hindi, including the use of Devanagari (Nagari as the script instead of the more prevalent Kaithi). It is from Alok's book that I learned that in the Hindi heartland each caste — Brahmins, Kayasthas and Banias — had its script before Devanagari emerged as the common script for all.
http://inet.vidyasagar.ac.in:8080/jspui/bitstream/123456789/2052/1/6.pdf

[23] During his time at Allahabad University, Tripathi (1952–2020) had produced a literary journal called *Parivesh*. In 1973, he joined JNU to study political science. Fluent in six languages, Tripathi went on from student politics with the SFI to a Rajya Sabha membership.
https://thewire.in/politics/dp-tripathi-obituary
Starting from the journal *Parivesh*, where his poems appeared in 1972, Shukla (b. 1950) has published seven major collections of poetry, besides an edited volume and a translation from Pablo Neruda. He holds an MSc and DPhil in physics from Allahabad University.
https://www.facebook.com/dineshkumar.shukla.77
Krishna Pratap Singh joined the police and died in an anti-dacoity operation

apart from his politics, he was a very fine poet. Most of them went on to make their mark in various ways. They considered me well-read on Marxism. But they thought of me as purely shushk — a dry political animal. And in any case, the CPI(M) did not have the romantic halo of armed revolution.

One day, I began discussing the poet and Marxist critic Christopher Caudwell's writings on culture with them. I thought of Caudwell as an original thinker of depth. I admired his writing on how culture developed as an integral part of the productive activities of the people, and his engagement with the philosophy of physics and science. I had found his views on the origin of music — how music synchronises collective labour, emotions and artistic content — quite original within the larger framing of the materialist view of history.[24] For the budding poets, the view that labour is not just the subject of poetry but also its source, a starting point of poetry and music, was a revelation. It was completely different from that of the neo-romanticism or Chhayavaad of Hindi literature. They also discovered that I could (if necessary) talk about culture, and was not a total alien in their poetic territory. That created a different level of engagement with them.

Though the introduction to Marxism via cultural theory and Caudwell helped, some of them still had reservations. They accepted the critical vision of Marxism but said that they were really worried by revolution, or what they called the violence of Marxism. There were two or three of them with me that day when

---

soon after.
Ramji Rai is a member of the CPI(ML). Writes for *Samkaleen Janmat*.
Vibhuti Narayan Rai (b. 1950) completed his MA in English literature at Allahabad University in 1971. He joined the police force in 1975 and retired as director general of police, UP. Apart from novels, satire and criticism in Hindi, he has written in English on communal conflict and the role of the police. His novel *Shehar mein curfew* was translated into English (*Curfew in the City*, 1998) by C.M. Naim. From 2008 to 2014, he was vice chancellor of the Mahatma Gandhi Antarrashtriya Hindi Vishwavidyalaya, Wardha.

[24] Christopher Caudwell, *Illusion and Reality*.
https://www.marxists.org/archive/caudwell/1937/illusion-reality/ch01.htm

I said, 'Let's go for a walk.' I took them past the railway station. Those days, at every railway station or place of worship, you would see a band of destitute people, some without limbs, eyesight, or just very old, begging. Common sights of the violence of a class society. This is what I thought and what I told my new friends: 'You don't usually see this everyday violence inflicted on so many people as violence because it is taken for granted, considered normal. But if people protest, start a struggle against the ruling classes, and blood is shed, you think that is violence.'

I wanted to shock my friends with the normalisation of the violence our society inflicts on the poor, which we do not register. They were sensitive poets and began to think of violence differently. I think it helped to break their mental barrier against Marxism. D.P. Tripathi joined the SFI in JNU, and the CPI(M), and was at the time of his death the general secretary of the Nationalist Congress Party. Ramji Rai joined the CPI(ML) Liberation and is currently a Politburo Member of the party. The others did not join politics. Vibhuti Rai — I did not know him well in Allahabad — became a police officer, and continued to write. His books on the Hashimpura killings and the communalisation of the police remain outstanding pieces of work.[25] Dinesh Shukla, who joined the railways, is also an eminent Hindi poet who still refers to the working people as the inspiration for his writings.

The party in Allahabad was very weak. There were a few members or close sympathisers, but that was about it. There were two leading Hindi writers in Allahabad then: Markandey Singh and Bhairav Prasad Gupta. Each ran a Hindi literary magazine, and I wondered why, with two such writers, we did not have a strong left literary movement or an organisation there. In my innocence, I asked Markendey Singh this question. He told me, quite kindly I remember, that Lenin's view of writers is that they will join the revolution, but only as the rear-guard. It is futile to

---

[25] *Hashimpura, May 22* (trans. Darshan Desai, 2016); Sampradayik dangé aur bharatiya police (1998).

organise them. I have tried, without success, to find out whether Lenin actually said this.

The Naxalite movement had drawn the leading sections of the CPI(M) in Allahabad who joined what became the CPI(ML) under Charu Mazumdar. Later they began returning to the CPI(M), starting with Professor G.P. Singh, who had a group of students and youth followers with him. One of them was Ranbir Singh Chauhan, who was already emerging as a student leader. He later fought the Allahabad University elections as a candidate of the left and was elected general secretary of the Students Union. Anugrah Narayan Singh, who was an important figure in the university, came close to the left briefly, but then joined the Congress. He remains one of its important leaders in UP.

I used to cycle all over Allahabad. I also introduced my progressive student friends to cheap Muslim restaurants frequented by the working population — rickshaw drivers and mechanics. We discovered that the food was cheaper and better than what we got in the more middle-class eateries. The places were not as clean as the middle class would like — and their clientele was not middle class — but the food was good. And if you ate buffalo meat, it was one-fourth the price of a meat dish — chicken or mutton — in a more middle-class place. We also discovered how we had unconsciously communalised food, believing 'they' were communal for not eating in Hindu eateries, and not 'we' who didn't eat in Muslim eateries.

After one year of course work, we had to do a Master's thesis. That called for some 'original' work that would attempt to solve a specific problem not solved before. In engineering research, this usually meant using a different method to solve a problem that had already been solved. It took a long time for me to understand that 'research' is primarily about finding problems to solve, and recognising a tractable problem for a Master's thesis. A bigger problem was best kept for a PhD, and the biggest left for a lifetime's work! Most students in Indian institutions face such problems in undertaking research. The reasons include not being trained to think originally from the school level upward, and being pushed instead into the learning-by-rote system.

Initially, I chose using a numerical method to solve a non-linear stress distribution problem. This led me to another major change in my life. I had to use this new and strange beast called a computer; there were only a handful of them in the country. But the beast became very much a part of my life, as I gravitated from solving mechanical engineering problems to computer controls of power plants, and then problems dealing with controls, optimisation, fault detection and simulation of power plants.

I had seen my fellow students learning FORTRAN programming. In those days all scientific computing was done in FORTRAN language, but I had not taken an extra course to learn to program.[26] I had no interest in learning programming then, but later tried to learn it on my own while solving nonlinear differential equations that I encountered in my Master's thesis. With very little background in the required mathematics and no knowledge of programming, this was a tough task!

People who use smartphones today may be shocked to hear that a typical smartphone is much more powerful than a supercomputer of that era — the IBM 360/75 that powered the computers that computed the Apollo moon launches.[27] Your smartphone has an onboard memory a million times that of the old supercomputers, and can compute 120 million times faster than a computer that was used for the moon landings! Let me briefly describe the card decks we used. Each card had one line of instruction which we had

---

[26] There were initially two commercially available computer languages, then meaning a language in which you could program a computer to execute a set of mathematical instructions: FORTRAN (FORmulaeTRANslation) for scientific and technological work, and COBOL for commercial applications.

[27] https://www.ibm.com/ibm/history/ibm100/us/en/icons/apollo/breakthroughs/

to punch into card-punching machines. Then we would give in our deck to run on the computer. If you were lucky, you could collect your results in a few days. No problem is ever coded correctly the first time. So if you were good and meticulous, you could finish your problem in a month or two. For people like me, error-prone by nature, and learning to program on the fly, it took much longer.

IIT Kanpur had a computer centre to which I had access as a Master's student. This gave me time to go to IIT Kanpur, give my card deck to be run, then spend time with friends I had made there, or sit in the library and read. And since it was Kanpur, I had a home and a political party. I also had access to my father's car as he had just retired and did not use it all that much. This was my Kanpur life.

But I grew tired of it. I had heard a lot about JNU. Devi Prasad Tripathi, who was already a friend, had joined the SFI in JNU, and he waxed eloquent about the student movement there, and about the teachers and the ambience of the campus. I had friends in Delhi, fellow students in BE College who had joined the Master's courses in IIT Delhi. I knew I could stay with them and also have access to a computer centre. I decided to go to Delhi and do my computer work for my Master's. Thus began the JNU part of my journey, which would change my life in many ways.

3. To Delhi and a Turning Point

I had come to IIT Delhi in early 1975, as there were only a few places where computers were available to students doing their thesis work. After submitting my card decks to the computer centre to run the program, I had to wait a week for the results. I would spend my week's 'vacation' in the JNU canteen, arguing about politics.

D.P. Tripathi was then a councillor. (He was later elected president of the JNU Students Union in the mid-term elections of December 1974.) I knew him from Allahabad, where he was a student before he joined JNU. Through him, I got to know the entire SFI leadership of JNU, including Ashoklata Jain, student councillor of the JNU Students Union (JNUSU); and Sitaram Yechury, Indrani Majumdar, Dinesh Abrol, Shakti Kak, A.D. Neelakantan, Sohail Hashmi and many others.[1]

The JNU part of the story is perhaps more well-known among my friends — particularly as it led to my arrest and a year in jail. But

---

[1] Sitaram Yechury's PhD in economics was interrupted by his arrest during the Emergency. There were many others among our comrades in JNU whose doctorates met the same fate, and not necessarily because of being arrested! Yechury is the current general secretary of the CPI(M).

Indrani Mazumdar studied history in JNU. She is a part of the Centre for Women's Development Studies and has been part of the women's movement as both a scholar and an activist.

Dinesh Abrol is professor at the Institute for Studies in Industrial Development, New Delhi.

Shakti Kak is professor and director at the Centre for Jawaharlal Nehru Studies, Jamia Millia Islamia, New Delhi.

A.D. Neelakantan was the unit secretary of the SFI. He later died, tragically, in a bus accident in Kerala.

Sohail Hashmi is one of the founding trustees of SAHMAT. He is a filmmaker, historian, columnist and urban conservationist based in Delhi.

To Delhi and a Turning Point

From left: D.P. Tripathi, Sitaram Yechury, Dinesh Abrol, a student, Ashoka, Hariram Murthy in JNU.

coming to Delhi for my Master's thesis was an equally important turning point in my life. After I began running my programs in IIT Delhi's computer centre, I realised that I had set up a problem in my thesis that was probably unsolvable, at least through the route I was trying. It was a dead end. Luckily, I had become good friends with J.K. Pal, who was in Engineers India Ltd., and an ex-student of Bengal Engineering College, where I had done my Bachelor's. He had very strong feelings of college solidarity and was an active member of the BE College alumni in Delhi. He was doing his PhD in electrical engineering under Professor A.K. Mahalanobis in IIT Delhi, while working full time at a job. He became my unofficial thesis guide, and taught me control theory. He also helped me find a suitable problem and a way to solve it numerically. In short, he helped me with the larger problem of finishing my thesis.

My choice of the new problem for my thesis was not governed by any serious interest in the subject. The area was digital control — using a computer to solve control problems. At the time, it appeared to be a minor decision; but it had consequences. In fact, it completely changed my professional trajectory. From a mechanical engineer, specialising in pumps and compressors (process machines), I ended up amid the simulation, optimisation and digital controls of power plants. As all control systems gravitated to digital controls later, I moved, along with this field, from the periphery of the discipline to its core.

As I said earlier, I learned that the world of research is littered with problems, but the question is to choose one that can be solved. Of course, there are exceptions. The most well-known is Stephen Hawking's doctoral thesis on 'Properties of an Expanding Universe' (1966), the last chapter of which is the big bang theory;[2] or as Sheldon in the sitcom *Big Bang Theory* would describe it, the universe starting from a space-time singularity. If that fires up your enthusiasm for an earth-shaking thesis, there is also the antidote of Einstein. In 1905, he published a series of papers on the special theory of relativity, the photoelectric effect (for which he was given the Nobel Prize) and Brownian motion. All of them whales of papers. His PhD thesis, on the other hand, was submitted only for the purpose of a doctoral degree and has been called a minnow among such whales.[3] This is what I tell students who work on their PhDs — that they should treat it like any other academic milestone, not the work of a lifetime. Unfortunately, I did not use the advice myself; nor did a host of my friends and comrades.

Because of J.K. Pal, I also came to know Professor A.K. Mahalanobis and Professor Dutta Roy in the Electrical Engineering Department of IIT Delhi. They were among the best minds in the country in their disciplines. Professor Dutta Roy also shared many of my larger concerns regarding science, technology and neo-

---

[2] This would probably have got him the Nobel Prize in 2020 but that he was no longer alive and the Nobel is not given posthumously. His book, *A Brief History of Time* (1988), has been called the most unread book of all time by the BBC.
http://news.bbc.co.uk/2/hi/uk_news/1078475.stm

[3] This is, of course, an exaggeration. Einstein withdrew his original submission in 1902 and submitted a 16-page thesis, *A New Determination in Molecular Dimensions*, in 1905 (from Berne where he was living) to the University of Zürich. It is a part of his much larger work on statistical mechanics.
https://arxiv.org/pdf/physics/0504201.pdf

colonialism.⁴ (Later on, I invited him to speak on some of these concerns on platforms that I became involved with.)

The new problem I chose involved computer work. After submitting my card deck at the IIT Delhi (IITD) computer centre, I had time on my hands, as IITD's computer was less powerful than the one at IIT Kanpur (IITK).⁵ Apart from some time at the IITD library — they had a wonderful history and philosophy of science section — I spent most of my time in JNU.

My real introduction to JNU happened in the students' canteen and the dhabas 'down campus', now no longer a part of JNU. Endless cups of tea and coffee with 'bread-omelette' or 'omelette-bun' accompanied intense debates on everything under the sun. A discussion on capitalism in Indian agriculture might seamlessly move to capitalism in agriculture in Russia, semi-feudal relations in pre-revolutionary China, along with heated debate on Althusser's *For Marx* (trans. 1969). For somebody whose Marxism was largely derived from texts and movements, I was pitchforked into lively debates on a much wider set of issues.

The faculty and students had an easy relationship, unlike the completely hierarchic and rigid atmosphere of Allahabad, and I remember the long discussions I had with Sudipta Kaviraj on Louis Althusser's debates with the British Marxists, John Lewis and E.P. Thompson.⁶ Politically, I regarded the British Marxists as revisionists, but I felt far more empathy with them on philosophy

---

⁴ His *Glimpses from a Lifetime in Teaching and Research* (2015) gives us only some 'glimpses' of his views on teaching, research and why he did not settle abroad like many of his colleagues.
https://www.inae.in/storage/2018/12/Sep-2015-Glimpses-from-a-Lifetime-in-Teaching-and-Research-by-Prof-SC-Dutta-Roy.pdf

⁵ International Computers and Tabulators Ltd.
https://www.computerweekly.com/photostory/2240108431/Well-known-computer-firms-of-the-past-where-are-they-now/10/What-happened-to-ICL

⁶ Sudipta Kaviraj is a scholar of South Asian politics and intellectual history. He teaches at the Department of Middle Eastern, South Asian and African Studies at Columbia University, New York.

than with Althusser.[7] Recently, I have read on some of these issues again, and I remain convinced of what I had then formulated. Marxism has two components, a science of society and the goal of a just society. Marxism as science suggests possibilities of change at a given point, but does not identify a particular path as inevitable. It tells us what cannot happen but leaves open possibilities in society, such as socialism, reconfiguring the status quo, or even descending into barbarism. It is we, as humanity, or as conscious movements, that have to fight for emancipation from the exploiting classes. Both put together tell us what is possible and what we have to fight for, but they do not prescribe the possible as predetermined,[8] which the Althusserian position would lead us to do.

This paralleled, closely, my exploration of the broader

[7] For the non-initiated, revisionists and reformists may be strange terms from a foreign language! Yes, today I too am amused at the amount of energy we put into putting people into these various pigeonholes. Revisionism, in the orthodox Marxist lexicon — and I am still an orthodox Marxist — means that Marx had a revolutionary understanding of society with labour at its centre. Production and its appropriation by various classes is the basis of class struggle. A revolution is when the system of production and the relations of classes to production is fundamentally changed. A reformist, as I have explained earlier, believes it can be changed incrementally through reforms. A revisionist is — in our books — somebody who changes a fundamental understanding of labour and the relation of classes to production but still claims to be a Marxist. To complete the Marxist lexicon, a left adventurist is one who believes that the subjective conditions for a particular form of action are there even when they are not. Most people who use these terms would also classify themselves as Marxist Leninist, not to be confused with parties who added ML to their names as a part of the Sino-Soviet split and sided with the Communist Party of China. To be dogmatic fortunately has the same meaning in English as it has in our Marxist dictionary!

[8] 'Men make their own history, but they do not make it as they please; they do not make it under self-selected circumstances, but under circumstances existing already, given and transmitted from the past.' *The Eighteenth Brumaire of Louis Bonaparte*, Karl Marx, 1852.
https://www.marxists.org/archive/marx/works/1852/18th-brumaire/
'Freedom is the appreciation of necessity . . . . Freedom does not consist in the dream of independence of natural laws, but in the knowledge of these laws and in the possibility this gives of systematically making them work towards definite ends.' *Anti-Dühring*, Friedrich Engels, 1878 (after being serialised in *Vorwärts*).

relationship between science and technology itself. I also compared the Althusserian overdetermination of contradiction as a zero-inertia state that we know of in physics, in which all forces balance in a way that a small change can produce big outcomes, changing trajectories in a new direction and creating a new state.[9] (Yes, I am often tempted to interpret social problems in the light of what I know best, science and technology.)

Social change needs knowledge of social laws — as consciousness — but also human action as mass movements to effect revolutionary change. The discussions as a young student in JNU have remained with me to read further, re-evaluate and refine for the rest of my life.

Coming as I did from Calcutta and Allahabad, both of which had a degree of violence associated with them — political violence in Calcutta and goonish violence in Allahabad — I discovered a very different student movement on the JNU campus. Every meeting of students of any organisation would be followed by questions and answers, often heated debates, which would spill over outside the meetings as well. And for the first time, I encountered open general body meetings, in which important decisions of the Students Union would be ratified by a vote in the general body of students.

The other major political development that came into my life in JNU was coming across a debate which did not exist, perhaps, in any other Indian university at the time. This was my first encounter with certain Marxist currents that were strong in the UK and France, and which I later found in Brazil as well. Foremost among these was the Trotskyist current, rooted in a different kind of debate than I had encountered before. While the Trotskyites had more splits than even the Maoists, all of them shared a view of Stalin as committing the original sin within the Russian revolution, and

---

[9] Later, chaos theory, or more simply non-linear dynamics, brought this out much more clearly. I regard Althusser's overdetermination of contradictions as equivalent to the butterfly effect of nonlinear dynamics.

viewed all communist parties as agents of the Soviet Union. They had an ambivalent relationship with the Maoists, regarding them as backward, but still a possible ally in Asia, since the Maoists had, by that time, begun calling the Soviet Union a social imperialist state.

My differences with the Trotskyist formations were very different from those I had with other communist formations I had encountered till then. The CPI and the various Naxalite streams all accepted Marxism-Leninism as the basis of their politics. Internationally, these trends may have been identified with the Soviet Union or the Chinese, but in India the divergence between the CPI, the Maoists and the CPI(M) originated within the undivided party right from the beginning. I was critical of various changes in the Soviet Union, and its formulation of a possible non-capitalist path to socialism for newly liberated countries. Similarly, I disagreed with China's characterisation of the Soviet Union as social imperialist, which again the various Naxalite streams adopted.[10] Both sides differed with us, but at least we had a common set of Marxist texts that neither of these two streams denied.

The Trotskyites were different as they went back to the 1920s, sometimes even further. That meant arguing virtually from first principles. Jairus Banaji, their vocal and charismatic figure, was one of the most well-read Marxists I have met. But he and his admirers were very much textual Marxists trying to map the Indian landscape to familiar historical analogies from which they could then work out the tactics to be adopted here. But there is no question that debates with them forced us to read the basic texts and our history much more thoroughly than we would ever have done otherwise. Their virtual demise on the campus was a loss to other Marxist currents as well.

[10] While I was critical of the Soviet Union's internal changes, I was also disturbed by its inability to change its structure of production to accommodate technology changes that were taking place at a rapid rate elsewhere. I was yet to formulate my own views on self-reliance, autarchy and inter-dependence of economies, which took another two decades.

The SFI also had a brilliant set of student leaders. Foremost was Prakash Karat, but it also had D.P. Tripathi and Sitaram Yechury, both of whom made their name in politics later. Among the faculty, Prabhat Patnaik, Utsa Patnaik, Anil Bhatti and Sudipta Kaviraj were already making waves, not only in their disciplines, but also as major intellectual figures of the left. As young faculty, they stood out even among other notable figures such as Romila Thapar, Bipin Chandra, Yogendra Singh, and many others who Vice-Chancellor G. Parthasarathy and Dean of Students Moonis Raza had put together as a stellar faculty.[11]

Though I had been in passionate *political* debates with Naxalites and the CPI, I had not encountered an *intellectual* Marxist debate on current issues. For me, the mode of production debate in the *Economic and Political Weekly*, or how to understand the growth of capitalist production in Indian agriculture, was a watershed moment. For the first time, I saw a concrete question being analysed by Marxists who had sharp differences. Interestingly, it was not simply a division between different ideological streams of the left — Ashok Rudra, Utsa Patnaik and Paresh Chatterjee — but also within each one. For example, Utsa Patnaik and N. Ram debated the same issue in the *Social Scientist*.

I had some rudimentary understanding of agriculture but little knowledge of the terrain over which this debate was taking place. Instead, I mapped it into the political debates I was already in. To the Naxalites, Indian independence had not happened and India was still semi-feudal, semi-colonial, and its bourgeoisie was completely parasitic or comprador. I disagreed with this politically, as also the CPI's understanding that the Congress was fundamentally changing Indian feudalism and travelling possibly towards a non-capitalist path. One grossly overestimated feudalism and the other underestimated capitalist forces in India.

To the Trotskyites, colonialism meant India was fully

---

[11] Neeladri Bhattacharya, et al. (Ed.), *JNU Stories: The First 50 Years*, Aleph, New Delhi, 2020.

integrated into capitalism and the Indian peasantry was no different from the peasantry in England. As I found later, Western Marxism, if we identify it as a geographical entity, underestimates the white supremacy undergirding Western imperialism. This led its adherents to believe that capital in a colony behaves similarly to how it does at home. They even argued that multinationals bring not only advanced technology but also a more advanced working class into the country.

The debate over the more technical aspects of Marxism as applied to capitalism in Indian agriculture — production relations, property relations, the juridical aspect of property relations — and how to analyse them concretely was most instructive. Utsa's incisive analysis, her grasp of India's agrarian economy and the sharpness of her writing, stood out among all others in the debate.

Jairus Banaji was, at the time, a proponent of Laclau's colonial mode of production, a formulation I was encountering for the first time.[12] My problem with a colonial mode of production was that I looked on classes and mode of production as analytical categories. Here, mode of production characterises the relationship between classes in terms of ownership of the means of production: between those who own the means of production and those who labour on it. The exercise of ownership is the means by which surplus is extracted from the fundamental producers. The two classes are antipodes as a fundamental contradiction exists between them during the process of production.

A colonial mode of production seems more of a descriptive category than an analytical one, since those who produced the surplus in the colonies were either peasants or workers, with their antipodes as feudal landowners or capitalists. In my view, the colonial mode of production used this formulation to cover the more complex relations of production, particularly of the peasantry, which was better characterised by Utsa Patnaik as semi-

[12] https://newleftreview.org/issues/i67/articles/ernesto-laclau-feudalism-and-capitalism-in-latin-america

To Delhi and a Turning Point

feudal in her mode of production debate referenced above.

While my computer work was progressing at a glacial pace, the politics in JNU had reached an intense phase with the midterm elections of the Students Union. The Union's Free Thinker president Anand Kumar was leaving for the US to work on his research. D.P. Tripathi was the candidate of the SFI for presidentship. Though the Free Thinkers represented a motley crowd of students whose primary identity was that they were not SFI, its political core was the Samajvadi Yuvajan Sabha. This core consisted of Anand Kumar, Ranjana Kumari, Rajaram, Digvijay Singh, Anil Mishra and others.[13] The election campaign was conducted by both sides through a series of high voltage public meetings at night in the hostels. These meetings would end in charged political debates during the question-answer sessions following the speeches. The Trotskyites were our chief inquisitors, with Jairus Banaji and Sri Prakash leading the attack, Prakash Karat and DPT responding to the questions.

One of the problems the Free Thinkers had was that after Anand left, they did not have a speaker of his quality. DPT, in contrast to the FT candidate, was an orator who could mix poetry and earthy metaphors with left politics in a way that few could match. On the other hand, when the FT candidate was asked in one of the meetings if he stood for the status quo or for social change, he replied, 'Of course, for social change.' Asked how such change would come about, he decided to outflank the SFI from the left and answered, 'Armed Revolution!' The next day, the SFI — I think it was Suneet Chopra's work — put up a series of posters with a boy and girl, standing arm in arm, with the caption 'Armed Revolution'; and another with a gramophone record captioned, 'It has 78 Revolutions per minute'.

---

[13] Anand Kumar was Professor of Sociology at JNU.
Digvijay Singh was an associate of George Fernandes of the Janata Dal and later the Samata Party. He served as a union minister in the Chandra Sekhar government (1990–91), and in Atal Bihari Vajpayee's NDA government (1998–2004). He passed away in 2010.

Many evenings, days and nights were spent in heated debates on Marxism with fellow Marxists belonging to different streams. It included the cut and thrust of debates in meetings, the passionate discussions outside, the occasional overflow of emotion but mixed with good humour as well. DPT won the midterm by a landslide and was the president of the Union through its most testing time, the Emergency that was soon to follow.

I was watching and learning a new kind of politics among the students. At the same time, major events were taking place in my personal life. For the first time, I was meeting young women who were not my cousins or friends' sisters. In those days, boy to girl ratios in the engineering colleges were something like 50:1. So, a friendly, normal conversation with girls was out of the question. JNU was a different world, where boys and girls met as fellow students and friends, discussing politics, films, books and pretty much everything under the sun. I learned how to have normal conversations with women, and build a sense of camaraderie irrespective of gender.

Not that gender was out of the equation, it never is. Some relations have a spark while others do not. Among all the friends that I acquired in the JNU canteen and dhabas, Ashoklata Jain was different. She was a students union councillor, and convener of the School of Social Sciences, by far the largest school in JNU. At that time, there were only four schools: International Studies, Social Sciences, Languages, and Life Sciences, with the School of Physical Sciences and School of Computer Sciences still to come up.

Ashoka had a small-town background and had done her MA in Bijnor, from Agra University. She had topped the university, joined the Centre of Studies in Regional Development (CSRD) for the MPhil/ PhD program, and was the first to complete an MPhil thesis in JNU on tribal distribution in India. Her PhD work, on regional aspects of the Bhils, was guided by Professor Moonis Raza.

Coming from a small town, then Agra University, one would

have thought Ashoka would find it difficult to navigate life in a university like JNU. That she became one of the leaders of the JNU campus was an indication of her mettle. In an essay on JNU entitled 'Heady, Informal, Inclusive: The Early Years', Atiya Habeeb Kidwai writes:

> When I look back, I am amazed at what CSRD [Centre for the Study of Regional Development] enabled the first batch of MPhil and MA students to achieve later in life ... I distinctly remember the admission interview of Ashoklata, a petite and charming young girl from the small town of Bijnor, Uttar Pradesh. She broke down when the first question was put to her in English. Even our persistent assurance that she would lose no marks if she replied in Hindi could not stop her tears, and I had to take her out of the room to console her. Within a span of four years, the same Ashoklata became the chairperson of the JNUSU Council, organised the Janwadi Mahila Samiti and addressed huge rallies on the lawns of India Gate.[14]

This was also testimony to the inclusive student politics of JNU. Politics played a major part in easing the entry of students from diverse backgrounds, as each student body competed with others to find activists and leaders. This is unlike other elite institutions that are far more hierarchic and driven by class. JNU became even more inclusive with major changes in the admission policy so that social criteria (caste/tribe), economic backwardness, and geographical background (backward regions) were given due weightage — through additional points to candidates for admission.[15]

---

[14] In Neeladri Bhattarcharya et al (ed.) *JNU Stories, The First 50 Years*, Aleph, New Delhi, 2020, p. 47.
[15] In 1972–73, the SFI-led JNUSU (with V.C. Koshy as president) advocated an admission policy which would pave the way for students from poorer backgrounds and backward regions to come and study in JNU. The struggle for the admission policy began after the Union's analysis of the admission

By the time we met, Ashoka was very much a leader on the campus. Her politics, her friendliness, and her mischievous eyes won my heart, and I set about wooing her. The problem was that I had no clue about how to do this. I had never 'wooed' a girl before, and I had no close friends on campus I could get advice from. So, it took me an excruciating length of time to get to the point. We discussed politics; then progressed to my teasing her, and her teasing me back. My only advantage was a glib tongue and that I could speak on almost anything thanks to my vast knowledge of trivia from reading a ton of pulp fiction. To add to my personality, I had even grown a beard while in Allahabad University. Competing with student leaders there with a minimum age of 30 required some compensatory advantage. In my case, it was a beard.

In this dance, the major impediment was how I was to pop the question. How was I to say the simple words, I love you, and I want us to be together? After a few weeks of this mental torture, I decided to take the bull by the horns. We were both sitting in the JNU library. I went up to her and asked her out for tea in the dhaba near the library. I guess I must have looked rather intense as I put this all-important question to her. She looked at me, hesitated for a brief moment and then said Yes. I knew then that I had a green signal. So, over tea, I hemmed and hawed and finally blurted out that we should be together. She said Yes, and smiled, a smile that

---

pattern in 1972 found that the admissions were skewed in favour of students coming from privileged strata — those from big urban centres, and those who had access to the better educational institutions. The campaign to refashion the admissions policy of JNU was the first major struggle led by the JNUSU. The result was a path-breaking admission policy using a deprivation point system that awarded a maximum of 20 deprivation points based on social, economic and regional backwardness. The admission policy was implemented in 1973 (six years before the Mandal Commission was set up), and the results were immediately felt, as the new batch of students came from far more diverse backgrounds. The final touch to this policy was given in 1974 when the Academic Council approved the union president's resolution for reservation for SC/ST students. See The JNU Students' Movement and the Struggle for Social Justice, August 30, 2017. http://sfijnuunit.blogspot.com/2017/08/?m=0

To Delhi and a Turning Point

made me walk on air for the next few days.

I decided that I would join JNU for a PhD. The reasons were now personal as well, since Ashoka was there. Delhi IIT was not an option as it was a politically regressive campus, with Subramanian Swamy as the major 'dissident'. Its atmosphere can at best be described as late colonial. IIT Delhi was set up under a UK-India collaboration and was deeply conservative in terms of its academic and social culture.[16] In contrast, it is not as though the SFI in JNU was active only on campus. They joined different actions, including workers' strikes, leaflet distribution in the city and even teaching children in the construction camps near JNU.

I had completed my thesis and submitted it to Motilal Nehru Regional Engineering College back at Allahabad for my Master's degree. On my return from Allahabad I applied for admission to the Science Policy Centre in the School of Social Sciences. I was admitted but was quite torn by having to move into social sciences from a science-technology stream. I suddenly discovered that

---

[16] In his INAE speech quoted earlier, Professor Dutta Roy traces the backward academic culture of IITD to the British influence and the way IITD was used as a dumping ground of incompetent British faculty.

however much I had neglected my studies, I still loved science and engineering, and was reluctant to face the impending divorce.

R. Sadananda had done his PhD in IIT Kanpur and joined the fledgling School of Computer Science in JNU. He suggested that I apply to join the School of Physical Sciences and if selected, I could opt for a PhD in computer sciences, where there was a scholarship available through an industry grant. That was how I joined the School of Computer Sciences in JNU and was its sole student that year.

By then, Ashoka and I had decided that we wanted to get married and we informed both sets of parents about our decision. Ashoka's parents had met me, and were not opposed to the marriage, but they did worry about its impact on their extended family in Bijnor. We, as a rootless family from East Bengal, did not have to consider whether my parents would lose face by my marrying outside 'our' community. I think this is one of the reasons that Bengalis and Punjabis have the most inter-state marriages in India.

There is an amusing story about how communities regard each other in the complex mosaic that is India. Ashoka had spent most of her school and college years in Bijnor with her grandmother, as her father was in the Provident Fund Department and had a transferable job. Her grandmother was deeply suspicious of me and asked Ashoka's parents how they could trust a Bengali, as, in her view, Punjabis and Bengalis were not trustworthy. When my mother heard this — I told her because I thought it was hilarious — she was outraged. Not at Ashoka's grandmother's distrust of Bengalis, but how we, as good Bengalis, could be clubbed with the deeply suspect Punjabis!

By this time, we had made up our minds that we were not going to wait on the slow pace of our families. We went to the Special Registrar's Office in Tees Hazari and gave the requisite one-month notice for a civil marriage. As part of this process, we also had to appear before the Additional District Magistrate, South,

To Delhi and a Turning Point

P. Ghosh. He did not have any objection to our marriage but had a lot to say about the militancy of the JNU students, particularly of the girls there.

There is a bit of back-story to this. During one of the general strikes just before the imposition of Emergency, the police and students had clashed outside what was called down campus on the Outer Ring Road. The police had tried to clear the road and had also fired tear gas shells in the campus. During this standoff, P. Ghosh, as the additional magistrate, and Ashoka, representing the students, had met for a negotiation across the boundary wall. We were sure Ghosh had recognised her and hence this 'inquisition' during a routine application for a civil marriage. But our personal affairs were actually proceeding smoothly, with both sets of parents accepting the marriage, only (predictably) fighting for a 'formal' (read religious) ceremony as well. Unfortunately for them, that was a battle they were not going to win.

But there was another battle before us, with the university — as well as the entire country — turning into a battlefield of sorts. We were on the brink of the infamous Emergency.

4. A University Under Emergency

How did the Emergency affect Jawaharlal Nehru University? The university was, after all, named after Nehru, Indira's father and the patron of democracy in India; Indira herself was its chancellor. JNU was a bastion of left student politics with an array of left formations. The Emergency was a test: how would such a university as an institution stand up to state terror?

At the outset, we need to be clear why JNU and other universities are attacked by authoritarian forces — whether during the Emergency, or now, during the BJP-RSS years. The rulers understand the strength of the resistance that can come from students and youth. Universities are places where new thinking and new knowledge is supposed to emerge. Critiquing the status quo, whether in knowledge or society, is an integral part of any university that seeks to generate new knowledge. This aspiration poses a threat to the hegemony of ideas that support the existing order: new thoughts and new movements tend to emerge from the universities. That's why the establishment considers universities dangerous places.

JNU is a small university by Indian standards, with about 8,000 students. But it has always been an intellectually vibrant place where everything is up for debate. It is a place where students and teachers sit together in the classroom or outside and discuss the most controversial topics without a sense of hierarchy or fear. In short, ideas and beliefs, whether those of the student or teacher, have to withstand critical analysis.

The student movement in JNU has always been about what is happening in the country, not just internal issues of the university. Yes, the struggle for hostels, better food and other facilities is part

A University Under Emergency

of the student movement on campus. But there has always been a vital connection to wider struggles — of the working class, and of women, Dalits and Adivasis in the country.

Even during the build-up to the Emergency, the students in JNU had participated in solidarity actions, during industrial actions by workers in the city or all-India actions like the 20-day railway strike of 1974. They were on the streets again in response to subsequent all-India calls. The government of Delhi, then only a union territory, worked directly under the central government. Once the Emergency was declared, it was clear that the government would meet any resistance with force and arrests. All protests were banned, and any marches or courting of arrest — the traditional, benign modes of protest — were met by invoking the Defence of India Rules as a minimum, and weeks, if not months, in prison.

With the Emergency, student unions in the universities were de-recognised. All the normal trappings of democracy were dispensed with, including the right to protest within the university. The SFI held sway in JNU at the time. We recognised that the Emergency was not a short-term measure and the normal, open methods of protest would expose our organisation to immediate state reprisals.[1] We organised ourselves for underground activities. As part of this, the SFI in JNU decided not to issue *calls for action* in its own name, but in the name of *The Resistance*.[2] The administration knew, of course, who *The Resistance* was. But they could not prove it was the SFI, and this gave us some nominal protection.

The Resistance was a cyclostyled broadsheet (this being the technology of the day). During the Emergency, we could no longer go to the nearby Munirka village where we usually produced our

---

[1] In a jail discussion, D.P. Tripathi, who was in Tihar along with me, characterised the protest that the SYS and ABVP organised as 'satyagraha', it made the task of the government very easy. Arrest the satyagrahis, identify the leaders, and put them in jail under DIR or MISA.

[2] A selection of these texts is available in JNU SFI's blog. http://sfijnuunit.blogspot.com/

pamphlets. We decided to buy a cyclostyling machine, cut the stencil on a typewriter and cyclostyle the pamphlets ourselves. Saumitra Chaudhuri, who later became a member of the Planning Commission, was quite often the writer, typist and cyclostyle machine operator all rolled into one. We would distribute these pamphlets at night, and this activity continued throughout the Emergency. The leading activists either stayed out of the campus or changed rooms every night.

Soon after the Emergency was declared, the campus had its first taste of terror. On July 8, there was a big midnight raid on JNU. Two of the boys' hostels on campus were cordoned off by the police, and there were mass arrests. In the police station, a masked figure identified those to be detained and charged under the Defence of India Rules, and those to be let off.[3] One of the more amusing sidelights of this midnight raid was when the policemen mistook Bob Marley, the Jamaican reggae singer and composer, for a dangerous radical. They picked up the student who had Marley's poster up in his room. The victim was B. Muthu Kumar, who later joined the foreign service and, as ambassador of India to Tajikistan, was one of those who engineered India's 'alliance' with Afghanistan's Northern Front and its charismatic leader Ahmad Shah Massoud.[4]

The Resistance pamphlet on this raid is now available on the Bodhi Commons site, from where I have reproduced other pamphlets — those of the Students Union and the SFI.[5] Ashoka and I were not on campus during the crackdown. For obvious reasons, we generally stayed out of the campus at night those days.

---

[3] Strangely, he remains a mystery man to this day in spite of a large number of JNUites joining the administrative services who presumably had access to the records.

[4] V. Sudarshan, 'How India Secretly Armed Afghanistan's Northern Alliance', *The Hindu*, September 1, 2019.
https://www.thehindu.com/news/national/how-india-secretly-armed-ahmad-shah-massouds-northern-alliance/article29310513.ece

[5] See http://bodhicommons.org/

A University Under Emergency

Soon after, the university administration brought out the prospectus for the admission of new students. The prospectus declared membership of the Students Union optional. It also required new students to sign a Code of Conduct that ruled out their participation in any activity not sanctioned by the University administration. The Code of Conduct was in the offing for all students, as was de-recognition of the Students Union. *The Resistance* brought out another pamphlet in late July or early August 1975 on these issues. This was to prepare the students for some form of protest action that we knew we had to undertake on the campus soon.

FIGHT THIS ATTACK ON THE UNION

Immediately, after the police raid on the campus on 8 July we had pointed out that this was only the beginning of a deliberate attack on the Students Union and the democratic forces on the campus. Nine students and one karamchari arrested in the raid have been charged under section 69 of the D.I.R. (Defence of India Regulations Act) on the totally false pretext that the students had held a meeting at Kaveri hostel on the 7th night. Everybody knows that this is a bogus charge and that no meeting was held or planned. We had pointed out in our first leaflet that the attack is concentrated on the Union, which the Government and the University authorities are bent on disrupting because they know it is the most powerful forum of the students expressing their united interests. The police action carried out under the Emergency exposes the character of the Indira Gandhi regime today. Who is the Emergency directed at? Is the Students Union right reactionary? Are the nine students falsely charged under D.I.R. right reactionaries?

Now the Vice-Chancellor at the behest of the Prime Minister's Secretariat has announced in the latest prospectus that Union membership will henceforth be voluntary. It is in order to cripple the Union and destroy its representative and democratic character that this move has been made under the cover of the Emergency. The V.C., willing stooge of the Congress that he is, has further published a brochure for the new students in which the infamous 'Code of Conduct' imposing an unacceptable discipline on the student community has been put forth. It is untruthfully claimed that this has been formulated in consultation with students and faculty. The General Body of Students and the Students Council not only rejected outright this contemptible code but condemned even the move to discuss it.

Nagchaudhuri and the authorities are playing with fire by adopting this course.[6] Unable to terrorise us by sending in 1200 armed police, they are now manoeuvring to undermine the Students Union constitution and put shackles on the student movement. The Union derives its legitimacy and sanction not from Nagchaudhuri or the University authorities, but from the democratic will of the students. Any attempt to tamper with the Union on the part of the VC is a threat to our democratic rights and will be met with stiff resistance, Emergency or no Emergency.

We call upon the students to prepare for a big struggle even at short notice to force Nagchaudhuri to end his nefarious activities. We warn those elements on the campus who support this Emergency and act as paid agents of the Administration to stop their conspiracies or they will also face the anger of the students.

ANY ATTEMPT TO IMPLEMENT THE VOLUNTARY MEMBERSHIP TO THE UNION WILL BE MET BY A FORM OF ACTION THAT THE STUDENTS CONSIDER NECESSARY TO DEFEND THEIR DEMOCRATIC FORUM.

— *The Resistance*

---

[6] Basanti Dulal Nagchaudhuri (1917–2006), physicist and second VC of JNU (1974–79).

A University Under Emergency

The admissions to JNU became the flashpoint between the university administration, led by its vice-chancellor, and the students. The students in JNU were proud of their role in the admissions process. A Student Faculty Committee — a committee where the students had elected representation along with the faculty — scrutinised the results and the tabulation of points, including compensatory points for social and economic deprivation. The university administration's task was to post the results and organise the admissions. But now the vice-chancellor and the university administration added an extra step: they would weed out those names blacklisted by the police from the admission list. The SFI and the Students Union brought out leaflets condemning the vice-chancellor for violating the agreement with their union, an agreement that had been passed in the academic council. At the same time, a pamphlet by D.P. Tripathi, president of the JNU Students Union, informed the students about the VC's arbitrary action.

> Students' Federation of India — Bulletin
> Welcome to JNU
> August 1975
> The new academic session has begun with a series of systematic and obviously planned manoeuvres attacking the democratic movement built over the last few years, and to curb the hard-won rights of the student community. The first of these manoeuvres was the arbitrary declaration by the Vice-Chancellor, in the prospectus, that the membership to the Students Union is voluntary. The Students Union in our University, unlike those in many other universities, is fully independent of the administration. It was formed and has been sustained by the strong democratic student movement in the campus. The affairs of the Students Union — including elections — are managed entirely by the students, and the

Students Union is responsible to the students and students alone. The Students Union membership is automatic to all bonafide students and *compulsory* (as per the agreement with the VC at the time of its formation) *as it is the only independent forum which reflects and caters to the democratic interests of the students*. To weaken the Students Union by making its membership voluntary is to weaken the democratic movement built up in this campus until now. The SFI condemns this act of the VC and shall strongly resist this move.

This move should not be seen as an isolated one. It is a continuation of the efforts of the VC to disrupt the democratic movement in the university. These attempts began with the so-called 'Code of Conduct' proposed by the Vice-Chancellor last year which was unanimously rejected with contempt by the General Body of students. The same 'Code of Conduct' we find has been printed and circulated this year titled 'norms of behaviour'. The SFI shall resist this move, which is yet another to weaken the democratic movement in the campus.

These attempts of the Vice-Chancellor have been followed up this year by blatant violations of the admission procedure as laid down by the Academic Council. There has been arbitrary intervention by the Vice-Chancellor in the functioning of the SFCs and we find that some names recommended by the SFCs have been arbitrarily struck off by the Vice-Chancellor. We wish to point out that the VC cannot reverse or nullify the procedure passed by the Academic Council and endorsed by the Executive Council. This we see as an attack on the academic freedom of the University and shall therefore resist it. We greet the stand taken by a considerable section of faculty in opposing this interference by the Vice-Chancellor. We, however, condemn that section which has objectively been playing the 'rear guard' of the authorities. It is interesting to note that those who ostensibly declare themselves as 'dedicated to the students' cause' have refrained from mentioning the attacks by the Vice-Chancellor on the democratic movement in the campus.

The SFI calls upon all democratic elements in the University to resist this two-pronged attack of the VC, one against all traces of democratic functioning on the campus and the other on the Students Union.

LONG LIVE STUDENTS, TEACHERS AND KARAMCHARI UNITY RESIST THESE ATTEMPTS BY THE VC & HIS COLLABORATORS AND UNITE TO DEFEND YOUR DEMOCRATIC RIGHTS

INDEPENDENCE DEMOCRACY SOCIALISM

SFI (JNU UNIT)

Jawaharlal Nehru University Students Union

August 7, 1977

Friends,

The Students Union wishes to inform the students of the University of the arbitrary action of the Vice-Chancellor in striking off names from the admission list which were recommended by various centres after evaluation. This is a blatant attack on the democratic rights of both the students and the teachers. The Students Union welcomes the stand taken by a considerable section of the faculty who are opposing this attack on academic freedom. Once again, we reiterate that these anti-democratic acts will not be tolerated by the students of this University. As far as the admissions of students is concerned, we do not accept this interference and violation of the democratic procedure laid down by the Academic Council.

We will not allow the Vice-Chancellor to prevent the admissions of Students simply because they do not meet a certain criterion which is completely extra academic and apparently mysterious. We demand that the Vice-Chancellor should at least abide by his own statement that no section of

the University community can infringe upon the democratic rights of any other section.
RESIST THIS ATTACK ON DEMOCRATIC RIGHTS
LONG LIVE STUDENT UNITY
— Devi Prasad Tripathi
President, JNUSU

Soon after, the president of the Students Union, D.P. Tripathi (or DPT as he was more usually called) and many others were denied admission. A Students Union meeting was held on August 19, 1975, and was chaired by Ashoka since DPT was among those who had been struck off the admission list. The meeting condemned these acts of the university administration. Here is an excerpt from the pamphlet issued by the Students Union and signed by Ashoka:

The time has come for the students to strike against the measures taken by the Vice-Chancellor to curb the democratic rights of teachers and students. Because of their political opinions, and despite their excellent academic performance, students have been victimised and denied admission. The University authorities launched this attack beginning with the President of the Students Union, Devi Prasad Tripathi.

Tripathi, a first-class student throughout, coming from a backward area, as well as an economically deprived background, was not given admission to the M Phil program. The Chairman of the Board which interviewed JNU students of the Centre for Political Studies, is said to have stated prior to the written test and interview that Tripathi would be eliminated. The older students will remember that this same Tripathi came first in the list for the MA program.

Two student councillors, Rajaram and Promod Kumar Mishra, again both first class students were recommended for admission by their respective faculties, who found them academically competent, but were denied admission by the VC. The reason again was that they hold certain political opinions which differ from those of the Vice-Chancellor.

A call for action was again given by *The Resistance*. This was for an academic boycott on August 22.

Urgent: Read & Circulate
Boycott Classes in Protest: 22 August
Students who have qualified for admissions and [been] approved by the Centres concerned have been struck off the lists by the Vice-Chancellor and the Registrar's office. They [the vice-chancellor and registrar] have been passing on the lists to the police and Govt. for screening. By this action they hope to crush the Union and keep students who do not toe the official line, off the campus. The president of the Union, Tripathi, has been denied admission in his own centre for M Phil by giving him ridiculously low marks in the viva and test. Two of the Union Councillors, Rajaram and P.K. Mishra have had their admissions annulled by the VC in their own centres and in the School of International Studies, after they had qualified. Similar cases exist in other centres: History: Sujata Madhok; Social Systems: Rabindra Ray; School of Languages: Ramesh Dixit; School of International Studies: Mohan Ram.

By this the University has struck a blow at the students and teachers on the campus, making a mockery of the admission system so carefully worked out in the past. They have interfered with the rights of the 'other components of the University'.

IN PROTEST ALL THE STUDENTS WILL BOYCOTT CLASSES, THE LIBRARY AND ALL ACADEMIC WORK ON THE CAMPUS ON 22 AUGUST, FRIDAY, TO EXPRESS THEIR PROTEST AGAINST THIS HEINOUS ACTION OF THE VC AND THE ADMINISTRATION.

We call upon the students to strictly observe the following:

1. All non-residents should stay at home on 22 August.

2. All residents should either stay in their hostels or go out of the campus for the day.

3. Spread the word of the boycott to your friends individually and explain the reasons for this action.

We make an urgent appeal to the faculty to observe this boycott and cooperate by not taking classes in protest against the dictatorial step of the VC. Let this be a joint action.

UNITEDLY GO INTO THIS ACTION BOLDLY;

REBUFF ALL ATTEMPTS TO SUPPRESS OUR DEMOCRATIC RIGHTS.

— THE RESISTANCE

Events continued to escalate. The university first suspended Ashoka. Then, a Court of Honour 'tried' Ashoka for challenging the university administration and expelled her from the university. This led to the call for a three-day strike, probably the first such mass action in a university during the Emergency. The Resistance called for a three-day class boycott, September 24–26, in protest against Ashoka's expulsion.

Urgent: Read & Circulate

Boycott Classes in Solidarity with Ashok Lata Jain on 24, 25, 26 September

Ashok Lata Jain, student councillor of the JNU Students Union and PhD student in the Centre for Regional Development has been expelled by the 'Court of Honour', set up by the Vice-Chancellor on trumped-up charges. This black deed is the worst act perpetrated on the student community since the foundation of the University. The authorities are continuing their offensive against the democratically elected students union. Coming on top of the order prohibiting Union elections, the expulsion of Ashok Lata Jain is an attack which the students will resist. Ashoka has been victimised for doing her elementary duty as an elected student representative and for upholding the democratic rights of students.

TO EXPRESS OUR TOTAL SOLIDARITY WITH HER ALL THE STUDENTS WILL GO ON STRIKE BY REFUSING TO ATTEND CLASSES, THE LIBRARY, AND OTHER ACADEMIC WORK FOR THREE DAYS BEGINNING FROM 24 SEPT.

Our students have been taught another object lesson about the real face of the Emergency: expulsion of left and democratic student leaders, denial of admission to them, and terror on the campus. The Vice-Chancellor having instigated this action has left for the United States to continue his intrigues with US imperialism on behalf of the Indira Govt. on the Indo-US Joint commission.

Let us make every effort to boldly convert the three-day boycott into a historic protest. We solicit the active sympathy and support of the teachers and employees in this just struggle of ours.

Withdraw the action against Ashok Lata Jain!

Unitedly we will fight for our rights!

— THE RESISTANCE

Before the three-day strike began, the students union called a General Body Meeting where they condemned the vice-chancellor but were careful not to openly endorse the strike called by *The Resistance*. At that time, the CPI and its different platforms had endorsed the Emergency as a move against the fascist movement of Total Revolution of which the RSS was a part. They believed Mrs Gandhi's 20-point program would create conditions for a non-capitalist path towards socialism. It was only when Sanjay Gandhi and his five-point program were on the ascendant, with family planning and tree planting as 'progressive' slogans, that they realised their mistake. But these were the early days, and the reality of the Emergency was yet to dawn on them. At the General Body, the AISF launched an attack on the SFI, accusing us of violating democracy through our secretive arm *The Resistance,* instead of giving an open call for a strike. They derided any argument about the curbing of democratic rights under the Emergency and the threat it posed to the students if an open call was given.

I still remember the bitter argument I had with one of the AISF stalwarts on the campus. I told him that identifying us as *The Resistance* would open us to attacks under the Emergency. He was completely impervious to any such argument — he claimed that we were fabricating the story of an Emergency in which civil liberties were lost. (Later, after my arrest, Kamal Mitra Chenoy, on behalf of the AISF, issued a pamphlet condemning my kidnapping and arrest, and he was promptly expelled for six months by the university. And even later, when Kamal was appointed to join the faculty in JNU, one of the objections raised against his appointment was his expulsion from the university as a student.)

I remember another heated discussion — this one with a rising star among the Trotskyites — when some of us were distributing leaflets for the three-day strike. He chastised us for being 'adventurists'. He accused us of inviting the armed might of the state into the campus, warning us that this would crush the student movement. The Trotskyites usually attacked us for not being socialist and revolutionary enough, so this was an altogether new tune. I remember being amused by the picture of the Indian state invading JNU with tanks and guns. Still, I guess my Trotskyite friend had the last laugh. The state did come in, a few days later, not in tanks but in one black Ambassador car.

On September 25, the second day of the three-day boycott, we stopped the 'crown princess' of the Emergency, Maneka Gandhi, from entering her class. Tripathi, Indrani Mazumdar and I were standing with a couple of others in front of the School of Languages building when Maneka Gandhi arrived to attend class. DPT told her a student had been expelled, there was a strike on, and she should go back. She left. It had seemed a fairly 'cordial' exchange.

A University Under Emergency

But according to the account of the Shah Commission,[7] Maneka went back to the PM's house and complained to her husband Sanjay Gandhi. Sanjay was the de facto ruler of Delhi at the time and, increasingly, he called the shots in the Congress. P.S. Bhinder, then deputy inspector general (range) Delhi and part of his coterie, turned up for his daily report to Sanjay. If everything was as it should be, Sanjay asked Bhinder, why couldn't his wife Maneka attend her classes in JNU?

P.S. Bhinder was not just the deputy inspector general of police in Delhi, he was the key police person in the Emergency administration of Delhi, along with Superintendent (CID) K.S. Bajwa, who supplied whatever 'evidence' Bhinder required.

(A curious and telling detail: Bhinder was involved in Sundar Daku's murder, a killing in cold blood by the police in 1976. He was indicted and spent some time in Tihar, apparently in the same ward my MISA colleagues and I had earlier occupied. The Sundar case was dropped after Mrs Gandhi's election victory in 1979. The point to note is that nobody asked whether Sundar was a dacoit or not. The only question asked was whether this was a case of extra-judicial killing by the police. This is in contrast to Ishrat Jahan in 2004 and many other cases today, when extra-judicial killings are justified on the basis of a person's alleged antecedents.)

To get back to Bhinder after his meeting with his boss Sanjay on September 25: He went directly from the PM's house to the police contingent posted outside JNU, commandeered the official car — a black Ambassador — of Superintendent (South) Rajinder Mohan, and drove into the campus in rather filmy 'commando style' accompanied by two constables and one deputy superintendent, T.R. Anand — hefty men, all. By this time, DPT had moved away. I was still standing in front of the School of Languages with Indrani

---

[7] J.C. Shah, former chief justice of India, was appointed in 1977 to head a commission to investigate the excesses of the Emergency. The Shah Commission submitted two interim reports, in March and May 1978, before the fall of the Janata Party government in July.

Mazumdar and a few others. Bhinder grabbed hold of me and began pulling me inside the car. I resisted. There was a scuffle for some five minutes. Indrani tried to help, quickly realised she was no match for the policemen, but noticed the car keys in the ignition. She tried to snatch the keys but was prevented. The details of my kidnapping are in the Shah Commission records. I reproduce extracts below of what Shakti Kak and Indrani Majumdar and Manoj Joshi deposed to the Shah Commission as their eyewitness accounts:

> (*Excerpts from Shah Commission Proceedings*)[8]
> He (Prabir Purkayastha) admits to have participated in the boycott as a form of protest on 25th Sept., 1975 against the expulsion of Ashok Lata Jain who was an elected member of the Students Union. He has stated that:
> At about 10 a.m. a black Ambassador car came, stopped nearby and four persons walked to the place where I was sitting, and one of them asked me whether I was Devi Prasad Tripathi, the President of the Students Union, and I said I was not. In spite of my protest, I was physically dragged inside the car after a couple of minutes of scuffling, and the car drove off. Shakti Kak and Indrani Majumdar, who tried to stop the car, were dragged some distance along with the car.
> (And) That I was taken to R.K. Puram, Sector 4, Police Post where the person driving the car ordered the policemen to take me away. The SHO of the Police Station informed me that the person driving the car was Bhinder, DIG. I was held there throughout the day, and I was given. The MISA warrant at about 11.00 p.m. at night.
> Kum Shakti Kak, a student of Jawaharlal Nehru university has stated that:
> On 25th Sept,1975 at about 10 o'clock in the morning I

---

[8] Available from the Ashoka University-Stranford University Archives. https://searchworks.stanford.edu/view/zk122by7435

was sitting on the lawn in front of the School of Languages with the petitioner and three other students. That at that time the black Ambassador Car No. DLE 5747 with four people inside stopped near us and one of them climbed down from the back side of the car and came to the petitioner and held him by the shoulder and asked him whether he was Devi Prasad Tripathi, he said no and I also said that he was not the person. Yet he pulled him and took him near the car. By that time three more persons got out of the car and tried to push him in the back seat. I along with other students, thinking that they were Goondas trying to abduct the petitioner went near the car to rescue him (petitioner). We succeeded in pulling the petitioner from the car. At that time two more persons came from the other side and pushed him into the car, they also got inside with him. He was caught by the waist while his arms and legs were out of the open car doors. The person who was driving the car immediately started it and the car sped away with doors swinging open. The persons who abducted the petitioner were rough with the students who were trying to rescue the petitioner.

This unheroic picture of my being whisked away — in Shakti's words — with my arms and legs waving in the air while my body was in the car, is not an image that I would like posterity to remember. In my defence, I was tall, skinny and mostly arms and legs those days.

In spite of my efforts and my fellow students', I was trapped in the car and whisked away to the RK Puram Police Station. Bhinder dropped me off there, telling the police to be careful with me since I had a history of escaping!

Indrani's attempt to snatch the car keys from the ignition had an amusing replay. During the Shah Commission hearings, Bhinder pretended there was no car, no kidnapping, and, of course, no mistaken identity; that the lieutenant governor of Delhi, Krishan

Chand, had told him there were three ring leaders on the campus, DPT, Ashok Lata Jain and Prabir Purkayastha.

This was the story he manufactured for the Commission: that 20–25 students had gathered on campus, raising anti-government slogans and physically preventing students and teachers from attending classes. But prohibitory orders were in force. So he and his police — quietly watching the proceedings — were forced to arrest me since I was one of the ring leaders of the gathering and identified by other students as Prabir Purkayastha, 'one of the three names on LG's list'. Bhinder completely denied the commando-style raid in a black Ambassador deposed by other eyewitnesses, including Indrani.

But during his cross-examination, a master class in the way it was conducted, Justice Shah asked Bhinder, 'Once you had arrested Purkayastha, why didn't you arrest D.P. Tripathi? There was a pending MISA warrant against him.'

Bhinder blurted, 'We would have been beaten up' and that the 'students did everything to pull him out, they tried to drag us out ... and there was a girl there, I do not know her name, who tried to snatch the key of the car out. They tried to lie down in front of the car.'

Shah responded in his usual soft-spoken style, 'So you had gone inside with a car!' Bhinder was silenced for a minute before conceding that he had indeed driven the car into the campus, and it was a black Ambassador as others had described. He essentially admitted the entire sequence that others had deposed was correct and what he had claimed initially was wrong.

I have often wondered how I could have been mistaken for DPT, who looked quite different. Perhaps one detail went against me. The previous night, I was trying to trim my overgrown beard when Ashoka offered her 'help'. The result was such an uneven scrub that neither she nor I could stop laughing. This forced me to shave my beard for the first time after I had grown it in Allahabad. DPT did not have a beard; so maybe if I'd had a beard, Bhinder might have realised his mistake sooner. But I did learn my lesson and never shaved off my beard again!

Another amusing story about the daylight kidnapping was that one of the three plainclothesmen accompanying Bhinder got left behind in the haste to take me away. The students surrounded him and he was on the verge of being beaten soundly. At that point, policemen with raised firearms entered the campus in a police vehicle. They asked the students to hand the person over to them. Told that he was one of the persons in the gang that had kidnapped a student, they said: 'We will take care of that, hand him over to us.' The students decided that they should lodge a formal complaint, though fully aware that the kidnapping was conducted by the plainclothes police. When they reached the Hauz Khas police station, they found the person who had been left behind was T.R. Anand, the deputy superintendent of police posted there.

This is what actually happened. Having kidnapped me, Bhinder drove the car he had borrowed from the superintendent (south) towards the RK Puram police station. On the way, he asked whether I was DPT. I said I wasn't and stated my name, but he asked for proof. In those days, we hardly ever carried a wallet or identity card. Reflecting back, I'm not sure I even owned an ID card. Even driving licenses were bulky documents which we, if we drove at all, left in the car. So, with no proof of not being DPT or who I said I was, I was dumped in the RK Puram thana.

The whole day at the thana was one of suspense. I didn't know if I would be released once the JNU authorities informed the police they had picked up the wrong student, or whether I would be charged with some specific offence. The answer came late in the evening, around 11 PM. I was served with the Maintenance of Internal Security Act (MISA), according to which you can be held in *preventive* detention if the state deems you have endangered

India's security. This was supposed to last four months, with an internal review and further detention if you were deemed a continuing threat.

Why did my MISA warrant take so long to be served? During the entire period of the Emergency, orders and reviews were carried out entirely mechanically, the additional district magistrates rarely disagreeing with the judgement of the police authorities. In my case, as the police had nothing on record against me, P. Ghosh, the additional district magistrate Delhi (South) who had to sign the MISA warrant, objected. Initially, the police claimed that I had been arrested as a result of a scuffle between them and the students, but when the Dean of Students K.P. Mishra and the Registrar of the University came to the police station after being asked by Ghosh, they said that there was no such scuffle as claimed by the police. Instead, the police had entered the campus in plainclothes in an unmarked car and had abducted a student who had just joined the university. When Ghosh confronted Superintendent Rajinder Mohan with the university's version of the story, he admitted that this was indeed the case. The Shah Commission Report says:

> ... the latter (the SP South, Rajinder Mohan) told him that Shri P.S. Bhinder had gone to the JNU to arrest Shri D.P. Tripathi because Smt. Maneka Gandhi had complained to Shri Sanjay Gandhi about the anti-Government activities in JNU and Sanjay Gandhi had summoned Shri Bhinder and had asked him to take drastic action; that Shri Bhinder had gone with the intention of arresting Shri D.P. Tripathi but had taken another student into custody in the mistaken belief that the student was Shri Tripathi.

He said, 'I really can't sign this warrant as you have nothing against him on record' and reported this to the district magistrate of Delhi, Sushil Kumar. Finally Sushil Kumar rang up P. Ghosh at night and told him: 'You have to sign the MISA Order as the

A University Under Emergency

PM's House' — meaning Sanjay Gandhi — 'is involved'. All this was placed on record by the Shah Commission. That's how I came to be booked under MISA.

P. Ghosh also deposed to the Shah Commission that the grounds on which the MISA order was to be signed didn't reach him till four or five days after it was signed. This was the norm during the Emergency: orders would be signed based only on the names that Superintendent (CID) K.S. Bajwa supplied, and the grounds for the order arrived days later. The CID took some time to 'prepare' the grounds, hence the delay. This was all the application of mind that additional district magistrates, the signing authority, were permitted; they signed orders for detention under MISA, depriving people of their right to liberty, without knowing why.

In my case, even the CID was hard-pressed to find anything incriminating. Whatever records may have existed were in Allahabad, and back in those days, as good as inaccessible to the Delhi police. Knowing that they had to fabricate the grounds for my arrest, they produced some rather purple prose on how dangerous I was. I cannot resist reproducing this prize quote:[9]

> He is a staunch SFI worker, who has got good influence in the SFI Unit of JNU. Though he took admission only in the year 1975, yet had attracted Miss Ashok Lata Jain due to his political image.

My dangerous 'political image' that could attract a leading student activist was reason enough to lock me up!

As the Shah Commission's documents and testimonies bear out, PM's House was a euphemism for Sanjay Gandhi, who held no constitutional position and, therefore, could not be named in official correspondence. Had the officers' notings in the files

---

[9] Shah Commission of Inquiry Papers: Subject File No. 23 (Part II), 'Students in the Emergency', South Asia Conflict Archive/Shah Commission Papers. https://searchworks.stanford.edu/view/zk122by7435

> "He is a staunch SFI worker, who has got good influence in the SFI Unit of JNU. Though he took admission only in the year 1975, yet had attracted Miss Ashok Lata Jain due to his political image."

revealed that they were taking their orders from Sanjay Gandhi, it would have been an admission that they were violating their service conduct rules; hence the coinage, 'PM's House'. Like Voldemort in the Harry Potter books (He-Who-Must-Not-Be-Named), Sanjay Gandhi became 'PM's House' in bureaucratese!

The Shah Commission's Report has a chapter on Delhi during the Emergency, where the activities of the key players are detailed. Though Krishan Chand, as lieutenant governor, was the titular head of the Delhi administration, the real players were Navin Chawla,[10] secretary to the lieutenant governor; Om Mehta, minister of state for home; P.S. Bhinder, deputy inspector general (range); Jagmohan (Malhotra), vice chairman of the Delhi Development Authority;[11] and superintendent of police (CID), K.S. Bajwa. All of them were close to Sanjay Gandhi, doing whatever he wanted and more — to please the crown prince of the Emergency.[12]

Why was there a reluctance to state the real cause of my arrest? Was it because it would have meant accepting not only that a student strike had broken out at JNU, but even the prime

---

[10] Though the Shah Commission had held that Navin Chawla was one of those responsible for the Emergency's 'excesses', he never suffered any consequences as the Janata Government fell soon after the Report's submission. He rose in the bureaucracy and became Election Commissioner in 2005, and Chief Election Commissioner in 2009 during Manmohan Singh's prime ministerial period. I guess an ambitious and a pliable bureaucrat is useful to any regime.

[11] Jagmohan, who later joined the BJP, was the key figure of the large-scale demolitions in Delhi. One major demolition was at Turkman Gate in April 1976, in which at least 12 persons died in police firing. (Shah Commission Interim Report II, Section VI).

[12] There was the case of 12 textile inspectors and customs officials who were arrested under MISA for their temerity in doing their job and inspecting a consignment of Mrs Amteshwar Anand's. Mrs Anand was Sanjay's mother-in-law (Maneka's mother) and ran a textile business.

A University Under Emergency

minister's daughter-in-law could not attend her class? I guess putting down the real cause, that we had stopped the crown princess from going to her class right in the capital city of the country, was too embarrassing for the Indian state to admit even in strict confidence, within the privacy of its files.

A postscript on P. Ghosh: He knew that Ashoka and I were engaged to be married. We had given our notice for marriage before P. Ghosh, and he had recognised Ashoka as a student activist. The strike that day was against her expulsion. His reluctance to sign my MISA warrant was possibly greater on this account. After my release, when Ashoka and I did get married, he was still the additional district magistrate and 'officiated' at our marriage. My father had invited him to join a small family dinner that evening. He came and even presented us with Regis Debray's *Prison Writings*. Regis Debray had spent time in jail in Latin America after joining Che Guevara's call for revolution.

I have met Ghosh — who later became Secretary, Department of Environment — at various conferences on environmental and climate change issues. He very proudly tells others, 'You know, I signed his MISA warrant and put him behind bars, and I also officiated at his marriage.'

The Shah Commission Report further details the PM House's interest in my arrest and subsequent incarceration. After I had spent nearly six months in jail under MISA, the Home Ministry wrote to the Delhi Administration (D.L. Vashishth's Demi Official or DO letter to Sp. Secretary Sailaja Chandra) to re-examine this case for revocation of the order. The Delhi Administration disagreed. After almost nine months in jail, Brahmananda Reddy, then home minister, wrote in my file that there was no reason to keep me in jail as there was nothing on record against me in the police files.[13] R.L. Mishra, joint secretary, wrote in a DO [Demi Official] letter to Sailaja Chandra (July 9, 1976),

> ... the role of Shri Pravir Purkayastha in organising the strike was very peripheral and for that he has already been punished by detention for nearly 9 months. It does not seem necessary to continue this detention any longer for effectively dealing with the emergency. I am, therefore, desired to request that the order of detention in respect of Shri Pravir Purkayastha may be revoked under intimation to the Ministry.
>
> This bears the approval of the Home Minister.

Om Mehta, the minister of state for home, wrote in the file (*overriding* the home minister's opinion) that the PM's house was involved and so the detention had to continue. Om Mehta was the de facto home minister, not Brahmananda Reddy, the official incumbent.[14] The lieutenant governor met Om Mehta and both of them concluded that the detention had to continue; this was what Krishan Chand, the lieutenant governor, noted in the file before sending it back to the Ministry of Home Affairs. (Many of these and other details are recounted in *The Emergency Chronicles*, an excellent and highly readable book by Gyan Prakash, who was a fellow student in JNU and a friend.)

Meanwhile, back on the JNU campus, *The Resistance* published a

---

[13] Shah Commission of Inquiry Papers: Subject File No. 23 (Part II), 'Students in the Emergency'.
https://searchworks.stanford.edu/view/zk122by7435

[14] Krishan Chand in his examination by the Shah Commission called Om Mehta as the executive Home Minister as he was the one in daily contact with the PM's house! Shah Commission of Inquiry Papers: Subject File No. 23 (Part II), Students in the Emergency, pp. 87.
https://searchworks.stanford.edu/view/zk122by7435

A University Under Emergency

response to my arrest as part of a call to continue a three-day class boycott. (I had been kidnapped from the campus on the second day of the boycott.)

> Fight this Police Terror Tactics Unitedly: Continue the Boycott on the 26th:
> Angry over the very successful beginning of the three-day boycott call on 24th by the students protesting against the expulsion of Ashok Lata Jain, the police in collusion with the University authorities have perpetrated a cowardly provocation against the students.
>
> After the ninety per cent boycott of classes on the 24th, on the 25th morning the boycott threatened to be total. An instance is the School of Languages where with over 600 students, only 3 entered the building in the morning. Since the 24th three police trucks were parked around the campus to intimidate the students. At 10:30 a.m. the police went into action. A black Ambassador car with 4 plain-clothes men was parked inside the campus. The men approached Prabir Purkayastha who was standing near the School of Languages and dragged him away to the car, and despite the resistance of some students they whisked him away. This fascist style attack has been launched on a totally innocent person. Purkayastha joined the University only two months ago and is senior fellowship holder in the School of Computer Sciences. This was a deliberate provocation as Prabir had been asked by the policemen if he was Tripathi [the JNUSU President] and he had replied in the negative.
>
> The VC (now safely ensconced in the USA) had informed the last Academic Council meeting that after the 8 July raid the authorities had assured him that the University would be informed within 8 hours of the names of the students arrested and the charges on which they are held. We demand that the

Rector and the Registrar get this information and get Prabir released immediately.

The students, teachers and employees have responded to this blatant provocative act with outrage and are determined to unitedly face such onslaughts.

REMAIN CALM AND CONTINUE THE BOYCOTT TO ITS SUCCESSFUL CONCLUSION ON 26th!

The JNU students' protests continued, with Sitaram Yechury and DPT being arrested in early November. DPT was arrested while walking up to the new campus from the old campus; charged under MISA, he joined me in Tihar.[15] Again an amusing sidelight was that the policemen who had arrested him also shared their problems with him. After the fiasco of my arrest and its worldwide coverage, the police had to wait in plainclothes *outside the campus* for more than a month in order to nab him on this deserted stretch of road. They complained bitterly of this long vigil on the mere off-chance of nabbing DPT one day. A raid on the campus was no longer an option!

The Resistance circulated a pamphlet on Sitaram and DPT's arrest:

The Struggle Will Continue!
13 November 1975
In the last four months the University authorities have in collusion with the police and government been launching one attack after another on the students of JNU and particularly the Union office-bearers. The students have been unitedly meeting these attacks and their determined resistance has foiled all these attempts to suppress the Union and the functioning of the left and democratic organisations on the campus. The latest round

---

[15] JNU then had two campuses. Old Campus, where most of the classes were held, and New Campus — which housed the hostels and a few of the smaller departments. The current JNU campus is the 'New Campus' of our times.

A University Under Emergency

of attacks began on the night of 4th November when Sitaram Yechury (student councillor) was arrested from his residence under Sec. 108 of Cr. P.C. On 6th November, the Registrar informed the Union of its 'derecognition' by the authorities. On the 7th they did not allow D.P. Tripathi, President of the Union and ex-officio member of the Academic Council to attend the Council meeting. On the same night Tripathi was served with an expulsion order from the University for six months. Finally, on the 11th evening, Tripathi was arrested by the police inside the campus in the notorious 'Purkayastha kidnapping' style. He has now been detained under MISA. All these reprehensible activities once again illustrate the hand in glove working of the Nagchaudhuri clique with the Congress bosses and the police.

Having failed to stamp out rising protest on the campus, one bunch of henchmen of Indira headed by Nagchaudhuri 'derecognised' the Union' seeing that it would not disrupt Union functioning, another bunch of henchmen headed by the DSP, Hauz Khas Police Station have resorted to arresting Tripathi. We salute Devi Prasad Tripathi for ably and courageously leading the students in the last four months at such great risk. We are confident that the students will continue to nurture and support the Union in his absence.

The main task of the student community is to preserve our democratic forum — the Students Union. It is our duty to see that the Union functions in a new way on a long-term basis in a situation characterised by severe repression. This will be the most effective rebuff to the gang of desperadoes ruling this country and administering our university. Their storm-troopers cannot stomach the fact that a strong leftist union continues to function in a university in the capital city. That is why in the past four months, 9 students have been arrested under DIR (including the General Secretary of the union); 2 students have been expelled from the university. For this record of black deeds the culprits in the University echelons will meet a just and fitting retribution soon.

Prof Nurul Hasan, Union Minister for Education, is visiting the campus on 14 November to attend the function being held to celebrate the tenth anniversary of the foundation of the Centre for Russian Studies. On this occasion to mark a venture in Indo-Soviet cooperation, we should like to remind the honourable minister and the pseudo-progressives on the campus that they are celebrating what Lenin called the 'barracks method in the treatment of students and liberal intellectuals.'

Concrete plans must be drawn up by mutual consultations amongst left and democratic organisations on the campus to keep the resistance to the dictatorial regime and in defence of our democratic rights growing and link them up with action elsewhere. We appeal to the students to continue to maintain their magnificent unity and unite with the karamcharis and democratic teachers to further strengthen our common struggle.

Nurul Hasan's speech that day was greeted with a walkout by the students who had strategically occupied the front rows. It was a visible mass action which showed that the will of the students had not been broken. The administration was not going to find it easy to respond.

Meanwhile, I was in Tihar Jail, in a general ward at first, before being transferred to the MISA ward. Over the coming months, I would meet many people, from criminals to political leaders, those of the left and right; I would read; I would exercise more than I have done at any other time in my life; I would learn to cook. And I would learn how to survive, especially by teaching my mind to focus on the day to be lived out, rather than some future point when I would be free again.

5. Life in Jail

TIHAR: THE PLACE AND THE PEOPLE

I was taken to Tihar at night, after the jail was locked down. This was unusual.[1] A lockdown means that every prisoner is in his cell and a head count of all the prisoners has been tallied against the numbers in the books. Since tallying the numbers with the books is a very important function — it is how they know if a prisoner has escaped — the jail rule is that no new prisoner is inducted after lockdown.

So there I was, one of the very few who entered Tihar after lockdown. At the time, male political prisoners were held in dedicated MISA wards meant for prisoners in preventive detention, or in wards meant for those charged under the Defence of India rules. Women political prisoners had a much harder time as they were kept with the general run of undertrial or convicted prisoners. Being an Indian prison, the jail also doubled up to house the mentally ill who had not found a place in mental asylums. The jail authorities did not take me to one of the MISA wards but one with non-political prisoners who were either undertrials or convicts.

This was my first introduction to jail. This particular ward had a set of separate blocks, each holding a set of individual cells. There was some open space between the blocks but no greenery. The cells were pretty basic, there's no other way to describe them.

---

[1] During the Shah Commission's investigations, the officers investigating my case did not believe me when I told them that I had been taken to Tihar after 10 PM. They later explained to me the jail rules and why they were so surprised. They did verify from the jail records that this was indeed the case.

Each prisoner had a slab of cement with a sheet and pillow. The lucky ones might get another sheet to cover themselves with. And in winter, we got a blanket. The 'toilet' was part of the cell. Luckily, my cell was single occupancy.

The day was structured in a predictable way: you were let out in the morning and locked up at night. The lights were always kept on at night, we learned to sleep with them on. The cell gates would be locked by evening, when the major jail event of the day was conducted — the headcount of the prisoners. I guess counting is important to all bureaucracy including the jail bureaucracy, an appropriate end-of-workday ritual, same as tallying the day book of every branch of a bank!

In this ward, I was with some people convicted of relatively serious crimes, and others who were under trial, waiting for bail or not eligible for bail due to the severity of the crime. I don't know whether there is any system of separating the undertrials from the convicts today, but at the time it was a mixed population. For the mentally ill, it took another 25 years for Justice J.S. Verma, chairperson, National Human Rights Commission, to direct governments '. . . to ensure that mentally ill persons are not kept in jail under any circumstances.'[2]

This brings back a particularly poignant story I witnessed. Three Sikh gentlemen charged with murder were awaiting their verdict. They had decided to expiate their sin by doing good deeds and earning punya, in the hope that god would look kindly on them and they would not be convicted. They looked after a mentally ill prisoner who was blind and also couldn't speak but only made some sounds. Perhaps the file of their good deeds didn't reach god's desk, for they were convicted. The whole ward was very sympathetic. I guess it had to do with the camaraderie among prisoners, along with appreciation for the way these three had conducted themselves

---

[2] See:
https://nhrc.nic.in/press-release/nhrc-directs-states-ensure-mentally-ill-persons-are-not-jailed-under-any-circumstances

Life in Jail

in prison. The only person who was happy at the outcome was the blind and deaf person they had looked after. He had been worried about losing his helpers if they won release.

There were some prisoners who were not really anti-government, but were being held as they were union leaders in an autonomous institution. The union was not politically affiliated to any party, and its leaders were close to the Congress. An officer in the institution who did not like their union activities had complained to the police that they were opposing the Emergency. Normally, they would not have been housed with common prisoners but with other political prisoners. They were at pains to explain to me that they did not wish to be lodged with prisoners from the political opposition, as they were not opposed to the Emergency; it was at their own request they were lodged with 'normal' prisoners.

This case also exemplifies the nature of the Emergency. Prisoners included people who had been put behind bars just because some factory owner or someone in a government department happened to dislike a trade union or its leaders. All they had to do was say that the named person or persons were opposing the Emergency. The administration could then charge them with being anti-Emergency, and quite often that was enough to hold them under MISA, or the Defence of India rules. The latter was a somewhat better fate since it allowed some room to fight in court, though you would still be locked up for a while. As for those being held under MISA, the Supreme Court laid down in its ADM Jabalpur verdict of 1976 that we had the right to life and liberty but we could not move the court to enforce this right. All MISA orders were meant to be reviewed every four months. Of course, we all knew this review was a farce, in the way internal reviews of government decisions almost always are.

Even the brief experience of being locked up with undertrials and convicts was enough for me to understand a couple of things. One was that food was, in a sense, a 'democratic' leveller. Everyone, but everyone, got really bad, almost inedible food. The other was that I saw first-hand the number of ways in which class protected people like me. I inspired a kind of respect simply because I was seen as 'educated' and 'political': *padha-likha ladka hai, political hai*. Even in jail, we were protected by class, something that is not normal in most countries. Leaving out the US jails, which appear to be particularly brutal (whether in the Hollywood version or in serious literature), even in Latin American countries, class did not protect you. From the stories of my Latin American friends who, or whose friends, were imprisoned by brutal dictatorships under Pinochet or other dictators, torture against political prisoners was 'egalitarian'. Unlike us, everybody accused of leftist views faced torture and a brutal prison regime. Of course, we also had the history of the independence movement, with yesterday's prisoners being tomorrow's leaders. But there is no question that class provides you a degree of protection even in jail.

I think I was in a general ward for five days before I was shifted to Ward Number 14, one of the two MISA wards. The other one was Ward Number 1. If my memory serves, the ward for those arrested under Defence of India rules was Ward 15.

WARDS 14 AND 17

Tihar Jail was a very large prison, occupying about 65 to 70 acres of land. There were low barracks in each ward, all single-storey, with some grounds attached to each one. Once the prisoners were let out during the day, we were not really cramped for space. In Ward 14, we were not in individual cells; it had two large barracks, with about 20 persons held in each and one bathroom per barrack.

There was some classification of prisoners who were divided into B ('better class prisoners'), and C, or 'ordinary prisoners'. In Delhi, all the political prisoners were in the 'better class' category. In the jails of UP, that was not the rule, as I discovered when I was taken to Naini Jail in Allahabad for my master's viva. Only a select few were designated 'better class'. As Indian jails carry significant

Life in Jail

class distinctions, particularly in the matter of food, it made a huge difference to the political prisoners detained in UP. Better class in Tihar meant we got somewhat better prison-issue clothing, two blankets and even warm clothes in winter; on the whole, better facilities.

At Tihar, we were issued with rations from the jail store, which we collected every day, and were also allotted convicts — from among those sentenced to serve with hard labour — to cook our food. We only had to supervise their cooking. There was a rota system for kitchen duties among us, which consisted of going with the convict labour assigned to the barracks to collect the day's rations from the store, and supervising the cooking. Some of our fellow inmates knew how to cook, so the food was not bad at all, particularly for someone like me used to long periods of hostel food! P. Ghosh, the additional magistrate who had signed my MISA warrant, was for a short period also supervising Tihar Jail. He asked the jail superintendent to arrange a meeting with me. During our talk, he wanted to know how the food was, and I told him it was better than JNU hostel food. The jail superintendent was very pleased, till I explained, no, it was not a compliment to Tihar but a commentary on our hostel food.

This is where I picked up some rudimentary understanding of cooking, not by doing any but simply observing how it is done. This was useful later in life, but of course, the doing is always different from knowing the theory!

Those who had been convicted to serve with hard labour found cooking for us a lighter duty, as they also shared our food. But the jail kitchen duty, cooking for two to three thousand people on an almost industrial scale in Delhi's summer was very hard indeed. And the food was bad, as the rations issued for the 'C Class' prisoners were very, very poor. As I had shared the same food that ordinary prisoners had, I knew how bad it was. The rice and wheat had stones and, from the smell, were clearly either rotten or stale. Again, the question of class, even in jail.

There is a difference between those who were under rigorous imprisonment and had to do labour and those who were either serving simple prison sentences or there as under trials. But again, class makes a difference. Even if you are convicted, you get 'better class' treatment in jail because of your status. If you were a graduate or paid income tax then you did not do hard labour. There was the famous case of an eye doctor, Dr Jain, who had conspired with others to kill his wife. He was convicted and was also assigned a prison duty. But his labour, his prison duty, was looking after the jail library.

Later, when I was shifted to Agra, I had to supervise the non-vegetarian cooking with another young student activist from Bihar. Neither of us knew how to cook, nor did the convict labour who had been assigned to us. It was then we had to start from scratch and work out how to cook by trial (and mostly error). Initially inedible — even our convict labour refused it — our food grew to be just about edible by the end, a huge improvement!

The two barracks in Ward 14 were segregated politically, more by voluntary action than by the jailers who had assigned our barracks. One was the RSS-Jan Sangh barrack (yes, there were people — though few — in the Jan Sangh who did not identify as RSS), and the other was a very mixed bag: everyone who was not RSS-Jan Sangh. It consisted of the Jamaat-e-Islami, and different shades of the left, including socialists, and those with no particular political affiliation who had been picked up in the police dragnet. This included Mam Chand, a newspaper vendor in Connaught Place, who stocked — as he told me — both the RSS mouthpiece, the *Organiser*, and CPI(M)'s weekly *Peoples Democracy*. Funnily enough, the publication he was arrested for stocking was not one of these 'subversive' papers, but Piloo Mody's English weekly, *March of the Nation*, which could hardly be called subversive.

Mam Chand's story also figures in the Shah Commission Report, as he, a sole breadwinner with nine children, was arrested because of a complaint by Arjun Das, a municipal councillor in

Delhi and one of Sanjay Gandhi's hangers-on. The authorities admitted that they had not read the 'subversive' literature discovered in his stall, but had signed the MISA order against him under instructions from the 'PM's House'. Possibly, putting a newspaper vendor behind bars was a warning to others not to keep any papers or magazines critical of the government.

Ward 14 housed some important prisoners: Nanaji Deshmukh, Kanwar Lal Gupta, Arun Jaitley and Murali Manohar Prasad Singh.[3] Later, D.P. Tripathi, the JNU Students Union president, joined us in Ward 14. Nanaji Deshmukh, a key RSS functionary, was the *de facto* second in command of Jayaprakash Narayan's Total Revolution movement, a position JP made official at the Ram Lila Maidan rally of June 25, 1975, declaring Nanaji the secretary of the Lok Sangharsh Samiti. This was also the public meeting at which JP asked government officials and military not to obey the 'illegal and immoral orders' of the government, providing Mrs Gandhi an opportunity to claim that he was openly promoting sedition.

It was the nature of the JP movement that it had no core set of beliefs but was riding on the wave of reaction to the Congress's perceived corruption, aided by Mrs Gandhi's drift towards a more authoritarian position. This was also the period of Sanjay Gandhi's emergence from a failed car-maker to a successful political entrepreneur, under his mother's umbrella. The open support of the Indira government to Sanjay's venture was not only a tale of violation of laws and government regulations — aided by Sanjay cronies like Bansi Lal — but also of the discord between Mrs Gandhi and her one-time private secretary, P.N. Haksar, as Jairam Ramesh details in his book *Intertwined Lives: P.N. Haksar and Indira Gandhi*.[4] The Sanjay gang in the administration retaliated against P.N. Haksar with a raid on Pandit Brothers on July 15, 1975. Pandit Brothers, owned by Haksar's uncle, had a landmark shop-cum-

---

[3] DUTA President during AIFUCTO strike of 1987.
[4] Jairam Ramesh, *Intertwined Lives: P.N. Haksar and Indira Gandhi*, Simon & Schuster, 2018.

showroom in Chandni Chowk and another in Connaught Place.[5] Officially, the raid and subsequent actions against the owner were for not displaying proper price tags. The 81-year-old uncle and a 72-year-old brother-in-law, K.P. Mushran, were arrested, though released on bail by the evening. The raid was organised by a special squad under the chief secretary.[6] The charges were framed under the Defence of India rules. Apparently, India's defence during the Emergency rested on having proper price tags in shops!

Ward 1, which was larger, also had a mixed bag of politics, mostly RSS-Jan Sangh and socialists. In Delhi, the RSS-Jan Sangh was the major opposition to the Congress and had the largest numbers. Again, it was a mix of MISA detainees, with inmates from the RSS-Jan Sangh family, such as Sundar Singh Bhandari (general secretary of the Jan Sangh), the former mayor of Delhi, Hansraj Gupta, and his son Prem Sagar Gupta who would be a future mayor; while the socialists included Surendra Mohan, Raj Kumar Jain and Vijay Pratap, Hansraj Rehbar, a well-known leftist Hindi writer, and Ram Nath Vij.[7] Srilatha Swaminathan and

---

[5] Haksar's uncle R.N. Haksar owned 80 per cent of the shares of Pandit Brothers, and Haksar's sister and his wife Urmila Haksar ten per cent each.

[6] Later, there were income tax investigations, even searches for contraband foreign goods at Pandit Brothers. The details are available in Urmila Haksar's book, The Case of Pandit Brothers, Urmila Haksar, Perspective Publications, 1978 and also in Shah Commission Interim Report I. https://docs.google.com/file/d/0B_lk5cgbo2uuMjZBTGU4YzdsNlU/edit?pli=1&resourcekey=0-oi_8Mw8liaIGeW1TtaM3gg

[7] Surendra Mohan (1926–2010), a trade union leader and an activist and leader of the socialist movement, became a Rajya Sabha member from the Janata Dal (1978–84), after declining the Morarji Desai government's offer to appoint him as a union minister.

Prof Raj Kumar Jai, a socialist (retired from Delhi University), remains an active columnist on socialist platforms.

Held in jail for 20 months during the Emergency, Vijay Pratap was a senior fellow at the Rajiv Gandhi Institute for Contemporary Studies in 2020. He is a socialist with a wide-ranging involvement in ecological and livelihood movements.

Hansraj Rehbar (1913–94). Rehbar's writings in Hindi and Urdu encompass novels, short stories, criticism and translation.

Ram Nath Vij is a professor at Hans Raj College, Delhi University.

Life in Jail

Maharani Gayatri Devi were in the women's ward, and though they had a small room to themselves, this wasn't a ward for political prisoners.[8] I used to meet Srilatha fleetingly, on the sidelines of the weekly visit, mulakaat, permitted to prisoners and got to know her much better later during the organisation of the World Social Forum 2004 in Mumbai.

I had been in jail for about a month when D.P. Tripathi (DPT) was arrested. This meant I had a companion whose position was similar to mine. At this point, we functioned as some kind of CPI(M) voice inside the jail. Our separate mulakaats netted us a range of information, so we were relatively well informed about what was happening.

Kanwar Lal Gupta was an ex-MP from Delhi. He was friendly and outgoing. He and Arun Jaitley would sit with us — Murali Babu, DPT and me — and have conversations on a range of topics including politics. Most of these were about the Emergency. As we were all starved of news, we pooled our information from the once-a-week mulakaats. Of course it also included a healthy dose of gossip and rumour, the staples of a censored society.

It might appear at first sight that the two barracks in Ward 14 were organised politically. But I discovered pretty soon that there was a deeper reason for this division. Our barrack — mixed politically — had one common factor, a non-vegetarian kitchen, while the other barrack had a vegetarian one. It meant that in our barrack, while both vegetarian and non-vegetarian food was cooked, in the other barrack's kitchen meat and eggs were strictly taboo. Food taboos go far deeper than politics: that is why they lend themselves so easily to the divisive use of food in politics that we are witnessing today. Not that this is new, as the RSS and its forebears had been trying to politicise food, particularly bovine —

---

[8] Srilatha passed away in February 2017. She continued to be in CPI(ML) Liberation till the end. Her father was the advocate-general of Tamil Nadu during the Emergency. The party then in power in Tamil Nadu was the DMK, and the state was relatively free of arbitrary arrests and DIR, MISA detentions.

both cow and buffalo — meat since the cow protection movements of the late nineteenth century.[9]

Since the other barrack, the RSS-Jan Sangh one, was strictly vegetarian, some of those from the RSS-Jan Sangh who were non-vegetarian used to come and eat with us. But the food that came during the mulakaats — yes, mulakaats meant that families could bring food for the prisoners — proved a problem for them. When the Jamaat prisoners had a mulakaat, we would get really delicious food: mouth-watering biryani, pasanda, kabab and kofta. I don't think I have ever in my life tasted food as delicious as what came during those mulakaats. A number of these items were *bada*, meaning either beef or buff. Most of those from the left had no problems with eating beef or eating with people who ate beef. But our RSS-Jan Sangh non-vegetarians had a problem. As one of them explained: '*Woh Bade wala jo hai na, woh hamse chalega nahi.*' Reluctantly, they turned vegetarian rather than eat with people who ate beef.

There was a jail canteen where you could buy some of the things you needed. For most of us who smoked, and I was a smoker at the time, it was cigarettes, paan, or beedis. The amount of money you (or your family) could transfer to your canteen account was very small, so we all switched to smoking beedis.

MULAKAAT: THE NEWS FROM OUTSIDE

Jail life for prisoners centred around two central issues: their release and their link with the outside world through *mulakaats*. If you were taken to far-off prisons, letters became important. In my case, since I was in Delhi and later on in Agra, letters were not crucial. Ashoka would visit me every week except those weeks

---

[9] Gyan Pandey, 'Rallying Round the Cow: Sectarian Strife in the Bhojpur Region, c. 1888–1917', CSSSC Occasional Paper No. 39. Calcutta: CSSSC., 1981.
https://opendocs.ids.ac.uk/opendocs/handle/20.500.12413/3241

when my parents made the trip from Kanpur to Delhi, and later Agra.

Getting permission to visit a prisoner was not an easy process. You had to apply to the additional district magistrate sitting in Tees Hazari, and collect your permit in the evening or the next day. Ashoka had shifted to her parents' place in North Delhi. So at least two days of every week had to be spent arranging a meeting with me. For people inside, this was very important, as it gave us a glimpse of what was happening and kept us anchored to the outside world. For those who have never been in prison, it is difficult to imagine how the loss of this lifeline affects those whose families are far away, or as in the Bhima Koregaon case, where various restrictions, including COVID-19, are used to deny visits to those detained under the Unlawful Activities Prevention Act. For the first few months, there were no mulakaats.

Once the mulakaat began, it quickly became one of the things that kept the MISA detenues going. I was lucky in this sense, the mulakaats had already started when I was arrested. Ashoka had earlier accompanied Com. Jaipal Singh's wife Usha-di to the Rohtak jail for her first mulakaat, as the party leadership wanted to know Singh's views on the Emergency as well as communicate its understanding of how to re-organise in view of the new situation.

We longed for news of what people outside were saying, news about the resistance to the Emergency — and we got it at our mulakaats. The left, the CPI(M) in particular, had decided that they were in for a long period of underground work. So we heard about the underground cells being put together as well as the overground activities, and how the two could function together. We also got news about the challenges they were facing, and of the brutality of the family planning program, and the many acts of wanton callousness and vindictiveness of the Emergency administration.

Some of the Maoists among us felt a little lost, as they were not getting this sort of news and support from the outside. Their organisation was not able to keep this living link with them. A few of them, including Murali Babu, joined the CPI(M) after they came out of jail.

We would also be a little mischievous, planting false information, claiming it came from our sources outside.

Within the Congress, there was a move towards introducing a presidential form of government. P.N. Dhar describes this proposal in some detail.[10] It originated with B.K. Nehru, India's high commissioner to the UK, and was then given shape by D.K. Barooah, Rajni Patel, A.R. Antulay, and Siddhartha Shankar Ray. Antulay was the major proponent of the presidential form of government and even drafted a document to this end, but it did not fly with Mrs Gandhi. She thought that such a drastic change could delegitimise her and cast the Emergency as a personal power grab. But one of its great supporters was Sanjay Gandhi, who thought — according to D.P. Dhar — that it offered a way of perpetuating the Emergency.

Once the prospect of a presidential form of government came up, the question was who would be the opposition candidate against Mrs Gandhi, since she would obviously be the Congress nominee. Various names including JP's were being floated, as possible candidates who could unite the entire opposition.

There was a rumour that JP had proposed Sheikh Abdullah as the common presidential candidate of the opposition. Sheikh Abdullah was a credible opposition candidate, a Muslim, someone who had spent time in jail, and a close friend of JP's. JP was, after all, a political maverick who had gone from being a socialist to moving very close to the Americans, and finally to the RSS on his Sampoorna Kranti journey. And Sheikh Abdullah would cut into the Muslim base of the Congress, voters who otherwise wanted to have nothing to do with the RSS. Nanaji's response to Sheikh Abdullah was sharp: '*Zinda makkhi hum niglengey nahi*' (We will not swallow a live fly).

[10] P.N. Dhar, *Indira Gandhi, the 'Emergency', and Indian Democracy*, Oxford University Press, 2000, pp. 334–37.

Life in Jail

(The idea of Sheikh Abdullah as a possible unifying candidate is not as farfetched as it might seem today. In 1983, Farooq Abdullah's coming together with other regional opposition parties and the left, would make him an all-India leader. It was an extremely short-sighted move of the Congress to dismiss his government in July 1984, by conniving with his brother-in-law, Ghulam Mohammed Shah, to drive home the point that a Kashmiri leader should not have all-India aspirations. What the Congress lost sight of is that Abdullah's elevation would have made the Kashmir Valley feel a part of Indian politics. Jagmohan of the Delhi demolitions fame was then governor of Jammu & Kashmir.

Kashmir lost that opportunity; instead, the lesson driven home was that any leader of Jammu & Kashmir exists at the sufferance of the central government. Jagmohan later joined the BJP. After the Turkman Gate demolition, he had stated that those displaced would not be resettled together as was done after other such demolitions. His argument, widely quoted, was: 'I did not destroy one Pakistan to create another.')

The Jamaat and the bulk of the Sanghis saw politics in a very narrow sense: for them politics was restricted to their narrow vision of society based on religious identities. With it came an odd fusion of caste, race and genetics that is peculiarly Indian. Science, and we know how this racialised science had no basis in reality, was used to argue the genetic superiority of the higher castes. They could not understand the larger view of society and history, as those did not exist if viewed from the narrow lens of their worldview; nor even politics in the larger context. They had no framework to analyse the larger currents. As Murali Babu used to say, a communist consciousness (or any radical politics) has to be developed. The Sanghis and the Jamaat have an advantage: their ideological consciousness is produced and reproduced within the family, from one generation to the next, as family values. It is a part of what you learn from your elders as aachaar: conduct, or the practice of good family values. (It is interesting that aachaar as good values, and achaar as pickles, are near homonyms. After all the aachaar they teach are indeed the pickled values of a society that refuses to change!)

After a few months, the MISA wards were getting overcrowded as there was a continuous inflow and no outflow. The jail authorities decided to add a new MISA ward, Ward 17, and made the offer that those who wanted to could shift there. When we — the leftists of different hues — found out that the socialists from Ward 1 were also shifting to Ward 17, we decided that might be more interesting for us. It was also a bigger ward with more space, so we could play more games, including volleyball. Ward 17 had two barracks and a row of cells. P.N. Lekhi, who later became government pleader when the Shah Commission was set up after the Emergency, was one of those transferred to Ward 17. The socialists there were, Surendra Mohan, Raj Kumar Jain and Lalit Mohan Gautam, among others.[11] Hansraj Rehbar, the writer, was also transferred from Ward 1 to 17.

I was very keen to study socialist literature. There were two major socialist streams: the Praja Socialist Party and the Samyukta Socialist Party — which broke from the Praja in 1955. The two parties merged and then split again a number of times. One of the key organisation men in the party and close to Dr Ram Manohar Lohia — the charismatic leader of the Samyukta group — once told us (he had joined us late in Ward 14) that his major problem with all the unifications and splits of the socialist parties was that every three years he had to start a new office from scratch: from buying typewriters to creating the membership list. He had barely set up a new office and organised it properly before a new unity/split meant he had to start all over again!

I asked the socialists in Ward 17 if I could read anything that

---

[11] Lalit Mohan Gautam — who died in January 2022, having contracted COVID-19 and dengue — had run a Delhi-based journal, *Resistance*, which printed only two issues before his arrest. He went on to defeat the Congress party candidate from the Okhla seat in 1977. Later, he set up practice as an advocate at the Delhi High Court.

they had, particularly *Ithihas Chakra* (Wheel of History, 1955) by Dr Lohia.[12] I was always a voracious reader and jail is after all the best place to read books, with relatively little distraction. Either because they themselves did not have it, or did not trust me to be suitably worshipful of their icon, they never gave me a copy of what they considered his iconic work. Though a number of his followers — e.g., Yogendra Yadav — have blamed other left currents, particularly the Marxists, of a conspiracy of silence in ignoring Dr Lohia, they seem to have done very little to make his works accessible.[13] Even today, it is not easy to get his books.

Surendra Mohan joined us in Ward 17 and became somebody I went on to meet on various platforms later. He was a lovable man with no airs about him and friendly with everybody. Before Ward 17, Murali Babu was the only one with an interest in chess, and he would play me. In Ward 17, both Surendra Mohan and Hansraj Rehbar played chess, providing me a larger group to while away time with.

During our detention under MISA, the issue of our ability to appear for examinations (in my case, my viva as a part of my M Tech Thesis defence), was discussed in the home ministry. As the Shah Commission brings out, the student detenues were considered high risk by the lieutenant governor of Delhi and by Navin Chawla, his secretary. It was only after the Delhi high court issued instructions on my case that I was taken to Allahabad for my viva. The Shah Commission's Report says,

> The attitude of Delhi Administration was particularly harsh in dealing with the requests from the student detenues for release on parole to enable them to take their University examinations. It has been intimated by the Delhi Administration that 17 students had applied for parole to appear in the examinations.

---

[12] http://164.100.47.193/dignitaries_file/Manohar_Lohia.pdf
[13] Yogendra Yadav, 'On Remembering Lohia', *Economic & Political Weekly*, Vol XLV No 40, October 02, 2010.

The records show that only one student, namely Shri Prabir Purkayastha, a PhD student of Jawaharlal Nehru University could appear [for his] examination. He could get this facility not because of any leniency on the part of the Administration but because the Delhi High Court had issued specific directions to the Administration to take him to Allahabad for his examination. Though the Ministry of Home Affairs had advised his release on parole, he was only transferred from Delhi to Naini Jail and taken there in handcuffs. He took his M.E. viva voce examination in jail.[14]

This order was passed by Justice S. Rangarajan, if I remember right, just before the court's winter break in December. That was one of the reasons the government could not file for an immediate stay in the Supreme Court, as they had done in other cases. Rangarajan suffered consequences for standing up to the central government on MISA cases. The MISA bench, consisting of S. Rangarajan and R.N. Aggarwal, had struck down the MISA order on Kuldeep Nayar in July 1975. They, like many other high courts in the country, had held that no citizen could be deprived of fundamental rights during the Emergency and any order for detention was open to judicial review. Justice Aggarwal was reverted to a sessions judge and Justice Rangarajan transferred from Delhi to Assam.

I, like many others, had filed a habeas corpus petition in the Delhi court. Ashoka had found out that leading left lawyers like R.K. Garg, most of whom were with CPI, were reluctant to take up the cases of MISA detenues. In the Pandit Brothers Case, Mrs Gandhi had asked Rajeshwar Rao, the general secretary of the CPI, to direct R.K. Garg not to appear for the brothers in the Delhi high court or Supreme Court, not even on income tax matters.[15] R.K. Garg refused to accept this. Given that we — the CPI(M) — did

---

[14] Shah Commission Interim Report II, p. 43
[15] Urmila Haksar, *The Case of Pandit Brothers*, Perspective Publications, 1978.

not have any senior lawyer in the high court, Ashoka approached N.M. Ghatate, who was very close to the Jan Sangh and the RSS, to take up my case. Ghatate was happy to do so, as it was a fit case to show how MISA was being misused. Ghatate later became a member of the Law Commission and also the biographer of Atal Behari Vajpayee.

After the court order, a group of policemen appeared one evening to take me to Allahabad. Since it was already evening, they decided to take me to the police barracks where they were staying and shackled me to the bed for the night. Next morning, in manacles, with an escort of eight armed policemen, I set out for the railway station. It must have made quite an impression on the public. This was the only time I immediately got a berth almost entirely to myself in an unreserved compartment, as the entire section of the compartment immediately emptied out! We reached Naini Jail by evening and I reached the MISA Ward in time for dinner.

Naini Jail was also where Jawaharlal Nehru had been imprisoned, I believe in the same ward that we were held. The ward had a huge compound and the barracks were not locked at night, we could walk in the evening till quite late. Nanaji Deshmukh had asked me to talk to Murli Manohar Joshi, the Jan Sangh leader who was in Naini Jail, and get his views on whether to take a stand and remain in jail or seek an early release by reaching out to the government. Murli Manohar Joshi talked to me for over an hour on a cold December night, explaining why we all needed to get out of jail, 'whatever might be the strategy'. To quote his words, '*kisi bhi tarah, kisi bhi tarah, yehaan se nikla jaaye.*' When I came back to Delhi, I gave his views to Nanaji, along with a letter for him that I had carried back. Nanaji heaved a sigh and said, '*Woh aurat maane tab na!*' As we know now, the RSS had made overtures to Mrs Gandhi without success. Two letters from Balasaheb Deoras, dated August 22, 1975 and November 10, 1975, to Mrs Gandhi are now public, offering to disassociate the RSS from the JP movement and support her 20-point program.[16]

The last slice of my 12 months in jail was spent in Agra Central Jail. It started with a major jailbreak from Tihar, where 13 life-term prisoners escaped by digging a long tunnel from their ward and under the jail wall. While this was interesting news for us, it was traumatic for the jail staff. On April 23, some of us were called to the jail's main office from our ward. I recall that Surendra Mohan, Murali Babu and I were among those summoned. We were asked to come with our bags packed, so we had an inkling that we would be transferred from Tihar to some other jail.

When we reached the jail office, we were all herded into the large quadrangle that forms the entrance to Tihar just within the jail gate. With us stood detenues from the two other MISA wards, Ward 1 and Ward 14. We discovered we were all to be dispersed in small groups to different jails, with a number of groups destined to be transferred to UP. I asked to be given a look at the warrant regarding my transfer, and told the jail staff that they should write the class of the prisoner being transferred, as different states had different rules on who was recognised as a B Class prisoner. The jail official was quite surprised to learn from me that UP jails did not treat all MISA/DIR detenues as the same and there were huge distinctions in UP jails between those they classified as B or C class, even when they were being held under the same detention order.[17] Only five of us from Tihar were transferred to Agra Central Jail, which we reached by the evening. Among those who were transferred was Professor O.P. Kohli from the Jan Sangh's teachers' wing, who was one of the leaders of the Delhi University Teachers Association, and who later became the governor of Gujarat; and B.S. Atkaan, a socialist and a long-time trade union leader.

[16] https://twitter.com/_yogendrayadav/status/1049745360506290183?lang=en
[17] Initially, all MISA detenues were treated as 'Special Class' in jails. Later they became 'A' for MLAs and MPs, 'B' for Better Class and 'C' for others. In UP, as I had found out, 'B' was given only after the detenues approached the court; or, in rare cases, by the jail authorities at their own discretion.

Life in Jail

The question on all our minds was the reason for the transfer, and why us? While the jailbreak was the immediate answer, MISA detenues were a small part of the jail population.[18] The other one — why us — was also discussed, although we had no more than an hour or two before being taken away to our respective destinations in UP, Haryana and Rajasthan. The common denominator was that we had all filed habeas corpus petitions in the high court, but it appeared a very petty reason for such a major step regarding detenues. After all, the ones who had been despatched earlier from Delhi were major leaders like JP, L.K. Advani, Madhu Dandavate, Jyotirmoy Basu, Biju Patnaik, Chandra Sekhar, Samar Guha, Major Jaipal Singh. There were few leaders of that stature among us, so why us?

(While JP was kept in Chandigarh, the others were sent to Hisar and Rohtak. A number of reports today talk about Advani and Madhu Dandavate being kept in Bangalore Jail for 18 months during the Emergency. These reports are not correct. Advani's book — *A Prisoner's Scrapbook* — gives the details of how, 25 days after their arrest, both he and Madhu Dandavate were shifted to Rohtak. Vajpayee was undergoing an appendix operation in Bangalore. He was in hospital during this time and was later allowed to go back to Delhi. He was interned in his house through most of the Emergency. There was a lot of criticism within the Jana Sangh-RSS about the 'deal' he had struck with Mrs Gandhi to be allowed to stay at home, committing himself not to participate in any anti-government activity.[19] This was also what we heard from some of the Jan Sangh-RSS fellow prisoners in Tihar, who were quite bitter about his role, though muted in their criticism.)

---

[18] MISA detenues in Tihar were about 200 as against the total prison population of 4,200. Shah Commission Interim Report p. 39, para 11.47.

[19] Subramaniam Swamy, *The Hindu*, June 13, 2000. (I was unable to negotiate *The Hindu's* archives successfully to this op-ed piece, but here is a link from Google:
https://groups.google.com/g/pesakkimuthucitu/c/uspNmTMBOvk/m/RBqMK6wD2nwJ

The Shah Commission Report (Interim Report II) gives us a glimpse of the pettiness of the Emergency administration in Delhi.[20] In retrospect, this is not surprising since it was run — as the Shah Commission concluded — entirely by Sanjay Gandhi and his trusted gang of officials. The jailbreak of a few criminals was used to settle scores with the MISA detenues who had dared to file habeus corpus writ petitions in the courts. These petitions were then making the rounds of various high courts, with a number of courts ruling that the MISA detenues had a right to approach court and the high courts did have jurisdiction in this matter.[21] The famous — or infamous — ADM Jabalpur judgement pronounced by the Supreme Court was still pending. It was passed a few days after our transfer, but possibly the government already knew about the split among the five judges hearing the case and the favourable verdict in store for the government.

Smt. Chandra, special secretary (home), has stated that some of the transfers were made because of 'awkward situations caused by Writs filed by the detenues', a version corroborated by J.K. Kohli, the chief secretary of Delhi, '...that some persons who had filed Writs, were transferred outside Delhi.' The lieutenant governor's version is even more telling: '...the conditions in Tihar Jail were not satisfactory and some detenues were sent to other places where they could lead a more comfortable life.'

Here is the full extract from the Shah Commission Report:

> 11.49 Transfer of MISA detenues presents an excess of its own kind. 200 MISA detenues including some prominent Opposition leaders were transferred from Tihar Jail to jails outside Delhi during the Emergency. Shri S.K. Batra has stated that the transfer of such persons involved great discomfort

---

[20] Shah Commission Interim Report II pp. 40.
[21] The nine high courts who had passed orders that MISA detenus had the right to approach the High Court were: (1) Delhi (2) Karnataka (3) Bombay (Nagpur Bench) (4) Allahabad (5) Madras (6) Rajasthan (7) Madhya Pradesh (8) Andhra Pradesh (9) Punjab and Haryana.

to the detenues because of the additional inconvenience and expense it involved to their relatives. He said that such transfers are always considered as penal measures in Jail Administration. Both Shri S.K. Batra and Shri R.N. Sharma have denied having made any proposals for the transfer of the MISA detenues. Shri R.N. Sharma [Tihar Jail Superintendent] had, in fact, suggested the transfer of ordinary prisoners to reduce the congestion in Tihar Jail, but it does not seem to have been accepted. Shri S.K. Batra has stated that many of the political detenues who had filed Petitions in the High Courts were transferred from Delhi during the period their petitions were being processed in the High Court.

Shri A.D. Sapra, Deputy Secretary (Home) who was also the DIG (Prisons), has stated that the names of the detenues and Places of their transfer were decided at 'higher level' and the job of the Home Department was only to process the cases. Smt Chandra, Special Secretary (Home) has stated that some of the transfers were made because of 'awkward situations caused by Writs filed by the detenues'. The transfers of the detenues were decided by the Lt. Governor who brooked no delay in their implementation. Shri J.K. Kohli, Chief Secretary, has also stated that he was not consulted in matters of transfers of MISA detenues. These decisions were taken by the Lt. Governor, and the officials of the Home Department used to get very short notice for making administrative arrangements for the transfer of the detenues concerned. The orders were informally communicated from Raj Niwas over telephone. Shri Kohli has also confirmed that some persons who had filed Writs, were transferred outside Delhi.

11.50 Shri Kishan Chander [lieutenant governor] has denied having made Shri Navin Chawla responsible for Tihar Jail in any manner as he already had a Jail Superintendent and the I.G. (Prisons) to look after the jail...He admitted that he knew that Tihar Jail was overcrowded and this fact was known to everybody in the Government. Discussions were going on to construct another building but no concrete steps were taken. About the transfer of MISA detenues, he said that the conditions in Tihar Jail were not satisfactory and some detenues were sent to other places where they could lead a more comfortable life.

So how comfortable were we after being transferred to Agra? Agra Central Jail was scheduled to be demolished, as it was set up in 1847 and was very old by now.[22] It had no plumbing or proper toilets, with convicts used for manual scavenging of the toilets.[23]

We were taken to a ward that had two rows of cells back-to-back, with each row opening out to a small strip of land in front and an iron railing between the two sides. Neither side could even see the other row. We were in the front row, while the back row was used for those detained under the 1974 Conservation of Foreign Exchange and Prevention of Smuggling Activities Act (COFEPOSA), the detention law that amounted to a MISA for economic offenders. The back row of the ward lodged Haji Mastan, the famous smuggler cum mafia don of Mumbai, and Lalit Dholakia, from a minor business family turned smugglers. For film buffs, Amitabh Bachchan's role in the mega hit *Deewar* was loosely based on Haji Mastan. While Dholakia's and other gangs were willing to smuggle drugs along with other contraband, Haji Mastan enjoyed some moral standing in Mumbai's crime world: Even though a smuggler and a don, unlike others he never smuggled drugs as he hated what they did to people and their families.

---

[22] The jail grounds were large and therefore quite attractive for real estate development. In fact, the demolished jail has become the key financial and business hub of Agra today. Ironically, it is called Sanjay Place after Sanjay Gandhi!

[23] Manual scavenging was not uncommon in our lives then, meaning it was around us much more visibly in that period. What strikes me today, after working with Bezwada Wilson and the Safai Karmachari Andolan (SKA), is how insensitive we all were to this issue.

We each had a cell that consisted of a block of two identical cells, one to be used for sleeping and reading, the other as a bathroom (no modern flush toilet but a dry toilet with manual scavenging), a small, walled quadrangle open to the sky and an iron door with a small window for the jail warder to look in periodically. After the first night, we were called into the jail office one by one the next morning, without any inkling as to why. At the jail superintendent's office, we were told that there were instructions from higher-ups (now we know they were from UP's inspector general, prisons) instructing that we be put under solitary confinement. We were not only in solitary confinement within the small block, but at night would be locked in the cell we were using as our bed/living room. Woe betide anyone who needed to use the toilet at night.

We were in solitary confinement for 25 days, before we were let out during the day to be locked up again at dusk. Others who had been transferred to Fatehgarh and Bareilly were also put in solitary cells, but they were let out after a week, primarily as these jails had other MISA prisoners who pressured the jail administration. As we were the only prisoners under MISA in Agra, we spent 25 days in solitary, which left me with enormous respect for the freedom fighters who had suffered solitary confinement and hard labour in the Andamans under the British.

The prisoners transferred to Haryana or Rajasthan were not put in solitary confinement. Why did the UP's inspector of prisons issue such an instruction? This is a question to which I have found no record or answer. Clearly, Sanjay and his close confidants running the Delhi administration and the home ministry would have indicated that we should be treated 'properly'. But why did the UP jail administration behave worse than others? After all, Bansi Lal in Haryana was as much a Sanjay henchman as the UP chief minister, N.D. Tewari. This is what, to me, characterised much of what are called the Emergency excesses. It was simply mindless, petty viciousness in the exercise of power, simply because you could. The belief in officialdom was that the Emergency was here to stay, and none of them would ever be held accountable.

Once we were put in solitary, we all started a hunger strike quite spontaneously. As the row of cells was large, we were separated from each other by an intervening empty cell (a cell block of two cells to be accurate). The only way to communicate was to stand on one side and shout at the top of your voice to your neighbour, a test of lung power. That is how we discovered that all of us were on hunger strike. I had not set any limit to my hunger strike and was concerned, as the sole representative of the left, that I should not be found wanting. So, I steeled myself for a long hunger strike. Fortunately, the others — being more practised in hunger strikes — had notified a 72-hour duration. After three days we broke our strike.

The next challenge was to survive solitary confinement. I had worked out a routine for myself: so many hours of studying engineering, so many hours of Marxist reading, the rest to be spent on exercise and walking around the tiny patch of cement which was our courtyard.

In between, the convict warders, who guarded us, would chat with us about their lives. Generally, they were long-time convicts, which in UP means dacoits. I learned from them about how they became dacoits, mostly from debt, lack of any work or occasionally a fight that led to them absconding and becoming dacoits. They uniformly denied their guilt in the crime for which they were convicted. They said, yes, we were dacoits, but we did not actually commit the crime for which we were convicted. The police — according to them — had simply made up the evidence! Mostly, it was a confession from somebody guilty who would be let off if they implicated their fellow gang members.

Four days after our transfer, the *Additional District Magistrate of Jabalpur vs. Shiv Kant Shukla* verdict, turning down our habeas corpus petition was pronounced by the five-judge Constitution Bench, with Justice H.R. Khanna as the lone dissenter. The majority judgement was passed by Chief Justice A.N. Ray, Justices M.H. Beg,

Y.V. Chandrachud and P.N. Bhagwati, all of whom held that under Emergency, we had lost the right to move courts on questions of life and liberty against government orders issued under MISA or under the Defence of India Regulations. The constitutional bench held that:

> In view of the Presidential order dated 27 June 1975, no person has any locus standi to move any writ petition under Article 226 before a High Court for habeas corpus or any other writ or order or direction to challenge the legality of an order of detention on the ground that the order is not under or in compliance with the Act or is illegal or is vitiated by mala-fides factual or legal or is based on extraneous consideration.

We might have our right to life and liberty but did not have the right to move the courts for its exercise. This is what Niren De, the attorney general, had argued, which the Supreme Court upheld!

It was only in 2017, 42 years later, that the Supreme Court in *K.S. Puttaswamy vs. Union of India* overturned the ADM Jabalpur decision. Justice D.Y. Chandrachud, (whose father, Y.V. Chandrachud, was one of the judges who passed the majority judgement in the ADM Jabalpur case) wrote the new majority judgement, striking down the ADM Jabalpur verdict, while confirming the citizens' right to privacy.

In solitary, time was the enemy, how to spend it? So I decided to write a petition to the Delhi high court on our being shifted to Agra and put in solitary there. I had a copy of my habeas corpus petition, and used large parts of the arguments from there, that preventive detention cannot be punitive, and how it was completely arbitrary, mala fide, and a 'colourable' exercise of administrative authority. All of it was derived from the habeas corpus petition. Since I was blissfully unaware of different kinds of writ jurisdictions, I 'filed' it under Writ of Habeas Corpus as this was the only legal 'book' I had. The court registry rejected it not because of the recent

Supreme Court judgement in ADM Jabalpur, but because it was filed wrongly as habeas corpus — produce the body. Since my body was only being mistreated, I guess its production was not the issue in law! In any case, the Supreme Court's verdict on MISA detenues had extinguished all our rights to approach the courts under any writ jurisdiction, leaving us entirely at the mercy of the government officials, even the pettiest ones — in disposition, if not rank.

(I have been involved in two more petitions since then, both to do with telecom. One of these was the 1996 auction of licences for landlines under Sukh Ram, with the conditions of selection being defined only after the price bids were opened. This was what was famously dubbed as a case-by-case consideration of the bids, with its associated image of suitcases of cash found in Sukh Ram's residence. The second was the change from fixed license fees to revenue sharing. I deal with these elsewhere, but the reason I mention them here is the commonality I discovered between law and engineering.[24] In both, we copy what has worked in the past. In law, these are precedents in judgements; in engineering, they are the standards and designs that work. The trick is to identify what works and what to copy. Except that knowing how to calculate and how to make proper drawings — in the days before software became the core of tech — is essential for engineers, and how to write English mixed with Latin for lawyers, the two disciplines are conceptually similar!)

While we were still in solitary, three detenues from Bihar joined us — Shankar Prasad Tekriwal, who was in the Jan Sangh then, a young activist from the JP movement, and a socialist.[25] Atkaan and I now had some additional socialist company.

One of the consequences of more numbers was an increase

---

[24] See below, Chapter 7, 'Living Politics'.
[25] S.P. Tekriwal had a chequered political career, travelling from BJP to RJD. He later left the RJD, highly critical of the way the Bihar administration was being run, even though he had been a part of it.

Life in Jail

of non-vegetarians. We had a separate kitchen run by only two of us, me and the young Bihari JP'ite, who had joined us. This was a real test of our cooking skills, as neither of us, or the convict labour allotted to be our cook, knew how to cook. We muddled along, refusing to give up our right to eat meat and eggs, even if we did not know any cooking. It was learning from the fundamentals, mostly learning how not to cook!

The transfer to Agra, Bareilly or Fatehgarh went hard, not with us so much as our families. They had to make long train or bus journeys, face the usual harassment that any jail procedure imposes, all in order to meet us all too briefly and then go back the same day. In Delhi, mulakaats were permitted every week; in Agra (as in all UP jails), we were permitted mulakaats only once a fortnight. Considering the hassles, it was a blessing in disguise: or our families would have had to make this tiring trip every week. O.P. Kohli's wife and Ashoka were both staying in North Delhi, and they would travel to Agra together.

For my parents, meeting me became more difficult, as they had to first come to Delhi to get permission to visit me in Agra jail, and then come to Agra before going back to Kanpur. My mother, who was a very strong woman, nearly had what we used to call a 'nervous breakdown'.

Ashoka would bring me books and the latest news. This was the height of Sanjay's family planning campaigns, particularly in the North Indian states. The stories of their excesses, government employees and school teachers not getting salaries if they could not produce evidence that they had motivated people to get themselves sterilised, to the outright brutality of forced sterilisation in 'family planning' camps. Regarding books, the jail administration was completely arbitrary: one book with Fidel Castro on its cover was thought to be too subversive, though Castro supported Mrs Gandhi during the Emergency. But Mao Tse Tung's Selected Works was accepted without a second glance!

After some more weeks in Agra, the jail routine became even

more relaxed, and we were not even locked up till late at night. We could visit the jail library, and participate in games like volleyball with other inmates in the barrack next to us. We also met with Haji Mastan when he had to go for his mulakaats, though these were only brief chats.

After Tihar, we had created a new routine for ourselves. Games, borrowing books from the jail library, exercising and playing cards: these became our daily routine. Prof Kohli was finishing his PhD on Hindi Literature and had an excellent library in his cell. Then there was the Agra Jail Library, full of dust-laden books, but again an excellent collection of classics, including Saratchandra Chattopadhyaya in Hindi translation. I was a devourer of any reading material I could lay my hands on, and my speed in reading Hindi soon rivalled that of my English, much to my own surprise. So much so that Prof Kohli was quite surprised at the speed at which I borrowed books from his library. Apart from Marxist classics and my engineering texts, I now had Hindi fiction to spend my time on.

I also learned some new card games, more as a means of socialising than out of any interest in the game itself. I have never liked games of chance, which is what my fellow prisoners were fond of. All this, including games in the evening with other prisoners — we were allowed to join them as our ward did not have any place for games — kept us fairly occupied.

This continued till the routine third review of my MISA Order took place. We had come to expect that these were mechanical bureaucratic exercises and meant very little. To my surprise, the review of September 25 arrived in Agra Jail, which said that I could be released, and my MISA Order was now revoked. Among the MISA detenues, I was one of the earliest to be released, a part of the small trickle that started then and led to most of them being released in January, precursory to Mrs Gandhi's January 18 announcement of the 1977 elections. Though the Emergency was formally revoked only in March 1977, for all practical purposes

Life in Jail

it ceased to exist after the announcement of elections. The only political prisoners left in prison were those of the Baroda dynamite case, in which the prime accused was George Fernandes. He fought the 1977 elections from jail and won from Muzaffarpur in Bihar.

I was let out of the Agra jail at night, with my clothes, a small amount of cash and my freedom. Having stepped out, I went straight to the railway station and bought a ticket on a slow train to Delhi. The only people who met me outside the jail — since no one knew about my release — were Haji Mastan's people, who used to supply him with home-cooked food, I suspect with the connivance of the jail staff. They were very impressed that I was in the same jail ward as Mastan, even though I had met with him only fleetingly. Even that elevated my status considerably!

I got on the train and was on my way to Delhi. The return to normalcy included the pushing and shoving required to get into an unreserved compartment in Indian Railways; a refreshing change from my cloistered life of the last 12 months.

6. The Last Chapter of Mrs Gandhi's Emergency

Once I was out of jail, I had to relearn life outside. From a completely structured life with a strict routine, I had to get back to what life actually is, with all its anarchy and movement. The first thread I needed to pick up was my personal life. Ashoka and I had been about to get married when I was arrested. We now had to give notice of our marriage again, and follow through quickly. The Emergency was by no means over. We were living with the threat of my getting arrested again, or of Ashoka getting arrested. We still didn't know what my release signified. Was it a precursor to the Emergency 'softening' and heading into elections? Was it a continuation of the Emergency rule with a gradual release of detenues, while all the other features remained the same?

Getting married meant we had to find a house first. We had to produce credible-looking people who would vouch for us. We decided that our good friend Saumitra Chaudhuri looked quite the venerable JNU professor (though he was the same age as Ashoka, and a student), and got him to vouch for us as a respectable couple.[1] Of course, the landlord did not need to know that we were yet to be married. With Saumitra providing us a good character certificate, Ashoka and I moved into a 'one room set' in Vasant Vihar, close to JNU.

---

[1] A JNU-trained economist, Saumitra Chaudhuri (1954–2016) was a close friend till he parted company with us politically. He, Gautam Navlakha and I even ran a small company, selling software products. He was an important figure in the economic world. In 2005, he became a member of the Prime Minister's Economic Council, and in 2009, part of the Planning Commission.
https://www.business-standard.com/article/economy-policy/economist-saumitra-chaudhuri-passes-away-116121900021_1.html

Negotiating with the two sets of parents proved less easy. Both insisted on a formal, religious marriage with a function for family and friends. They conceded that we could keep it simple. As a small compromise in return, could we not accommodate them? Ashoka and I refused, and reminded the parents that it was our marriage, not theirs. Both sets of parents finally accepted there would be no religious ceremony. It would be a 'court marriage', with the ADM officiating. We, in turn, agreed to a request from Ashoka's father — that he would host a formal dinner.

While these changes were taking place in my personal life, I also had to enrol as a student again; given the bureaucratic ways of any university, including JNU, this was not exactly easy. And, of course, after the suspended animation of jail, I had to get back to a social and political life. These three aspects of my life after jail went hand in hand with what was happening in the capital and the country. We also began to re-examine whether the structure of political activism that had evolved during the Emergency — working in small groups and not holding large organisational gatherings — should continue. We were trying to tackle the question predominant in all our minds: What did the softening of the Emergency regime mean?

Slowly, as more prisoners were released, public political activities were resumed. For us on campus, this could mean the return of simple things — such as a protest against the university administration. As political activity on campus grew more visible, I had to decide to what extent I should participate. I was not in the forefront, but if I joined a demonstration I would carry the faint but unmistakable halo jail had given me, a halo that was entirely the state's doing. I promptly received a warning from a 'well-wisher' to be very careful as I was being watched.

CHANGES IN THE POLITICAL SCENARIO – NEW ALIGNMENTS, NEW FORMATIONS

I was released from jail at the end of September, and elections were announced about three and half months later, on January 18. This was an object lesson in how quickly political scenarios can change.

In jail, we had had heated discussions on what would happen if Mrs Gandhi were to lift the Emergency and call for elections. Though the life of the existing Parliament had been extended by a year, Mrs Gandhi would either have to face elections in March 1977 or extend the life of the Parliament once again. What should the opposition political parties do if she called for elections? Settle amongst themselves for seat adjustments? Contest as an alliance with their existing identities but a common program? Would they fight independently? Or would they, as JP wanted, merge the non-communist parties into one opposition party?

As we now know, JP was trying to get the four major non-communist parties — Bharatiya Lok Dal, socialists, Congress (O) and the Bharatiya Jana Sangh — to merge into one party. The process of opposition unity had begun with JP's unconditional parole on health grounds, on November 12, 1975.[2] JP was also in dialogue with the government on how to restore normalcy and lift the Emergency. In his book *Indira Gandhi, the 'Emergency', and Indian Democracy*, P.N. Dhar relates that JP had told Sugata Dasgupta that if elections were announced and he was freed, he would 'try to support the opposition'.[3] JP said, 'I would try to so arrange matters that there is one candidate from each constituency. The BLD, the JS and Congress (O) should give up their identities and merge.'[4] JP later included the socialist streams in his plan to

---

[2] M.G. Devasahyam, 'Jayaprakash Narayan: An Idealist Betrayed', *Frontline*, October 11, 2018.

[3] P.N. Dhar, *Indira Gandhi, the Emergency and Indian Democracy*, Oxford University Press, New Delhi, 2000. Sugata Das Gupta was the director of the Gandhian Institute of Studies, Varanasi, of which JP was the Chairman.

[4] P.N. Dhar, 2000. Chapter 12, 'My Experience of the Emergency', p. 311.

work toward a unified non-communist, non-Congress opposition party.

In Tihar jail, we had had long conversations with Surendra Mohan on the opposition unity JP was promoting. As a socialist, Mohan explained why they should join a merged party, even if all the three component parties were reactionary. He said the socialists had been completely divided, not just into the two socialist party streams of the Praja Socialist Party (PSP) and the Socialist Party/ Samyukta Socialist Party. There were also socialists such as Ashok Mehta in Congress (O);[5] Chandrasekhar, originally with Lohia's Socialist Party, and Mohan Dharia, with the PSP, were now in the Congress. There was also a section of socialists in Charan Singh's BLD. Surendra Mohan's view was that if all these socialists got together, that would make for a strong socialist element within a united opposition party. In other words, the united opposition project was also a grand socialist unity project.

Paradoxically, the suggestion of a merger divided all parties. Rakesh Ankit has used archival material to give us an idea of the discussions that took place at the time.[6] The Congress (O) was the strongest holdout. This was not so much for ideological reasons, but because of their fight in court on which formation of the Congress, the Congress (I) or Congress (O), should inherit the property of the undivided Congress. When the party was divided, each of the two factions had captured Congress properties depending on their strength in different states. The court was yet to decide which one would inherit the symbol, the name, and various properties held by the Congress. The Congress (O) was worried that merging all parties in a new formation would weaken their case. They suggested that all parties should instead merge themselves in the Congress (O). Needless to say, the suggestion had no takers.

---

[5] Ashok Mehta was the general secretary of the Congress (O) at that time.

[6] Rakesh Ankit, 'Janata Party (1974–77): Creation of an All-India Opposition', *History and Sociology of South Asia* 11 (1), pp. 39–54, 2017. As Ankit clarifies, he drew heavily on the JP and Brahmanand papers, held at the Nehru Memorial Museum and Library, New Delhi.

(Surendra Mohan thought the Congress (O) was being venal in worrying about property if they gave up the Congress name. And Murali Babu wisecracked that the Congress (O) was quite right, since politics was finished for them in any case.)

Finally the court decided that the Mrs Gandhi-led Congress was the legal inheritor of the Congress Party. History shows that this proved no solution to the socialist fracturing: later, when the Janata Party split, the socialists scattered into every one of the resulting factions and splinter groups. Even today, all the leaders of the socialists are in different parties. Murali Babu was right in his prediction that merging the Congress (O) with the Janata Party would mean its end. Of course, he could not have foreseen that the merger would net its leader, Morarji Desai, his life's ambition of becoming India's Prime Minister!

JP had initiated the process of opposition unity, but the going was slow while elections appeared to be a distant prospect. A meeting called in May 1976 for parties to unite did not prove productive. According to Ankit, it was a hastily called meeting with very little preparation. In a letter to JP, Charan Singh said the meeting was a case of 'putting the cart before the horse' since 'we did not know what we or the new party would be standing or fighting for.'[7]

For opposition unity to happen, there had to be some sound reason why disparate parties, with their fractious leaders, should come together. The parties had differences on how the Emergency should be fought and what their attitude to Mrs Gandhi should be. There was a range of opinions within the opposition. George Fernandes had decided that only physical resistance would defeat the Emergency. Other leaders were holding discussions with Mrs Gandhi, on how they could come out of jail, and expressing their willingness to work with her.

The RSS belonged to the camp that wanted to come out of jail

---

[7] R. Ankit, ibid.

The Last Chapter of Mrs Gandhi's Emergency

and work within the limits set by Mrs Gandhi, but her will was what counted. We know today from Deoras' letters from Yerawada jail in Pune that he had signalled his willingness to compromise with Mrs Gandhi and the Emergency. (These letters were placed in the Maharashtra Assembly.) I have also written (in Chapter 4) about the message Murli Manohar Joshi conveyed to Nanaji Deshmukh, and Nanaji's response to Joshi's plea about getting out of jail at any cost. Subramanian Swamy has written about the willingness of the RSS to compromise and sign what he calls a 'document of surrender'.[8] R.V. Sharada Prasad, the son of H.Y. Sharada Prasad — Mrs Gandhi's media advisor and one of her very few close confidants — has also written in *The Print* about this same document:

> In November 1976, over 30 leaders of the RSS, led by Madhavrao Mule, Dattopant Thengadi and Moropant Pingle, wrote to Indira Gandhi, promising support to the Emergency if all RSS workers were released from prison. Their 'Document of Surrender', to take effect from January 1977, was processed by my father H.Y. Sharada Prasad.[9]

Getting out of jail on the strength of a compromise, while keeping its long-term goals in mind, was nothing new for the RSS.[10] They had done this earlier, after Mahatma Gandhi's assassination, by claiming that the RSS was only a cultural organisation. At the same time, they had set out to found a new party, the Bharatiya Jana Sangh, from Savarkar's Hindu Mahasabha, and filled it with young pracharaks from their ranks. The Hindu Mahasabha was also tainted in the eyes of Indian people, given the perception

---

[8] 'Unlearnt Lessons of the Emergency', *The Hindu*, January 13, 2000.
[9] https://theprint.in/opinion/rss-leaders-deserted-jayaprakash-resistance-during-indira-emergency/448294/
[10] A.G. Noorani, 'Basic instinct', *Frontline*, March 26, 1993. https://frontline.thehindu.com/editors-pick/basic-instinct/article33046787.ece

of its complicity in Mahatma Gandhi's assassination. Among these pracharak recruits were Atal Bihari Vajpayee, Deen Dayal Upadhyaya, Sundar Singh Bhandari, Nanaji Deshmukh, and many others who would play leading roles in the Bharatiya Jana Sangh and, later, in the Bharatiya Janata Party.

The Jana Sangh leaders were working with JP for a united opposition party, while the RSS was petitioning Congress leaders — Mrs Gandhi at the centre, and S.B. Chavan, chief minister of Maharashtra — to lift the ban on the RSS and release its leaders and members, in exchange for an offer of full cooperation with the government.[11]

As we know from M.G. Devasahyam's account in *Frontline* (October 11, 2018), JP looked to the Jana Sangh cadre to provide the organisational base of the new party. This was the argument he had used when he joined hands with the Jana Sangh and made Nanaji Deshmukh the second in command of his Total Revolution. Perhaps JP was of the view that India should move towards a two-party system like the UK and the US, with all other parties being marginal. At any rate, he appeared to consider the domination of Indian politics by the Janata Party and Congress a desirable goal, while marginalising regional parties and the communists. We may sympathise with JP's eventual disappointment with Jana Sangh leaders who had promised there would be no dual membership of the Janata Party and the RSS, but we can hardly be surprised at the RSS going back on its word by transforming itself into a 'cultural organisation'. It is clear to those who understand the RSS that it is the mother organisation of the Parivar; the associates, or other members of the family, comprise its front. The Parivar's political party, whether the Jana Sangh or the BJP, is essentially a mass electoral front of the RSS, which views itself as more than a political institution. After choosing to ignore the character of the RSS and its relationship with its various front organisations,

---

[11] A.G. Noorani, 'RSS & Emergency', *Frontline*, August 03, 2018. https://frontline.thehindu.com/politics/rss-emergency/article24440187.ece

including its electoral front, the other partners in the coalition later precipitated the dual membership issue, leading to the split of the Janata Party in July 1979.

But to go back to when the Emergency was still in place: political discussion had begun to be audible, but it did not have an urgent tone as yet; elections seemed quite far away. Most people, including the major opposition parties, had taken for granted that the Emergency was the new normal, and they still had to come to terms with how to work under these conditions. Yes, there was deep-seated anger among the people, especially against the vasectomy camps. Government officials and school and college teachers were assigned sterilisation quotas, and if they failed to meet them, their salaries would be stopped. People spoke in hushed tones in public, even when making an oblique criticism of the government. On the surface, things were quiet. This misled a section of the Congress into concluding that the Indian people were passive; even the opposition shared this sense.

While following political developments, I was also trying to solve three problems of my own: get married, get back to studenthood in JNU, and start my research activities again. Ashoka and I had by now moved into our one-room apartment, our kitchen a part of the bedroom. We had a small courtyard, where we could also wash the dishes. I quickly volunteered for the washing up as Ashoka's culinary skills outstripped mine. After the jail diet in Agra, Ashoka's cooking was indeed culinary heaven. We had just finished all the social rounds that post-marriage couples have to undergo when, on January 18, 1977, quite out of the blue, Mrs Gandhi declared elections.

ELECTIONS ARE ANNOUNCED

There are two questions about the Emergency that have been asked before and will probably be asked over and over. The first is why Mrs Gandhi declared a state of Emergency in the first place. The second question is why she declared elections in 1977.

Much has been written about why Mrs Gandhi declared the Emergency. It has been ascribed to her authoritarian instincts. It has been linked to the 'seditious' potential of JP's call for Total Revolution, and his asking government officials not to accept the 'illegitimate orders' of the government. Even the possibility of a coup planned by the US has been suggested. The possibilities go on in this vein.

Actually, the 'foreign hand' in a possible coup does not seem quite as farfetched now as it did then. After all, Mujibur Rahman[12] and Zulfiqar Ali Bhutto[13][14] were killed in army coups backed by the US. The Pinochet coup against Salvador Allende in Chile, as well as other military coups worldwide — orchestrated by the US — were a fact of life for many global leaders.[15] If we take the major

[12] A lot of material is now available on the US involvement in the assassination and overthrow of the Mujibur Rahman government. The key texts are: Lawrence Lifschultz, *Bangladesh: The Unfinished Revolution*, Billing & Sons Ltd., London, 1979, Christopher Hitchens, *The Trial of Henry Kissinger*, Verso, 2002.

[13] Ramsey Clark, the former attorney general of the US, had said, 'I do not believe in conspiracy theories in general, but the similarities in the staging of riots in Chile and in Pakistan are just too close.' In Sadia Navin Bilgrami's book *Duped*, Xlibris US, 2015

[14] 'Bhutto was removed from power in Pakistan by force on the 5th of July, after the usual party on the 4th at the U.S. Embassy in Islamabad, with U.S. approval, if not more, by General Zia al-Haq.' Ramsey Clark, 'The Corruption of Covert Actions', *CovertAction Quarterly*, Issue Number 65, Fall 1998, p 7.

[15] If we take the major leaders on the non-aligned movement, Prime Minister Nkrumah of Ghana was deposed in 1966 in a military coup, as declassified US government documents show (https://mronline.org/2021/02/25/how-did-a-fateful-cia-coup-executed-55-years-ago-this-february-24-doom-much-of-sub-saharan-africa/), the 1954 attempt to assassinate President Nasser in Egypt using Muslim Brotherhood, the military coup in 1965 against President Sukarno which brought General Suharto in power and led to massacres in Indonesia of communists and leftists on a scale which still lies largely unexplored. An estimated one million people were killed, including the bulk of the members of the half a million strong PKI, the Communist Party of Indonesia. See Vincent Bevins, *The Jakarta Method: Washington's Anticommunist Crusade and the Mass Murder Program*

The Last Chapter of Mrs Gandhi's Emergency

leaders of the Non-Aligned Movement for instance: declassified US government documents show Prime Minister Nkrumah of Ghana was deposed in 1966 in a military coup.[16] There was the attempt to assassinate President Nasser in Egypt in 1954 using the Muslim Brotherhood. Then there was the military coup in Indonesia in 1965 against President Sukarno, bringing General Suharto to power and leading to a massacre of communists and leftists. An estimated one million people were killed, including most of the members of the half a million strong PKI, the Communist Party of Indonesia.17 Along with Nehru, and President Tito of Yugoslavia, Sukarno, Nasser and Nkrumah were the leading lights of the Afro-Asian countries, and the founders of the Non-Aligned Movement.

Despite the fears — external and internal — that led Mrs Gandhi to declare the Emergency, the more interesting question is why she declared elections. The life of the Lok Sabha had been extended by another year in November 1976, so there was no constitutional requirement for declaring elections. Why did she do so in January 1977 and virtually lift the Emergency?

Technically, the Emergency continued till March 21, 1977, but for all practical purposes it was over with the announcement of elections. In her short speech on All India Radio on the evening of January 18, Mrs Gandhi not only promised the release of political leaders and activists (some of whom had already been released), but also promised 'to permit all legitimate activity necessary for recognised parties to put forth their points of view before the

---

that Shaped Our World, PublicAffairs, New York, 2020. Nehru, Sukarno, Nasser and Nkrumah were the leading lights of the Afro-Asian countries and founders of the Non-Aligned Movement, along with President Tito of Yugoslavia.

[16] See https://mronline.org/2021/02/25/how-did-a-fateful-cia-coup-executed-55-years-ago-this-february-24-doom-much-of-sub-saharan-africa/

[17] See Bevins, *The Jakarta Method*.

people.'[18] This was not a fake manoeuvre, as some suspected.[19] Clearly, Mrs Gandhi wanted the elections to restore the legitimacy she sensed she was losing, whether at home or abroad. She said:

> Let us go to the polls with the resolve to reaffirm the power of the people and to uphold the fair name of India as a land committed to the path of reconciliation, peace, and progress... Anyone can see that the nation is more healthy, efficient and dynamic than it had been for a very long time. The question before us is how to restore substantively those political processes on which we were compelled to impose some curbs... Legally, the present Lok Sabha can continue for another fifteen months. But we also strongly believe that Parliament and Government must report back to the people and seek sanction from them to carry out the programs and policies for the nation's strength and welfare. Because of this unshakeable faith in the Power of the People, I have advised the President to dissolve the present Lok Sabha and order fresh elections. This, he has accepted. We expect polling to take place in March...[20]

To understand the mind-set of Mrs Gandhi as well as that of the opposition, we need to look at how the Indian people perceived Emergency rule. There had been a sullen acceptance of the Emergency. The people adjusted to the demand for conformity. Resistance of even the normal kind was not really visible in public or at the workplace. Yes, there was simmering anger among the people

---

[18] Ravi Visvesvaraya Sharada Prasad, 'Why Did Indira Gandhi Call for Elections in January 1977?', Guest Column in *Open Magazine*, January 23, 2022.
https://openthemagazine.com/special/indira-gandhi-call-elections-january-1977/

[19] Inder Malhotra writing in *Indian Express*, talks about Congress (O) leaders, 'S.K. Patil: Indira has Laid a Trap for Us But We Must Not Fall into It.'
https://indianexpress.com/article/opinion/columns/the-abrupt-end-of-emergency/

[20] R.V. Sharada Prasad, *Open Magazine*, January 2022.

The Last Chapter of Mrs Gandhi's Emergency

— as we learnt during the course of the election campaign, but till that point it was not easily perceptible, even to astute observers.

The absence of visible resistance may have led Mrs Gandhi to believe she could legitimise her rule through an election and establish an order which would be a reset — not quite what we had from 1947, but not an Emergency regime either. She may have been misled by the people around her that she would win. Or she was willing to take this gamble since she felt that any other course lacked internal and external legitimacy. There was also the Sanjay Gandhi factor: as the emerging power centre in the Congress, he was setting India on a completely different course — both internally and externally — than the one that Jawaharlal Nehru (and she) believed in.

To what extent did each of these reasons weigh on her mind when she announced the elections? People today may miss the fact that the Nehruvian elite was international in a way that today's green card holding parochial expatriates are not. They located themselves as global citizens while being Indian. Mrs Gandhi was aware that if she did not have internal legitimacy, she would not have external legitimacy either. While that may not have been the sole or even a determining factor, it certainly would have weighed on her mind. She wanted both the internal and external legitimacy that only a free and reasonably fair election could give her.

In his book on the Emergency and Mrs Gandhi cited earlier, P.N. Dhar suggests possible reasons for the decision to hold elections: Sanjay Gandhi's capture of the Congress apparatus via the Youth Congress; reports of the degree of coercion involved in the 'family planning' program, and the deep anger of the people in response; and Mrs Gandhi's inability to control Sanjay. Indeed, Sanjay Gandhi and his coterie wanted a new constitution, the suspension of parliamentary democracy and the continuation of the Emergency regime.[21]

---

[21] Dhar talks about Bansi Lal's proposal of setting up a new constituent assembly whose main purpose would be to make Mrs Gandhi president for

Most analysts think Mrs Gandhi was misled about the 'positive' reaction of the people to Emergency rule. A ruler surrounded by sycophants hears only what she wants to hear: this was what they believe happened to Mrs Gandhi. It cannot be denied that a set of advisors must have assured her that the Emergency was extremely popular and she would sweep the polls. An authoritarian leader — having declared Emergency Mrs Gandhi was certainly one — is not going to hear unpalatable truths. Intelligence reports also predicted that she would sweep the polls.[22] In any case, Emergency or not, the officers of intelligence agencies prefer to serve up reports that further their careers rather than provide real intelligence to the political leadership. It is unlikely Mrs Gandhi did not know this simple fact of governance, or that she would have taken such assessments at face value.

I asked P.N. Haksar whether Mrs Gandhi declared elections because she was misled into thinking she would win. Or did she take this risk because she wanted the legitimacy of an electoral verdict despite its risk? PNH was no longer a confidant of Mrs Gandhi during the Emergency — Jairam Ramesh has described what happened between them in his book — so he may not have known her mind then as he would have earlier.[23] But PNH knew Mrs Gandhi as very few people did. And he did not believe that she was lulled into overconfidence by sycophants. He also pointed out that those close to her included a number of southern politicians, and she did indeed sweep the polls in the South.

---

life. *Indira Gandhi, the Emergency and Indian Democracy*, OUP 2000, p. 342.

[22] According to R.K. Dhawan, who said that the IB reports indicated she would win 340 seats. India Today TV interview with Karan Thapar, 'Remembering 21 Months of Darkness: Indira Gandhi's Aide R.K. Dhawan Tells of Her Huge Relief at Losing the 1977 Election', Karan Thapar, *Daily Mail*, June 25, 2015.
https://www.dailymail.co.uk/indiahome/indianews/article-3138052/Remembering-21-months-darkness-Indira-Gandhi-s-aide-R-K-Dhawan-tells-huge-relief-losing-1977-election.html

[23] Jairam Ramesh, *Intertwined Lives: P.N. Haksar & Indira Gandhi*, Simon & Schuster, 2018.

The Last Chapter of Mrs Gandhi's Emergency

Do I have a theory on what made her declare elections? When people close to her have failed to produce a decisive argument one way or another, I don't think I have any special insights either. I would conclude that it was not one specific reason that led to her decision but a combination of reasons. Having tasted popular success and international respect, she did not want to be known as the one who had converted India to an autocracy like many other newly independent countries. And she must have been uncomfortable with Sanjay Gandhi's attempts to continue the authoritarian regime with some tinsel cover of constitutional reforms that would effectively do away with electoral democracy.

Did Zulfikar Ali Bhutto's announcement of elections in Pakistan on January 7, 1977 — 10 days before Mrs Gandhi's announcement — play a role in her decision? In an interview with Jairam Ramesh, I asked him why Mrs Gandhi lifted the Emergency. He asked, in response, if I thought Bhutto's announcement of elections in Pakistan had any role. Ramesh did not suggest it did, but clearly his question meant he was citing it as a possible cause. I doubt that Bhutto's announcement would have had any impact minus the other reasons we have looked at. Yes, she may have had a sense of rivalry with Bhutto, both of whom were in Oxford at virtually the same time, both leaders of their countries, both with a strong sense of destiny. It may have catalysed the timing, but I believe that the decision was already in the making.

THE 1977 ELECTIONS AND THE DEFEAT OF THE EMERGENCY

Once the elections were announced, the entire political scenario changed, almost overnight. The question the opposition had to grapple with was whether they should participate in the elections. Did they have any chance of winning? If Mrs Gandhi won (with the opposition parties contesting) would they not be helping to legitimise Emergency rule? Should they, the opposition, boycott the elections as suggested by people like S.K. Patil?[24] To address their questions and doubts, the political leadership had to probe the pulse of the people, determine whether they had indeed acquiesced to the Emergency.

The detained political leaders began to be released almost immediately after the election announcement. In less than a month, most of the remaining detenues were out of jail. Public meetings and rallies were permitted, preparatory to holding elections. We were returning, slowly, to the business of politics in practice: once again, there were open discussions, rallies and marches. As these 'acts of normalcy' grew, the pace quickened.

Within five days of the call for elections, the formation of the Janata Party was announced. The various organisations that had come together in the JP movement had agreed to JP's demand that they fight the elections under a common banner. The formal merger of the parties and a new organisational structure were, however, not effected till after the announcement of the election results.

But the defining moment of the 1977 elections came two weeks after the announcement of elections. Stalwarts such as Babu Jagjivan Ram, Hemavati Nandan Bahuguna and Nandini Satpathy left the Congress to form the Congress for Democracy (CFD). They decided to fight the elections opposing the Congress(I) (as it was still known); and entered into an alliance with the Janata Party. The CPI(M) issued a call to avoid splitting the anti-Congress vote, calling for seat adjustments against the Congress. Suddenly, opposition unity was for real. The anti-Emergency forces had acquired momentum.

For Mrs Gandhi, the election campaign message was simple:

---

[24] Inder Malhotra wrote: 'Many of those who heard her broadcast concluded that Gandhi had some trick up her sleeve. Among those who thought so was S.K. Patil, a leader of the Congress (O) and a master tactician himself. After his and other opposition leaders' release from jail, he told his colleagues: "Indira has laid a trap for us but we must not fall into it."' 'The Abrupt End of Emergency', *Indian Express*, August 4, 2014.

The Last Chapter of Mrs Gandhi's Emergency

there had been a real threat of a breakdown of law and order. JP's call to disobey the government was a call for insurrection, and the state had needed to be stabilised through the discipline imposed by the Emergency. This is what Vinoba Bhave had said, in effect, when he claimed that 'The Emergency is *anushasan parva*.' (It is probably what earned him his title of *sarkari sant*.) Having re-invigorated the state through the Emergency, normal politics could be revived, hence the elections. In other words: if she won the legitimacy of a people's mandate in the elections, Mrs Gandhi would have a free hand to either continue with the existing constitutional structure, or consider alternatives.

The spin behind presenting the Emergency as bitter but necessary medicine was effectively destroyed when some key figures in the Congress came out against the Emergency. Jagjivan Ram's departure was a body blow to the Congress (I), followed by H.N. Bahuguna, who had led the Congress (I) in the most populous state that sent the highest number of MPs to the Lok Sabha. A number of other leaders followed. Mrs Gandhi's claims of restoring order sounded hollow when even her close associates began to desert her. It confirmed what was, in any case, common knowledge: the 'excesses' of the Emergency, and the rise of the extra-constitutional power centre centred around Sanjay Gandhi.

Of the Congress leaders who left the party, Jagjivan Ram was the most important figure. A major Dalit leader, he had been in Nehru's cabinet continuously since 1946. Indeed, he deserves to be remembered more than he is, which is why I am going to digress a little here. Jagjivan Ram was one of the most brilliant speakers I have heard. He was electrifying in the way he could relate to any audience, whether they were left, liberal or religious. He could speak in their idiom, their terms, and appear to be one of them. He was extremely intelligent and widely read. His oratory was great not in terms of demagogy, but in his being able to relate to an audience and bring out his vision in their context. That's a very, very rare skill. I would rank Jagjivan Ram and Hare Krishna Konar (whom I idolised as a public speaker) as the most convincing speakers I have heard in my life.

Ashoka's father was a complete acolyte of Jagjivan Ram after hearing him speak in a Jain Sabha with complete authority and erudition on the Jain Shastras. Much to Ashoka's anger, her father was preparing to campaign for the Congress (I) in spite of my being jailed. Bitter fights followed between father and daughter. Then Jagjivan Ram left the Congress. What Ashoka could not do to convince her father of the Emergency 'excesses', Jagjivan Ram achieved with his departure from the Congress.

Of course, any praise of Jagjivan Ram cannot be unqualified. Questions have been raised about his 'not remembering' to pay his income tax, and leaving behind considerable property, apparently acquired on the strength of a modest government salary. Again, he did not stand up during the Emergency when senior leaders needed to do so. (The story goes that he said he was willing to stand up and be counted, but his knees weren't up to it.)

On a different level, he did not espouse Dalit politics despite his background, which left him, arguably, somewhat unmoored. So, despite all his accomplishments, the Nehruvian Jagjivan Ram doesn't find a place in our pantheon of towering national leaders, either as a national leader or as a Dalit leader. All the same, Jagjivan Ram has never been properly assessed in our political life. We also tend to underestimate the powerful message conveyed when he switched over from the Congress (I) to the opposition. Was it that one moment which decided the outcome of the elections? No, there was a much larger groundswell. Did the moment help to build the groundswell? I would say it definitely did.

Though the formal lifting of the Emergency took place only after the elections were done, almost all political leaders of the opposition as well as MISA detenues were released once elections were

The Last Chapter of Mrs Gandhi's Emergency

announced. Only those charged in cases of sedition and violence remained in jail — George Fernandes and his associates in the Baroda dynamite case, for instance. (George Fernandes, however, contested from Bhagalpur jail, for the Muzaffarpur constituency of Bihar, and won by a huge margin.) Most of the Naxalites, too, were released only after the Emergency was lifted.

With the release of the leaders and political activists, the political processes lost during the Emergency were revived with public meetings and rallies. Slowly but surely, the sullen anger of the people transformed into participation, hesitant at first, then increasingly active. Their pent-up anger against the Emergency was channelled into support for the opposition in order to defeat the Congress (I) and deliver their verdict on the Emergency regime.

The newspapers too slowly opened up their columns to criticism of the government. Doordarshan — then the only TV channel — along with All India Radio, remained completely faithful to the government. But more than any instrument of mass communication, it was people on the ground at this point who spread their message against the Emergency. So much so that it was exhilarating to see the sands of politics shift under the Emergency regime before our eyes — and in the scant 50 days between the announcement of the elections and the vote itself!

The anger against the Emergency had swollen into a veritable tsunami of a poll in all regions except the South of the country. The Congress was wiped out in North India, and in West Bengal and Orissa in the East; in Maharashtra and Gujarat the results were mixed. In the South, most of the seats went to the Congress, partly because the southern Congress chief ministers had not come down as heavily on the people as in the North, which was directly under the ubiquitous PM's House. Compared to the North, coercive family planning and its excesses were far less evident south of the Vindhyas. The fledgling Janata Party plus its allies — if we count the seat sharing arrangement that they had with the Akalis and the CPI(M) — ended up with 326 seats. The Janata Party alone got an absolute majority with 295 seats. The CPI(M) garnered 22 seats, the bulk of them in West Bengal, where it had a seat adjustment with the Janata Dal. The Congress was completely wiped out. In Kerala however, it was the CPI(M) that drew a complete blank, while the alliance of the Congress (I), the CPI, the Indian Union Muslim League and the Kerala Congress swept the state. The Congress also swept Andhra Pradesh and Karnataka. The DMK managed to dent the Congress' success in the South a little, by capturing five seats in Tamil Nadu against the 34 won by the Congress (I) and its allies.

India was changing as the votes were counted and the election results declared, starting from the evening of March 22, 1977.

Unfortunately, I was at home with a high fever and missed experiencing, first-hand, the gamut of emotions felt by those gathered in front of the newspaper offices that had put up scoreboards of the incoming election results. There was an initial fear that Mrs Gandhi could still come out on top. This changed to jubilation as each round of counting revealed that the Congress was being routed in most states, with the exception of the South. The crowds increased as news came in of the Congress defeat, and the jubilation took on the flavour of a festival.

I heard this thrilling news in detail only when Ashoka came home late in the evening. Remember, we had no internet those days, and no mobile phones. The radio and TV were completely controlled by the government. Anyone listening to the radio would have believed that there was a ding-dong battle going on; in reality, it was clear that Mrs Gandhi and her party were losing by a huge margin. Finally, at 3 AM on March 22, All India Radio conceded that the Congress (I) was losing the elections, and that Mrs Gandhi herself had lost her seat in Raebareli by a margin of 55,000 votes. My only regret was that a spoilsport fever had robbed me of participating in the mass festival being celebrated in front of newspaper offices, from the likes of *The Times of India*, *The Indian Express*, and *Jan Satta* on Bahadur Shah Zafar Marg to the *Hindustan Times* office in Connaught Place.

The Last Chapter of Mrs Gandhi's Emergency

As one of her last acts as prime minister, Mrs Gandhi withdrew the Emergency. And finally, the nightmare that had lasted 21 months was over.

7. Living Politics

RELEARNING NORMALCY

There is an old Chinese curse of doubtful provenance: May you live in interesting times! The tumultuous 'interesting times' that we were 'cursed' to live through had passed with the lifting of the Emergency. (All these years later, the curse of interesting times seems upon us again.) The formation of the new Janata government headed by Morarji Desai meant that the old political processes, once taken for granted, and suddenly lost to us, could now resume. We no longer had to work in secrecy. People who had forgotten what 'normalcy' was had to relearn it, bit by bit. A lesson accompanied this learning: we realised that we value everyday normalcy only when we lose it. Its return felt like a weight had been taken off our shoulders — and our politics.

Making the argument that governments in nine states where the Congress had been defeated in the 1977 general elections had lost the confidence of the people, the Morarji Desai Government dismissed all nine. The Congress lost the subsequent elections in every one of those states, with the Janata Party winning in seven, the Left Front led by the CPI(M) winning in West Bengal, and the DMK in Tamil Nadu.

For us in JNU, the big change was that the students council, which had been virtually locked up by the administration, became active again. The students in JNU had not seen elections for nearly two terms. There was an upsurge demanding immediate elections, even though such an elected body would have only a few months in office, the tail-end of its term. For reasons that sounded good to us at the time, the SFI suggested postponing the elections to the next session, which was imminent anyway; but the students, keen to enjoy the newfound delights of political normalcy, were having none of it. What could be better than union elections, with heady late-night debates and discussions on not just the university but every topic in the universe? The two batches of students who had joined the university during the Emergency were eager to participate in an exciting event they had heard much about, while the older students were swayed by nostalgia for the open atmosphere of JNU student politics.

The SFI lost in its attempt to postpone the elections to the next session, but it won them convincingly with Sitaram Yechury as the new president. In fact, he won the student union presidency three times between 1977–78.[1]

Other prospects opened up as well, to participate in events beyond the campus. In 1978, the World Youth Festival, generally held either in the Soviet Union or the European socialist-bloc countries aligned with it, was held for the first time in Havana, Cuba. For most of us, Cuba, its leader Fidel Castro, and Che Guevara, were inspirational. There was great excitement when the team of students from India included Ashoka, Indrani Majumdar and D.P. Tripathi, all from JNU. The team also included the artist Vivan Sundaram, who was familiar to us. The JNU SFI had hosted his exhibition.[2] Vivan had also participated in a poster exhibition we had organised during Mrs Gandhi's by-election from Chikmagalur, after she lost in Raebareli.

Ashoka had an interesting story from her visit. She asked the guide, who was from the youth wing of the Cuban party, to

---

[1] The first time was with the delayed election of March 1977, held to make up for the 1976–77 session when elections did not take place. The second was the 'normal' election for 1977–78, held in September. The third election came about because Sitaram sought a renewed mandate after our failed attempt to remove the VC and his close associates in the Emergency administration.
[2] The exhibition was titled after Luis Buñuel's film, *The Discreet Charm of the Bourgeoisie*, the first time I came across Buñuel.

(L to R) Dr. Vithal, a Cuban comrade, Ashoka and Vivan Sundaram in Cuba.

take them to a poor locality. There they interviewed the poorest householder they could find. Ashoka even had a photograph of this 'poor' house, which looked middle-class to us. It was striking that Cuba had not just alleviated general poverty, but its poor had a level of livelihood that would be considered middle-class in India. Even today, the kind of abject poverty we see in India is not to be seen in any Latin American or Caribbean country. Cuba had, of course, achieved this much earlier, as they had abolished the rich landed estates and got rid of the mafia-Batista axis that ran Havana.[3]

As the seventies came to an end, both Ashoka and I, in very different ways, began to get more involved in causes and organisations beyond the campus. In Ashoka's case, there was

[3] Fulgencio Batista (1901–73) was part of the cabal that ran the government from behind the scenes till 1940 when he was elected president of Cuba. His defeat in the 1952 elections seemed imminent, but he led a military coup with help from the US government and installed himself as president. Political rights were withdrawn, communists were brutally repressed, and Cuba's sugar industry, as well as 70 per cent of the country's arable land, were handed over to US owners. He was finally overthrown in 1959.

greater involvement with party activities. In mine, it was starting my journey on the path to learning how, post-Emergency and post-university campus, I could live politics. There were several milestones along the way, but the most important one was the discovery that I had three 'passions' I would always live with: science, technology, and, of course, politics. How these three would come together over the next four (and more) decades became clearer only with time. It is hard to compress the years of youthful discussion and argument and learning that formed the foundation of what I would become, and continue to be: a science activist.

I had always been passionate about science and technology. Even before the Emergency, a number of students interested in the history and philosophy of science had formed a discussion group around contemporary issues in science. It included Dinesh Abrol, Rajendra Prasad, Usha Menon, K.V. Krishnamurthy (KVK as we called him, a civil engineer associated with the communist movement in his youth), and several others. I had not yet joined JNU — I was still completing my Masters in engineering — but I would hang out in JNU with this group. We felt we needed a formal structure, and decided, possibly without thinking it through, that a periodical would be the right start. I blame Lenin for this. He set us a wrong example with *Iskra*, leaving us budding Marxists following recklessly in his footsteps with no sense of the pitfalls ahead!

To broad-base such an effort, we tried to get together the old Association of Scientific Workers of India (ASWI) that had been founded in 1947. As a young engineer, KVK had actively worked in the *Vijnan Karmee*, the publication of the ASWI.[4] Though

---

[4] KVK was one of the first engineers to work on building dams. He led a strike of the workers while heading a hydro-electric project, and was then sent to the UN where it was assumed he could do little mischief. He became a major spokesperson for the third world view on hydroelectric projects and river water sharing, in which the UN was a major player. On his return to his parent department in India after nearly 35 years, he was with the Central Water Commission, with his office just across from JNU.

constituted as a trade union, and as part of the World Federation of Scientific Workers — regarded as being close to communists and the Soviet Union — the ASWI had a large constituency in India. The nationalist and leftist scientists had come together in the national movement, and this was visible in the Congress Planning Committee headed by Jawaharlal Nehru. It had figures like Sahib Singh Sokhey,[5] very much to the left, as well as Nehru, who identified himself as a socialist. Nehru also became the first president of the ASWI, perhaps the only head of a government to head a trade union!

Discussions on the magazine immediately ran into philosophical issues. In our innocence we had wanted to call it *Peoples Science*. A section of those participating in the discussions wanted to know what that meant. And shouldn't there be an apostrophe in *Peoples Science*? Did the term mean science done by the people in their everyday lives? Or only big science done in institutions and laboratories? Even more fundamental questions were raised: Who does science belong to? Indeed, what is science? Some of us tried very hard to argue that all these positions could be discussed in the pages of the magazine. What we didn't understand yet was the Indian intelligentsia's love for abstract thought and discussion, not necessarily supplemented with productive activity! All these goings-on had come to a halt with the Emergency; once it was over, we picked up the thread to hold a seminar on self-reliance, in 1978. The follow-up was that in the same year, instead of further discussions on 'peoples science', we constituted a public interest organisation, the Delhi Science Forum (DSF), to address science and technology policies, as also to popularise science and

---

[5] Major General Sahib Singh Sokhey (1887–1971) was a biochemist and military physician who went on to serve in the Rajya Sabha from 1952 to 1957. He was instrumental in securing Soviet assistance in 1953–54 to establish a large pharmaceutical plant in India, today known as Indian Drugs and Pharmaceuticals Ltd (IDPL). For more on the history of the left in Indian science, see Prabir Purkayastha, *Knowledge as Commons: Towards Inclusive Science and Technology*, LeftWord Books, 2023.

work out what people's science would mean in practice.

A MILESTONE SEMINAR ON SELF-RELIANCE AND THE FORMATION OF THE DELHI SCIENCE FORUM

A large section of the Janata Government did not believe in either self-reliance or planning. For them, as for a section of the Indian bourgeoisie, planning was socialism; while science and technology could be bought just as we buy potatoes and onions in the market. This was also the way 'mainstream' economics viewed technology, simply as a factor of production like any other.

As science activists, we hoped that bringing together scientists, engineers, economists, and scientific workers would create the nucleus of a science movement in Delhi. This seminar, the first of its kind in the post-Emergency period, examined the Janata Government's trajectory through a larger leftist lens. While the Janata Government was dominated by the right, it also had various shades of socialists, from George Fernandes, Madhu Limaye and Madhu Dandavate, to older socialists like Ashok Mehta who had drifted more or less to the right. How would they react to the very pro-capitalist views of Morarji Desai and H.M. Patel, his finance minister?

Morarji had handpicked H.M. Patel for the finance ministry. Both men rejected Nehru's economic vision and were pro-US in their view of the world. Given the coalition nature of the Janata Party, Morarji and Patel could only somewhat dilute India's planning model and the public sector. The biggest blows both for and against foreign capital came, strangely enough, from the socialist George Fernandes, then industries minister. He advocated that no foreign company should have a majority share in an Indian company. This was accepted by the Janata Government; IBM and Coca Cola would depart from India after refusing to dilute their shareholdings. But Fernandes was also the force behind what was called a 'strategic alliance' between India's successful power sector undertaking, BHEL, and the German multinational equipment manufacturer, Siemens.

The core issue of self-reliance is not to stop at building steel plants, power plants and fertiliser plants with imported technology, but acquiring the ability to upgrade the technology that goes into building a new generation of plants. Merely setting up plants is not enough. Indian planning had envisaged gaining the capability to build the next generation of plants. With the 1974 Pokhran explosion, India had been cut off from technology imports in the nuclear sector. What many theorists on policy today do not realise is that the sanctions went far beyond the nuclear sector. A whole range of industries are considered dual use, for instance, steam turbines or heat exchangers. Here, BHEL stepped into the gap, producing the low-pressure steam turbines required for the nuclear power plants. Heat exchangers and distillation columns, key to the heavy water projects and India's nuclear energy program, were developed by Bharat Heavy Plates and Vessels. The heavy water plants became a part of the fertiliser plants, since ammonia is used for both.

The success of the self-reliance experiment threatened the same MNCs who had earlier denied technology to India. Their new strategy was to offer the latest technologies to Indian state-owned companies, hoping to seduce the Indian state into abandoning its independent development of new technologies. To neoliberal economists, technology was something that could be bought in the market, and self-reliance was economically 'not optimal'. To technologists, self-reliance was a question of developing the technology further. The BHEL-Siemens deal was a battle in the much larger war against India's self-reliance. Ashok Rao, who was then in BHEL, was an important part of the internal resistance to the BHEL-Siemens deal, and was central to linking the Delhi Science Forum with this resistance.[6]

---

[6] Ashok Rao later went on to become the President of the BHEL Officers Association and the National Confederation of Officers' Associations of

Living Politics

This was the backdrop of the self-reliance seminar. KVK advised us to hold the seminar in the Indian National Science Academy and make it into a big event. He taught us that it does not matter if you are small; if the idea behind an activity is big, nothing prevents you from thinking big! Indeed, we young science activists looking to carve out a new path for ourselves benefitted a great deal from our interaction with the earlier generation of thinkers on science, technology and development. These included A. Rahman, then head of planning in the Council of Scientific and Industrial Research, P.N. Haksar (PNH), Krishnamurthy, and, later, Arun Ghosh and M.K. Sambamurthi.

In this first major organising work in the public sphere, we managed to bring together organisations like the Kerala Sasthra Sahithya Parishad (KSSP), trade unions, old leftists or Nehruvian science and technologists to join us. This success led to the formation of the Delhi Science Forum soon after, with K.V. Krishnamurthy as our first president, and Dinesh Abrol as the general secretary.[7]

The 1978 conference also highlighted some differences among the activists who would go on to form the core of the people's science movement. Some of us were more engaged with policy issues, particularly self-reliance. Others focussed on what is loosely called scientific temper: What does science for the people really mean? Still others focussed on the popularisation of science. The Kerala Sasthra Sahithya Parishad (KSSP), in existence since 1962, was a pioneer in the country's science movement, including popularising the teaching and communication of science in the mother tongue.[8] The KSSP also gave the call for science through arts, the use of kala jathas, the jatha (travelling troupe) form

---

Central Public Sector Undertakings.

[7] We registered as a Society later. Though KVK was our first president, P.N. Haksar was the founding president of the registered Society of the Delhi Science Forum.

[8] For more information on the history of the KSSP, see: https://kssp.in/about-us/

inspired by Samudaya, a progressive cultural group in Karnataka.

I still remember my discussions with M. Parameswaran, who was already a major figure in the KSSP, on his paper at the seminar. He distinguished between high science in the universities and science as practised by the people in their everyday lives, and how our focus should be on the everyday science of the people, rather than the high science of the Bhabha Atomic Research Centre, Tata Institute of Fundamental Research and other science institutions. My disagreements with Parameswaran (MP as he is called in the people's science movement) have been lifelong, and while we remain friends and comrades, we argue for our different perspectives on science and development even today![9] For me, and many of us in the science movement, development of the people cannot be separated from advances in science and technology, and without such advances comes the prospect of falling back into dependence on other countries.

BALANCING POLITICS AND PROFESSION: THE EARLY YEARS

Meanwhile, Ashoka and I were mapping our day-to-day political involvements. Both of us took part in activities outside the campus. One such incident was the bus-fare hike in Delhi, which led to an agitation, and that led to my spending a few days again in the familiar accommodation of Tihar. True to police efficiency, only a few among those arrested were protesters. One of them was Ritu Jerath, a young student of JNU in the School of Languages. Unfortunately for the police, her father was the first secretary in the Indian embassy at Washington, and this led to a lot of questioning of the arrests.

Another one picked up at random from the protest site was a

---

[9] One difference was on the Silent Valley Hydroelectric Project, with M.P. and DSF on opposite sides. Today, I will admit I was wrong on that one. But on issues such as homeopathy, I continue to believe that there is no such thing as allopathy and homeopathy, only modern medicine!

young man in banking intelligence. He went with his family to meet the divisional commissioner — or was it the district magistrate? — to explain that he was not party to the protest but merely on his way to office when he was hauled in to make up the numbers. It appears that the DM spent most of the interview talking about what a problem I was, and how whenever they arrested me, they landed in trouble. Possibly he was facing some heat for arresting a senior diplomat's daughter and others who had nothing to do with the protests. This was also when the Shah Commission on Emergency excesses was at work. Along with Bhinder, the DIG who had arrested me, many others including this DC/DM were under the shadow of the Shah Commission. What was interesting was the official's concluding line: '...the next time we get him, we will fix him properly!' (I recall this now and wonder if after all these years his prophecy is coming true? Will they be third time lucky?)

Ashoka had begun to get involved in the larger party activities in Delhi. My own PhD was going nowhere. Or if it was getting somewhere, the pace was glacial. I've mentioned those punched cards for writing programs, where if you made a mistake, the calculations would go haywire. All you could do was try your luck in the next run — till the next mistake. On the whole, it was a time-consuming process before you got any meaningful results. I had two problems. One was that I had chosen a computational-intensive project: optimisation of power plants. The second was that it was in an area — control engineering — where I had no training. In other words, I was learning two different skill sets from scratch while trying to finish my PhD. Worse, I was trying to do all this on my own as Professor Sadananda, my official guide, was a friend and well-wisher who knew computer science, but not control systems.

Ashoka and I now faced a different kind of choice. Both of us had a middle-class background. If one of us was to become a full-time party worker (in our language, a 'whole-timer'), the other would have to be a wage earner. Both of us wanted to become whole-timers, but that was simply not possible, given the whole-timer wages. Most whole-timers are supported by their families, usually their partners. There was already an economic argument for me, as an engineer, to take up a job. Then Prakash (Karat) came up with an important argument for why Ashoka should become the whole-timer, not me. He pointed out that 'traditionally', the husband becomes a whole-timer, and the wife the wage earner. For me, that was a clincher. I was not going to follow the time-worn path of patriarchy for whole-timers. Another good reason was that we were in Delhi, and Ashoka was from the Hindi belt; of course, she would be more valuable for the party.

Having settled that question, I had to find a job. It helped that I had taken up computer science, and my choice of digital control of power plants helped provide an easy entry. These were the very early days of control and monitoring of plants, including nuclear and coal-fired power plants, as well as other industrial plants. The National Thermal Power Corporation (NTPC) wanted engineers with a computer control background for their computer-based data acquisition systems of power plants. The only two candidates were I and another person with a similar background, who was working in the Bhabha Atomic Research Centre. Both of us got selected. This started my long journey in control systems for power plants and my becoming one of the first in the field. In the late 1980s and '90s, I ended up participating in a number of international conferences on this subject. What was an accident of choosing a topic for my dissertation, became a career choice and resulted in my being one of the early practitioners in this field, and later an 'expert' in many government committees.[10]

One of the first international conferences I attended, IFAC

---

[10] I was a member of the Expert Group, Ministry of Electronics and Information Technology (MeitY) on Industrial Application for almost three decades, and served as the head of other Project Review Committees. I also became a regular participant in the International Federation of Automatic Control (IFAC) conferences on Distributed Computer Control Systems.

Distributed Computer Control Systems, was held in Monterey, California, in 1985. Our local hosts were the Lawrence Livermore Laboratories, the nuclear weapons lab that Edward Teller had headed for building the hydrogen bomb. IFAC was an unusual institution as it had both western technologists as well as those from the Soviet bloc. In spite of the cold war, all the participants were given a tour of this nuclear weapons lab. We also saw the most advanced laser of its time, which was called the Eye of Shiva, a reference to Shiva's third eye and, I guess, Oppenheimer's still lingering influence on the US weapons community.[11]

I also remember an awkward incident from the conference. We had a Japanese participant at one of the dinners, who was cornered by the wife of one of our hosts. She wanted to explain why the Americans had dropped the atom bombs: only to shorten the war and save lives. She wanted to know whether the Japanese people understood the 'humanitarian' reasons for dropping these bombs which had killed 110,000 (low estimate) to 240,000 (high estimate) within a year.[12] The Japanese colleague could only shake his head woodenly in a noncommittal gesture which could mean anything. No US President has apologised to the Japanese people for the two nuclear bombs dropped on Japan, even though there was no military reason to do this and Japan was on the verge of surrender. They were, in fact, the first salvo of the new cold war.

My long-term problem in NTPC was that it could not confirm my appointment! In public sector undertakings, the police verification takes place after your appointment. Once the Shah Commission had given its verdict that my arrest and imprisonment was a fit case to prosecute those who were responsible, it was difficult for the police to say that I should not be employed. But to give me a clean chit was near impossible, as P.S. Bhinder, who

---

[11] On witnessing the detonation of the first atomic bomb, Oppenheimer, who was leading the atom bomb project (Manhattan Project) quoted from the Bhagavad Gita, 'Now I am become Death, the destroyer of worlds.'

[12] Alex Wellerstein, 'Counting the Dead at Hiroshima and Nagasaki', *Bulletin of the Atomic Scientists*, August 4, 2020.

was responsible for my arrest, was now the police commissioner of Delhi. So I was in limbo: I could neither be sacked nor confirmed. Also, along with a few colleagues, I had started an engineers' union/association in NTPC, which did not endear me to the NTPC bosses.

I began looking for another job. I quickly got one in DESEIN, a consultancy organisation which had been started by O.P. Gupta, one of the batch of engineers sent from the Damodar Valley Corporation to the Tennessee Valley Authority (TVA), to train as power plant engineers. This was a part of Nehruvian policies: train a core team along with importing technology. The Indian steel plants, power engineers, oil engineers, were all sent for long periods of training, along with collaborations to import plants and technology.

I started my DESEIN stint on January 1, 1983. Meanwhile, my parents had moved to Delhi from Kanpur, where my father had stayed since his retirement as we never had a family home anywhere — one of the consequences of the 1947 partition. Unlike in Western India/Pakistan, where there was an agreement for a virtual exchange of populations, with refugees being rehabilitated, in Bengal it was decided that refugees were to go back. Most did not and were eventually rehabilitated, but it was done in a slow, piecemeal fashion, nowhere near the scale of Punjab. Another contrast was with the riots in Punjab, which were on a much larger scale, unlike Bengal, where Gandhi's presence in 1947 stilled the fires of communal conflagration. Gandhi had thought, as did many others, that after the Calcutta Killings and the Noakhali riots of 1946, East Bengal would be the epicentre of the riots. He, like many others, was proved wrong as the famed Punjabiyat gave way to communal forces.

We were staying in Sarvapriya Vihar, while my parents were in Masjid Moth. Ashoka had taken on more party responsibilities, becoming a member of the North-East Delhi local committee and a member of the Delhi State Committee. She, along with Brinda

Living Politics

(L to R) **Brinda Karat, Capt. Lakshmi Sahgal, Mrs Shadiram ('Chachi'), Ashoka, Ranjana Narula, Asha Lata and a comrade at the first State Conference of JMS in June 1980.**

Karat, still known in the Delhi party largely as Rita, her nom-de-plume from her underground years during the Emergency, was among the founders of the Janwadi Mahila Samiti (JMS) in 1980, with Brinda as the general secretary and Ashoka as president. It was a hard physical grind for Ashoka, as we were staying in South Delhi and her party work took her to North-East Delhi. There were no metros then, the bus service was undependable, and there was always the harassment women face using public transport in Delhi. The JMS office was in Vithalbhai Patel House, which acted as the hub of the women's movement, particularly in Delhi's resettlement colonies for the poor. JMS was (and still is) very much rooted in working with the urban poor and working women. And in 1981, Ashoka was part of the setting up of the All India Democratic Women's Association (AIDWA).[13]

As for me, becoming a professional meant that I had to change from the informal chai-table mode of functioning in the

---

[13] This mass organisation of women is now active in 23 states. Of its current membership of more than nine million, about two-thirds are from the poor, both rural and urban women.

university, to which we were all accustomed, to a more structured mode of life, of having to attend office every working day. Not an easy change for most of us, used as we were to our anarchist JNU lifestyles.

But we managed, especially Ashoka. She was JMS president; she was a central executive committee member of AIDWA; and in December 1981, she was elected to the Delhi state committee of the CPI(M), becoming its youngest member. In 1983, we were also preparing to become parents. Our son Pratik was born on the eve of Independence Day. It was a moment of great joy. Life was full for the new family.

But the moment was taken away from us in a shocking, unexpected tragedy. On the night of October 3, she had a spontaneous cerebral haemorrhage. Death came instantaneously.

The tributes came pouring in. But at the time they were just words, and for a long while it remained hard to make sense of what had happened.

Even now, after four decades, it is difficult to believe that a life so full and brave, so devoted to larger causes of the people, could be cut short at the age of 31. But so it was. I will not attempt to find words to describe the grief or loss; that was and is impossible. Besides the loving support of family, friends and comrades, two things kept me going. One was the political commitment, the belief in movements, that had brought Ashoka and me together. The other was the more immediate and critical task, a combination of joy and anxiety, my infant son. Even as I learned how to be a father, I would have to learn how to be a single parent.

Life went on, as it does, demanding that I adapt to a new routine of child-rearing, professional work and political engagement.

1984: RESPONDING TO AN ATROCITY IN DELHI

Mrs Gandhi's assassination by a Sikh bodyguard on October 31, 1984, was a traumatic event for the horrific Sikh pogroms

Living Politics

that followed in Delhi and other places. This was the fallout of a train of events in which the Congress had initially played footsie with radical Sikh elements in order to weaken the Akali Dal.[14] It culminated with Bhindranwale taking over the Akal Takht and Indira Gandhi launching the botched Operation Blue Star.[15] The damage to the Akal Takht had enraged the Sikh community, even those who did not support Bhindranwale, and led to Sikh insurgency and the call for an independent Khalistan. While it was a shortsighted Congress game in Punjab that led to the events that followed, the demand for Khalistan, or a homeland for the Sikhs, had come up even earlier.

I had mixed feelings when I heard the news of her death; after all, I had spent one year in jail as her 'guest'. But there was also foreboding as we heard reports the same night of attacks on Sikhs in different parts of the capital. By the next morning, the killings in Delhi had started, with attacks on Sikh localities, houses, taxi stands, the stopping of trucks, and their being set on fire along with their drivers.

At the time, my parents and I were staying in the DDA Flats in Munirka. Also staying there was Saumitra Chaudhuri, who later became a member of the Planning Commission. At that time, he was still a part of the CPI(M). On the morning of November 1, Saumitra and I decided to set out on his motorcycle for Vithalbhai Patel House, where the Delhi state committee's office was located. The streets were all deserted, with the burning wrecks of trucks and taxis on the road, and smoke rose from different parts of the city. When we reached there, reports were pouring in from different areas of Delhi, of violent mobs led by Congress leaders and local goon squads attacking Sikhs and their property. Wherever there was a concentration of Sikhs, there were massacres taking place.

---

[14] Hartosh Singh Bal, 'The Shattered Dome', May 01, 2014, *Caravan*. https://caravanmagazine.in/reportage/shattered-dome
[15] Mark Tully, Satish Jacob, *Amritsar: Mrs Gandhi's Last Battle*, Rupa Publications, 2016.

Prakash Karat was in the office, and we heard him give directions to all those who rang up: Form local groups and protect the Sikhs; if sufficient strength exists, confront the groups as they try to enter various areas and attack the houses of Sikhs.

We — Saumitra and I — decided to return and do something in Munirka DDA flats. Soon after we returned, we had our first test. A mob from the Munirka village was trying to enter the DDA flats area. A few of us, no doubt protected by our identity, resisted them. Saumitra went to inform the nearest police station, only to find that they had no interest in protecting the Sikhs. By that time, Sikh policemen, who formed at least 20 per cent of Delhi police, had been taken off duty. Worse, even the houses of Sikh policemen were being torched. Saumitra found out that there was a military detachment at the IIT Gate Crossing. He went there and found the officer in charge, who told him that his orders were, unfortunately, only to assist the civil authorities. As the concerned civil authorities — sub-divisional magistrates and additional district magistrates — had done a no-show, the army could not move on its own. The army had been deployed but its hands were tied. Saumitra did not stop there, he went to see a senior officer in the chain of command. The officer told him the same story, they had orders to 'assist' the civil administration and could not act on their own; otherwise, they could stop the riots within two hours.

Saumitra, I and many others did what a number of colonies in Delhi were doing: organise locally and protect the Sikhs living in our localities. We also learned directly of the police's role: a police inspector on a motorbike came and told us how the Sikhs were gathering in gurudwaras with guns and other weapons. Saumitra shouted at him for helping to spread riots. We learned the hard way why riots happen and why they are not stopped.[16] They are engineered by political forces who want to polarise communities and are not stopped because those running the state want the riots

---

[16] PUDR and PUCL Report, *Who Are The Guilty*, 1984. Nilanjan Mukhopadhyay, *Sikhs: The Untold Agony of 1984*, Tranquebar Press, 2015.

Living Politics

to continue. Riots in India (as elsewhere) are a continuation of politics by other means.

The scars of Mrs Gandhi's ill-fated flirtation with Bhindranwale, and, later, Operation Blue Star, led to her assassination; the anti-Sikh riots had the tacit support of Rajiv Gandhi. 1984 remains a blot on the nation's consciousness.

The role of the RSS-BJP is quite often overlooked in this story. It has been forgotten that L.K. Advani and Atal Behari Vajpayee sat on a dharna asking for armed forces to be sent into the Golden Temple.[17] The RSS cadre supported the Congress and participated in the anti-Sikh riots.[18] The RSS supported the Congress in the 1984 elections. According to an RSS pracharak, it is the first time the *Hindus had acted as Hindus* post-independence, and so the RSS felt that Hindu consolidation — as a consequence of the Anti-Sikh riots — required a vote for Rajiv Gandhi and the Congress. This Hindu consolidation would help them later.

THE SCIENCE MOVEMENT GROWS APACE

I quit my job in DESEIN in the early nineties, and set up a company with two partners, Saumitra Chaudhuri and Gautam Navlakha. Sagrik ran from 1993 to 2003. Later, while I worked as a consultant with Steag, I set up a small news portal, NewsClick, in 2009. I would commute every day from Gurgaon where I lived to the office at Noida, and to Malviya Nagar in the evening to NewsClick before returning to Gurgaon late at night. Later, I joined the software company Thoughtworks, then owned by the tech wiz Roy Singham, in 2013, and worked there as a consultant till 2017.

But I am getting ahead of myself. To go back to the 1980s and

---

[17] This was on May 03, 1984.
https://twitter.com/AmbedkarCaravan/status/1127898895558819840?lang=en

[18] See, for instance:
https://caravanmagazine.in/politics/rss-bjp-sangh-sikh-appeasement-1984

'90s and lay the foundation of my own science activism side by side with the growth of the science movement: After a few years as the president of the Delhi Science Forum, Krishnamurthy suggested that we approach P.N. Haksar to take over in his place. We were very doubtful that PNH, who was one of the major figures in the country, would agree to be the president of an organisation which had little pedigree. Its only strength was its agenda: building a science movement in the interests of the people, standing up for self-reliance, and scientific temper. We were quite surprised when PNH readily agreed to be our second president. He became the DSF president in 1983 and continued till his death in 1998.

Contradictory as it sounds, Haksar Saab was passionate about scientific temper; if he had a religion, it was probably his belief in science.[19] He may have enjoyed meeting with a bunch of young people. Perhaps it reminded him of his student days in the UK, when he was part of a young group around Rajani Palme Dutt (1896–1974), then the leading figure in the Communist Party of Great Britain. Haksar had participated in the International Students Union and was an active member of the Krishna Menon-led India League in London; it follows that he was regarded by the Americans as a 'fellow traveller'. His house in Shanti Niketan (Delhi) was always open to us, as to many others. He was not only easily accessible but always willing to engage with us. Arguing with him, we never felt that we needed to be conscious of his age or eminence. For him, reason, questioning, and understanding was not only a philosophy, but integral to the way he lived.

Haksar Saab remained a Marxist all his life. He combined his Marxism and readings in modern science with knowledge of classical Sanskrit texts, a combination that our generation did not have. He was quite contemptuous of the Jana Sangh-RSS-BJP

---

[19] P.N. Haksar and P.M. Bhargava were the driving force behind the 'Statement on Scientific Temper' released on July 19, 1981 at the Nehru Centre, Mumbai, and signed by a galaxy of leading scientists of that time. It was printed in *Mainstream*, July 25, 1981 pp. 6–10.

trend in Indian politics, not only for their toxic communal politics, but also their ignorance of both modern science and classical texts.

The Bhopal Gas Tragedy took place in December 1984, soon after his taking over the presidency. The Delhi Science Forum produced a detailed set of reports on the way Union Carbide had let the plant run down, how it had under-designed the safety systems, and on the extent of the leak and the possible long-term effects of methyl isocyanate.[20] The DSF also exposed the double standards of Union Carbide by underlining the difference in the safety systems of the West Virginia and Bhopal plants.[21] Jayaprakash, a part of the DSF, has been fighting the legal cases arising out of the gas leak, including opposing the unfortunate settlement reached by the Government of India and Union Carbide in 1989, under the aegis of the Supreme Court.[22]

The Bhopal Gas Tragedy helped us develop our ideas on what we were going to do as science activists. As the secretary, Dinesh Abrol chose what has always been dear to his heart, to be in the thick of action and work with all groups. I chose to focus on how I could use my technical expertise to analyse the plant failures, particularly of the protection system, instruments and alarm systems. This was my future trajectory, using the specific knowledge I already had and was acquiring, and combining it with my politics: why capitalism and its greed will always downgrade people's safety unless checked by workers' and people's movements.

---

[20] 'Delhi Science Forum Report: Bhopal Gas Tragedy', *Social Scientist*, vol. 13, no. 1, 1985, pp. 32–53. JSTOR.
https://doi.org/10.2307/3517242. Accessed June 2, 2023.

[21] Prabir Purkayastha and Barry I. Castleman, 'The Bhopal Disaster as a Case Study in Double Standards', in Jane H. Ives (ed.), *The Export of Hazard*, Routledge & Kegan Paul, London, 1985.

[22] See N.D. Jayaprakash, 'Perilous Litigation — The Leak Disaster Case', *Economic and Political Weekly*, March 24, 1990, and more recent articles.
https://www.epw.in/journal/1990/51/roots-specials/perilous-litigation-leak-disaster-case.html
https://thewire.in/rights/why-victims-of-the-1984-bhopal-gas-tragedy-are-yet-to-find-closure and https://thewire.in/rights/bhopal-gas-tragedy-curative-petition

Bhopal was a classic example: just to save a few dollars, even the chilling system necessary to keep the methyl isocyanate (MIC) tanks below temperatures that could otherwise lead to a runaway reaction was shut down, and a number of instruments were faulty through not being maintained. The city of Bhopal paid a huge price so Union Carbide could save a few dollars in running costs. Amit Sengupta led a medical team to survey the nature of the injuries people had suffered. Raghu (D. Raghunandan) became the go-to guy for us on environmental law and standards. Both Raghu and Dinesh looked at descaling technologies so that more value addition could be done closer to the producers without losing quality: in pottery, vegetable tanning, and later in food processing. To varying degrees, all of us were following up on how to bring our personal expertise to bear on the politics we believed in.

There was one major issue that I got involved with later, as a fall-out of the Bhopal Gas Tragedy. This was civil liability: Who would bear the costs of the loss of lives, and how would this liability be calculated? At the time of the Bhopal Gas Leak, the liability laws in India had yet to be fleshed out by judicial pronouncements. A number of legal opinions were aired, to the effect that without a well-developed jurisprudence on liability — a law of torts — in India, the headquarters of Union Carbide in the US made that a much better place than India to sue the corporation. With the help of US lawyers, a number of Indians had filed suit against Union Carbide, who wanted India as the place to fight such suits as they felt Indian tort law gave them a better chance of a lower liability. The Supreme Court headed by Justice Bhagwati was quite aware of this gap in Indian liability jurisprudence. The Oleum leak that happened in 1985, from the premises of Sriram Food and Fertilisers in Kirti Nagar, Delhi, gave the Supreme Court the opportunity to set the principles of liability such that it would not allow Union Carbide to avoid responsibility. M.C. Mehta, one of India's leading environmental lawyers, had already filed a case against the Union of India asking that the Sriram Fertiliser's oleum plant be shut down and shifted out of Delhi.

My involvement came about as M.C. Mehta needed technical people as witnesses in the Supreme Court, regarding the risk of storing oleum in a densely-populated locality and the risk to the people in case of a leak. The Supreme Court allowed M.C. Mehta to set up an expert committee, which consisted of G.D. Agarwal, T. Shivaji Rao and me.[23] After the Union Carbide plant, this was the second hazardous plant I was examining for safety. We brought up the fact that given the atmospheric conditions of early winter in northern India, what is called a temperature inversion, pollutants do not disperse easily. This is Delhi's famous winter smog, in which temperature inversion is the primary culprit, though stubble burning and vehicle exhausts are contributory ones. A simple calculation showed that under such conditions — a temperature inversion — if an oleum leak took place from the Sriram Fertiliser storage tanks, the impact in the densely populated areas close to the plant would be devastating.

The Supreme Court had taken up the oleum leak case to pronounce on the basis of compensation when a disaster occurs in a plant storing hazardous material. Even Sriram was forced to accept that oleum was a hazardous gas, and there was always a possibility, however remote, of leakages from the plant. It was, after all, an actual oleum leak from their plant which had led to the Supreme Court taking up the case. The Court's intention was to bring the Indian law of liability up to date from the 100-year-old Strict Liability judgement of 1868 in the *Rylands vs Fletcher* case in England. Through the oleum leak case — *M.C. Mehta vs Union*

---

[23] D.G. Agarwal was a professor at the IIT-Kanpur, and a member-secretary of the Central Pollution Control Board (CPCB). He was a passionate defender of the environment who died on October 9, 2018 after a 111-day fast on his demand for a clean Ganga. Shivaji Rao was a professor of civil engineering, and also worked on sustainable development.

of India — Justice Bhagwati's bench established the jurisprudence of 'absolute liability', holding the owners of the plant responsible, without exceptions, for any damage arising out of their hazardous industry/activity.[24] It was the reason Sriram Fertilisers decided to close down its Delhi plant and accept relocation elsewhere. It also meant that a stronger legal basis of holding Union Carbide liable for damages was established. Otherwise, Union Carbide's defence of having done due diligence, which was also Sriram Fertiliser's line of defence, would have had some legal legs. Unfortunately, the 1989 judgement by the R.S. Pathak bench, agreeing to the settlement of $470 million between the Union of India and Union Carbide, which was within the insurance limit of Carbide, grossly underestimated the extent of the injuries and the long-term costs to the victims, in terms of lowered life expectancy, medical bills and disabilities.[25]

While the Delhi Science Forum was more focussed on the policy issues of science and technology, there was a larger science movement in the country. Starting out as an organisation of Malayalam science writers in 1962, the Kerala Sasthra Sahithya Parishad expanded its initial objective of bringing science to the people in their mother tongue to become a movement of science for the transformation of society. There were also the Marathi Vigyan Parishad, Ekalavya, Karnataka Rajya Vignana Parishat, Delhi Science Forum and many others already active in the science movement.

The movement saw several major developments: the Jan Vigyan Jatha (peoples science jatha) in 1987; the formation of the All India People's Science Network (AIPSN) in 1988; and the Bharat Gyan Vigyan Jatha (jatha for total literacy) in 1990.

The sheer scale of the two jathas, their pan-Indian journeys,

---

[24] Supreme Court judgement on M.C. Mehta vs Union of India, page 7. https://main.sci.gov.in/jonew/judis/9120.pdf

[25] N.D. Jayaprakash, 'Bhopal Gas Leak Disaster: UCC's Heinous Crime and Response of the Indian State', *The Marxist*, XXVI 2, April–June 2010 https://cpim.org/marxist/2010-02-%20Bhopal-JP.pdf

Living Politics

starting from various corners of the country and congregating in Bhopal, were landmark events in the history of the science movement. It was an attempt to bring to both science activists and the people the message that science is not an activity reserved for scientists and technologists, but is also funded by society and scientists/technologists must be accountable to the people.[26] It also meant that decisions which have an impact on people need their participation, possible only if science is demystified and its social dimensions popularised. I am quoting below from the document of the 1987 jatha, its grand plan:

> You probably know already that the Bharat Jan Vigyan Jatha, a unique and historic nationwide event in science communication, is about to begin — on October 2, Gandhiji's birth anniversary, reminding us of the continuing need to struggle for self-reliance. Five zonal Jathas or mobile groups of scientists, teachers, artistes and PSM activists will be traversing over 25,000 km, holding performances at over 500 locations and converging on Bhopal to a rally of about 4000 scientists and teachers on November 7, the birth anniversary of Prof C.V. Raman. In addition to these Jathas, local-level programs will be organised continuously, thus reaching directly an estimated 50 lakh people all over the country.[27]

The 1987 Jan Vigyan Jatha not only created an all-India science movement, but also new science organisations in various states. Most of them were aware of KSSP's jatha form, combining different cultural forms or kala, with the message of science

---

[26] I am deliberately using science as a popular shorthand for science and technology, in spite of my great reluctance to club science and technology as if they are identical.

[27] National Organising Committee Bharat Jan Vigyan Jatha, 1987. https://archive.org/details/bharatjanvigyanjatha1987bjvs/page/n7/mode/2up?view=theater

and social change.[28] (KSSP was, in fact, even more radical in its slogan: Science for social revolution!)

The jathas also saw Raghu and Dinesh take on major responsibilities. Professor Udgaonkar (Tata Institute of Fundamental Research), was the chairman, M. Parameswaran was the convenor, Raghu was the organising secretary of the national organising committee. Dinesh led the Northern Jatha.

After the success in 1987, all the groups who had participated in the science jatha met in Kannur in 1988 to found the All India Peoples Science Network. M. Parameswaran became its president, and Raghu the general secretary. In 1990, the AIPSN and a newly-formed body in whose creation AIPSN played an important role, the Bharat Gyan Vigyan Samiti (BGVS), jointly undertook to conduct a literacy jatha covering the entire country. Wherever the jatha went, it would help create local-level total literacy campaign bodies. BGVS would create the content and provide organisational support to the mass literacy campaign by involving local organisations and well-known individuals.

The 1990 Bharat Gyan Vigyan Jatha, campaigning for total literacy, was ambitious. It was to initiate total literacy campaigns in each district on the model of what Ernakulam had already achieved.[29] Instead of the usual adult literacy projects, the difference was to organise a campaign involving school and college teachers and students, by first training them and then setting up groups

---

[28] Though we became familiar with the jatha form of public communication through KSSP and its use of Kala Jathas, it was Samudaya in Karnataka who had initiated the jatha form for their theatre performances. KSSP extended it much further, and the science movement used it extensively in its various campaigns.

[29] 'Operation Floodlight', completed in February 1990, had made Ernakulam the first district in the country where everyone between the ages of five and 60 was literate. Over 22,000 volunteers were involved, and the project was backed by the KSSP. See:
https://www.indiatoday.in/magazine/indiascope/story/19900228-successful-literacy-mission-creates-awareness-in-kerala-813696-1990-02-28

in towns, districts and villages to make people literate. Again, the model was what KSSP had pioneered — mass campaigns and use of volunteers.

As a part of the BGVS 1990 jatha, I was the convener of the Delhi Saksharata Samiti with Lalita Ramdas (or Lolly) as its chair. Since then, Lolly and her husband, Admiral Ramdas, have been dear friends of mine. During the literacy campaign, both of them would interact with us as equals, even if there was a large social distance between us activists and the serving chief of the Indian navy and his wife! Lolly had also been a major figure in the civil society protests on the anti-Sikh riots, so activism was (and is) very much a part of her life. After the 1998 nuclear bomb test in Pokhran, Admiral Ramdas, who had retired by then, joined the anti-nuclear weapon movement. He was in the company of other major international military figures who have made public their opposition to weapons of mass destruction.

Both the jathas greatly widened the base of the science movement in the country, not only in terms of their reach but also in building relations with other organisations who normally do not work with the left and would themselves be considered purely social movements (or in today's terminology civil society). Science and literacy were relatively neutral grounds, although we certainly considered science and technology very much a part of the larger political struggle, both the ideological and the physical one of who controls the resources and decides on the benefits of development.

One of the themes of the science jatha was peace, focussing particularly on nuclear disarmament. N.D. Jayaprakash, besides being one of the founding members of the Delhi Science Forum and fighting a 30-year long legal battle in the Union Carbide case, has also written and created an archive on nuclear disarmament. During the 1987 jatha, he created an exhibition on the theme, which we brought out as a publication, calling it the *Darkness of a Thousand Suns*, contrasting it to the once popular book *Brighter Than a Thousand Suns*, by Robert Jungk, on the atomic scientists and the Trinity test of the Manhattan Project. We also produced a slide show and film on the nuclear bomb and disarmament. All this became important 11 years later when India conducted the second nuclear bomb tests in Pokhran, in May 1998. The Delhi Science Forum became a ready source of information for journalists and others, on the nuclear bomb, the global disarmament movement and the arguments against the bomb.

PUBLIC SECTOR AND PUBLIC INTEREST ISSUES

By the 1990s, my earlier confusion and 'dilemma' about balancing science and technology with politics was resolved. It was no longer a question of 'balance' or trying to 'bring together' different aspects of my life. As far as I was concerned, my politics lived in the same place as my involvement in various forms with science and technology. Over the years, I helped organise a number of programs on self-reliance, sovereignty, and scientific temper.

I was very much involved in activities related to the telecom and power sectors, including helping the relevant trade unions. We also fought a number of public interest cases — on telecom and on pharmaceuticals, some of these in the Supreme Court. In the case of power sector 'reforms', the Electricity Act 1948, drafted and steered by B.R. Ambedkar, was transformed into the Electricity Act 2003. The backstory to this includes the Enron Deal's Dabhol power plant initiated in 1992, which meant that independent power producers (IPPs) would enter the market with power purchase agreements (PPAs). Enron's was the most notorious of these: the deal showed us, in vivid and lurid detail, what privatisation really is. 'In late 2001, the global giant, Enron, filed for bankruptcy in US courts. With assets strewn across the planet, Enron's collapse impacted almost everyone, for greater or lesser.'[30] In countries like India,

---

[30] Prabir Purkayastha and Vijay Prashad, *Enron Blowout: Corporate Capitalism and Theft of the Global Commons*, LeftWord Books, 2002.

Living Politics

[. . .] greedy politicians went into alliance with Enron to 'rehabilitate' public enterprises, mainly in the energy and water sector. Abandoning the sensible policy of keeping within the public sector such crucial components of socio-economic life as power, water, education and health, states like India, the Philippines and Argentina went in for 'privatisation,' via the fire-sale of state-funded assets for very low costs to rapacious global corporations whose only interest is in an increased profit margin not the liberation of the marginal.[31]

The spectre of privatisation continued to allure the Indian government at the cost of public interest. In 1994, the move to privatise telecom services led to the auction of licenses; the DSF fought a case on the matter. Nandita Haksar was my mentor on how the left should look at law and the courts: not as a substitute for movements but a complement to them. I learned a lot from her about law as a part of political work.

In 2009, on the 2G license issue, I wrote on 'the great spectrum robbery':

To recapitulate the spectrum swindle, the all India license and the spectrum for additional cellular operators (2G operators) was given away on a first-come-first-served basis at 2001 prices. The Telecom Regulatory Authority of India, experts within and outside the government, had all stated then that there was no justification for using 2001 prices when there were barely 4 million mobile subscribers as against 300 million subscribers in 2007. Sitaram Yechury wrote to the prime minister on this issue (letter dated February 29, 2008) cautioning the government that this was simply giving a huge largesse to new operators.[32]

---

[31] Ibid.
[32] Prabir Purkayastha, 'The Great Spectrum Robbery: Raja Must Quit', Delhi Science Forum, November 11, 2009.

DSF again went to court on this issue, this time with Indira Jaising as our lawyer. The breadth of her social and political vision, combined with her meticulous attention to detail was, for me, a political education. In both my interventions, I was not operating as a 'lone ranger'. Rather, I was helping the power sector and telecom unions.[33]

Another area of concern was that of the World Trade Organisation's trade-related intellectual property rights (TRIPS), which came into being in 1994. We had opposed India's joining the TRIPS agreement as this would adversely impact our 1970 Patents Act and our ability to manufacture generic drugs. The DSF was part of the All India Drug Action Network (AIDAN), and later the Peoples Health Movement, in which Amit Sengupta played a leading role. This engagement led naturally to addressing two issues of intellectual property rights — brand names versus generic names, and patents — raising the question, 'Did patents and copyright work to diffuse knowledge or appropriate it? The question naturally led to resisting the MNCs' control over knowledge...'[34]

The earlier Patents Act — the 1970 Act amended in 2002 — had a clause which made it difficult to patent software. India had a 10-year window in the 1994 WTO agreement, to bring the Indian Patent Act in line with the TRIPS agreement. The 2004 Draft Patent Bill, introduced by the BJP-led NDA, tried to modify the 3(k) clause of the Act to patent software, and also create a strong patent regime via 3(d) that would favour Big Pharma. There was a long stretch of negotiations with the UPA — which had replaced the NDA as the ruling coalition — in which the left played an important part in parliament. This led to India's Patents Act in

---

https://delhiscienceforum.net/the-great-spectrum-robbery-raja-must-quit/

[33] Two figures in the telecom sector who provided significant insights and support were D.K. Singhal, Secretary, Department of Telecommunications, and S.M. Agarwal, Secretary of Communications.

[34] Introduction, Prabir Purkayastha et al (eds), *Political Journeys in Health, Essays by and for Amit Sengupta*, LeftWord Books, 2020.

2005. The MNCs, both the software and pharma MNCs, were very unhappy. They have been trying to dilute the Patents Act ever since, using the Patent Manual as a tool to bypass legislative intent in the case of software, and filing cases in court as on the 3(d) clause over the issue of pharmaceutical patents.

The free software movement stemmed from the larger commons movement, treating copyright and patenting as an attempt to fence in the knowledge commons. It had started with what is called the Gnu license, which allows the software code to be modified freely, provided it is released to others under the same license. The free software movement was global and arrived in India as well. A workshop organised by Knowledge Commons and others in 2010 raised the question of whether the networked world carries 'new possibilities for alternate structures of creating knowledge and innovation';[35] and whether the notion of the 'commons' can be expanded to help such processes develop. The background paper for the workshopmade a case for the free software movement:[36]

> The patenting system originated in the days of the lone inventor and the need to protect his/her invention. Historically, the lone inventor has given way to large corporate or State funded research laboratories in the early twentieth century. Increasingly, institutions of scientific and technological research, have tended to duplicate the manner of working of global corporations, locating the production of knowledge in a framework premised on private profit. The Bayh-Dole legislation[37] facilitated the adoption of this model by publicly

[35] Delhi Science Forum, 'Science Commons: Collaboration, Not Competition To Promote Scientific Advance', Abridged Background Paper, January 1, 2009.
https://delhiscienceforum.net/science-commons/
[36] Ibid.
[37] The Patents and Trademark Law Amendments Act, passed in the US in 1980, is better known as the Bayh-Dole Act. In essence, it permits private players to

funded science in the US. In India, as elsewhere, a similar trajectory is gaining ground. Interestingly, this is also a time in which alternate models of generating knowledge and innovation have gained ground. The free software movement has shown that networked and open collaborations of 'hackers' can produce software of far better quality than what the best of well-heeled corporations working in isolation can manage.

THE NUCLEAR DEAL AND VARIOUS MILITARY AGREEMENTS

The India-US nuclear deal (2005–08) polarised the country dramatically. On the one hand, the yea-sayers insisted the deal was essential for India's progress. On the other hand, many of us, including foreign policy experts and former diplomats, had some sharp questions: How will the deal affect our independence in foreign policy, defence, and even in the field of nuclear technology? Was acquiring technology from the likes of Westinghouse and GE helpful or harmful? Would it undermine the self-reliance we had built over the last 30 years?

The left parties cautioned the UPA government — which they were supporting at that point — saying that, first of all:

> [. . .] binding India to the US on foreign policy would have serious consequences for India . . . Second, the US would shift goalposts in the process of converting the agreement into actual laws . . . any lifting of sanctions would be hedged by many conditions, and in any case the bulk of the sanctions would not be lifted. The price of this limited lifting of sanctions in the nuclear field would be extracted in the field of foreign policy — apart, of course, from the economic cost of buying

---

acquire exclusive rights over patents generated via public expenditure, and to defend these exclusive rights in court. The effect of the Act was to redefine the benefits of knowledge, away from universal progress and towards being a prerogative of wealth and profit.

nuclear technology, materials, and reactors...[38]

It is clear, then, that the problem was also economic. The costs were simply too high to import 16 reactors. Nuclear power plants imported from the US companies GE and Westinghouse, and the French company Areva, would bankrupt the Indian power sector. Ironically, all these three companies subsequently collapsed. They proved to be too expensive to run, even for the West.[39]

BUILDING A NETWORK OF MOVEMENTS

Politics, however passionate about it you are, cannot be limited to certain disciplines. In addition to groups and movements linked with science and technology, I was inevitably part of various broad-front movements over the decades. Just two examples out of many will suffice. After the demolition of the Babri Masjid in 1992, many of us came together to fight against communalism. One of these campaigns was called the People's Movement for Secularism. These campaigns had to be strengthened after the 'riots' in Gujarat in 2002. Earlier, after the Pokhran nuclear test in 1998, a committee for nuclear disarmament had been set up. The Movement in India for Nuclear Disarmament (MIND) remains committed to universal nuclear disarmament.[40]

Perhaps the culmination of the 'broad front' in my experience was the World Social Forum. I was among those involved in organising the Asian Social Forum in Hyderabad in 2003 and the

---

[38] Prabir Purkayastha, 'Coming Out of the Nuclear Cold' in Prabir Purkayastha, Ninan Koshy and M.K. Bhadrakumar, *Uncle Sam's Nuclear Cabin*, LeftWord Books, 2007. A.K. Gopalakrishnan, former Chairman, Atomic Energy Regulatory Commission (1993-1996), provided us with considerable technical and legal insights, especially with respect to US law and regulations.

[39] See, for instance
https://www.newsclick.in/westinghouse-bankruptcy-nuclear-energy-story-nearly-over

[40] Preamble, Movement in India for Nuclear Disarmament.
https://www.angelfire.com/mi/MIND123/

World Social Forum in Mumbai in 2004. Both saw an extraordinary number of people coming together to discuss issues ranging from dalit rights and women's rights to freedom of information and free software. The participants in their thousands represented varied social movements, trade unions, NGOs, peace and anti-imperialist groups, environmental movements — and all manner of networks of those usually excluded. The Forum's banner and its words remain unforgettable: *Another world is possible*. It is yet to be achieved, but certainly still part of the plan of action!

I am as old as the Indian republic. In my life of more than 75 years, I have learnt a thing or two, maybe even three. To put it simply, I have learnt how I can be part of my rich, diverse country, and, equally, part of the fascinating, complex larger world. All I need to do is fight for a better world for all.

Living politics needs, of course, a firm commitment to struggling for equality — in the broadest emancipatory sense — and justice for all, both within the country and among countries. But on a day-to-day basis, living politics means sustained work to build movements; to build a strong network, an alliance of movements. This, in sum, is what I have learnt over more than five decades. People's movements provide the larger world with its only rays of hope. And for me, in my life, they have taught me meaning and given me purpose.

Acknowledgements

This book began as a series of conversations with Githa Hariharan. The book could not have been written without her guidance, even if it was occasionally stern. Once again, Salim Yusufji performed his editorial magic; Sudhanva Deshpande and Vijay Prashad of LeftWord Books supported the book even before it was written; and the entire LeftWord team, and Vinutha Mallya, worked overtime to bring out the book. Rajesh Kalithody and Chandan Gorana provided logistical assistance. Most of all, this book — or more to the point, my life — owes more than I can say to several individuals, groups, organisations and movements over the years. I thank them all.

Annexure 1
From the Shah Commission Report

V. Detention of Shri Prabir Purkayastha[1]

11.134 Shri Prabir Purkayastha, a student of Jawahar Lal Nehru University (JNU) was detained under MISA on September 25, 1975, under the orders passed by Shri P. Ghosh, the then Additional District Magistrate (South), for his alleged active association with Students Federation of India (CPM) and for his alleged prominent role in organising the students' strike started by the SFI w.e.f. September 24, 1975, against the JNU Administration and the Government. Records of the Special Branch of the Delhi Police show that Shri Purkayastha had, in a meeting held on August 26, 1975, criticised the Vice-Chancellor for suspending Kum. Ashok Lata Jain and supported the call to fight against the alleged repressive policy of the University authorities. The report also states that in response to the call of the SFI for a strike in JNU he was noticed preventing some students from attending classes on September 24, 1975.

11.135 Shri Prabir Purkayastha has stated that he had joined JNU in early September, 1975, for his Ph.D. Degree; that he was a participant in the three-day boycott of classes in JNU from September 24, 1975, in protest against the expulsion of Kum. Ashok Lata Jain who was an elected member of the Students Union; that on September 25, 1975, when he was sitting in the lawn outside the School of Languages with three other students, Saraswati

---

[1] From 'Shah Commission Of Inquiry Interim Report II', pp. 56–59. https://archive.org/details/ShahCommissionOfInquiryInterimReportII

From the Shah Commission Report

Menon, Kum. Shakti Kak and Kum. Indrani Majumdar, at about 10 a.m. a black Ambassador car stopped nearby, and one of the four occupants of the car asked him whether he was Devi Prasad Tripathi, the President of the Students Union; that he said that he was not; that despite his protests, he was dragged inside the car after some scuffle, and all efforts of his companions to rescue him failed and the car drove off; and that he was taken to R.K. Puram Police Post where he learnt from the SHO that the person driving the car was Shri P.S. Bhinder, the then DIG (R). Kum. Shakti Kak and Kum. Indrani Majumdar, who were eye-witnesses to the incident have corroborated the statement of Shri Purkayastha. Kum. Shakti Kak stated that it was a black Ambassador car No. DLE 5747.

This car is found to be the official car of the then Supt. of Police (South) Shri Rajinder Mohan. According to their statements, the person who first came and asked Shri Prabir Purkayastha whether he was D.P. Tripathi was left behind in the campus and was later mobbed by the students who wanted to find out his identity and also to know where and by whom Prabir Purkayastha had been taken. He was 'rescued' by some police officers, who told the students that they would take care of their complaint. This officer was Shri T.R. Anand, Dy. Supt. of Police. Shri Purkayastha, Kum. Shakti Kak and Kum. Indrani Majumdar have stated that Smt. Maneka Gandhi, wife of Shri Sanjay Gandhi, who was a student of JNU, had gone to the University in the morning of September 25, and was stopped by the students including Shri Devi Prasad Tripathi from attending the classes, and was also asked to join the boycott. She did not attend the class and went away. According to Shri Prabir Purkayastha, his detention and the manner of his arrest could have been the result of this incident relating to Smt. Maneka Gandhi. Kum. Indrani Majumdar has stated that since Smt. Maneka Gandhi had also come in a black car, 'there was a lot of speculation later on as to whether the car was the same car which had taken Prabir away later on'.

11.136 Shri T.R. Anand said that he and Shri Rajendra Mohan were standing outside the JNU on the morning of September 25, 1975, when Shri P.S. Bhinder came there and made enquiries about the situation and particularly about Shri D.P. Tripathi, President of the Students Union, against whom a MISA warrant was pending execution. Shri Bhinder then decided to arrest Shri D.P. Tripathi himself and though Shri T.R. Anand told him that he did not know Tripathi and could not identify him, Shri Bhinder insisted on Shri Anand accompanying him. Shri Anand stated that he went inside the Campus along with Shri Bhinder and two constables in plain-clothes in motor-car No. DLE 5747 driven by Shri Bhinder himself; that Shri Bhinder arrested Shri Prabir Purkayastha on the suspicion that the latter was Shri D.P. Tripathi, though Shri Prabir Purkayastha said that he was not Tripathi and other students also said so; that Shri Bhinder was saying that he had to arrest Tripathi under MISA warrant but had taken Prabir Purkayastha into custody 'suspecting that he is Tripathi and he is concealing'; that subsequently Shri Bhinder had told the officers that Smt. Maneka Gandhi, who was stopped from attending the classes on September 25 had gone back to the Prime Minister's house and Shri Bhinder had gone to the JNU under instructions from the Prime Minister's house. Shri Rajinder Mohan has stated that Shri Bhinder had 'come straight' from the PM's house and had entered the University campus saying that he would go and arrest Shri D.P. Tripathi; that later Shri Bhinder told him that he — Shri Bhinder — had arrested one student who was not D.P. Tripathi but was one of the agitators and he should be detained under MISA; that it was at that time when he — Rajinder Mohan — 'came to know the name of the student who was arrested by Shri Bhinder'; that he told Shri Bhinder that the name of Shri Purkayastha did not figure in the list supplied by the CID and he did not have any grounds for detaining him under MISA; and that Shri Bhinder still told him that 'a decision has been taken and you will get a warrant from the Additional District Magistrate and it has to be executed'.

From the Shah Commission Report

11.137 Shri P. Ghosh, Additional District Magistrate (South) has stated that he had reached the Police Station Hauz Khas in response to the wireless message from the SP (South) and learnt from Shri T.R. Anand and Shri Harpal Singh, Dy. S.P. that a scuffle had taken place involving some police officials and JNU students; that on his request the Dean of the Students and the Registrar of the JNU came to the Police Station and told him that some police officials had 'entered the campus and kidnapped a student'; that when he confronted Shri Rajendra Mohan with his version, the latter told him that Shri P.S. Bhinder had 'gone to the JNU to arrest Shri D.P. Tripathi because Smt. Maneka Gandhi had complained to Shri Sanjay Gandhi about the anti-Government activities in JNU and Sanjay Gandhi had summoned Shri Bhinder and had asked him to take drastic action'; that Shri Bhinder had gone with the intention of arresting Shri D.P. Tripathi but had taken another student into custody in the mistaken belief that the student was Shri Tripathi; and that when Shri Rajendra Mohan insisted on the issue of MISA warrant against this student he went to the District Magistrate and brought all the facts to his notice and sought orders, but the District Magistrate felt that since the matter involved Shri Sanjay Gandhi, he would consult the Lt. Governor and seek his orders.

11.138 Shri Sushil Kumar has admitted that Shri Ghosh had brought the facts relating to the arrest of Shri Prabir Purkayastha to his notice and had sought his administrative advice. He categorically stated that Shri Ghosh had told him that it was a case of mistaken identity and that Shri Bhinder had acted under instructions from the PM's house, or from Shri Sanjay Gandhi, and had arrested Shri Prabir Purkayastha 'in place of' Shri D.P. Tripathi. Shri Sushil Kumar has admitted that since the matter involved the PM's house, he thought it necessary to discuss it with the Lt. Governor before he gave any orders to Shri P. Ghosh. Shri Sushil Kumar has also stated that he had brought the details of the case of

Shri Purkayastha to the notice of Lt. Governor and had told him that it was a case of mistaken identity and the police were insisting on the issue of MISA warrant against Shri Prabir Purkayastha. The Lt. Governor told Shri Sushil Kumar that he would let him know as to what was to be done about it. According, to Shri Sushil Kumar, the Lt. Governor told him on telephone later in the evening that 'the request made by SP (South) to the Additional District Magistrate for the issue of MISA detention order should be complied with'. Shri Sushil Kumar has admitted that he directed Shri Ghosh to act accordingly and Shri Ghosh issued the detention order which was served on Shri Prabir Purkayastha late at night. Shri Ghosh received the grounds of detention from the SP (South) after several days but the grounds were pre-dated.

11.139 Shri Rajendra Mohan has corroborated Shri Ghosh by saying that though he got the detention orders on the same day, i.e. September 25, 1975, he prepared the grounds from an unsigned note received from the Special Branch 4–5 days after this incident. Shri P. Ghosh admitted that though he had no evidence against Shri Prabir Purkayastha and that in fact found the story of the University authorities regarding Shri Purkayastha's innocence credible, he issued the detention orders, on the directions of the District Magistrate because 'in those days the practice was not to issue detention orders on the basis of subjective satisfaction of Magistrate but to issue them on the directions of our official superiors'. Shri Ghosh also admitted that the arrest was not made on the basis of grounds which were a mere formality and the date on which the grounds were signed were also a formality.

11.140 Shri P.S. Bhinder has admitted that he had arrested Shri Prabir Purkayastha from inside the University campus on September 25, 1975. He has admitted that he had gone into the JNU Campus with Dy. SP Shri T.R. Anand and two constables

From the Shah Commission Report

in plainclothes in the motor-car of Shri Rajendra Mohan which he himself was driving. He has said in his defence that the JNU was a centre of agitational activities and sometime either before the arrest of Shri Prabir Purkayastha or after a massive raid was carried out in the JNU and 8 to 10 students were arrested.

According to the statement of Shri Bhinder this was done under the directions of the Lt. Governor and he (Lt. Governor) was very happy about it. According to Shri Bhinder, three persons still remained to be arrested and Shri D.P. Tripathi and Shri Prabir Purkayastha were among them; that the Lt. Governor wanted these persons also to be arrested and was making daily enquiries in this regard; that he had gone to the JNU in the morning of September 25, 1975, after learning that some students were stopping others from attending classes; that he took Shri T.R. Anand, Dy. SP and two constables and went inside the campus where he found '10 to 15 boys' shouting anti-Emergency slogans, but he could not say what these slogans were; that these boys were preventing others from attending classes and Shri Prabir Purkayastha appeared to be the leader of the group; that he enquired about his name from another group of students and learnt that it was Prabir Purkayastha; and he remembered that Prabir was one of the three students still wanted, as directed by Lt. Governor, and he arrested him. The story of Shri Bhinder does not appear credible.

11.141 Shri Krishan Chand has admitted that Shri Sushil Kumar came to him on September 25, 1975, and told him that he had learnt from Shri Ghosh that under instructions from the PM's house Shri Bhinder had gone to the JNU and had arrested one or two students; but he said that Shri Sushil Kumar did not tell him that it was a case of mistaken identity. Shri Krishan Chand also stated that he found Shri Sushil Kumar puzzled because he did not know on what grounds that student was arrested and that he told Shri Sushil Kumar, 'I will find out and give you a reply.' He also stated that before Shri Sushil Kumar met him, Shri Bhinder had seen and had told him that they had found, a 'goldmine' because he had arrested some students and that the arrests would help the situation in JNU, but Shri Bhinder had given him no details nor had he felt any curiosity himself to ask for any further details, that he did not know that Shri Bhinder had himself gone to make this arrest nor was he told so by Shri Bhinder; that after discussion with Shri Sushil Kumar he consulted Shri P.S. Bhinder either on the same day or the next day, and later told Shri Sushil Kumar that 'if the information is from the PM's house and Mr. Bhinder says that this is correct then it would be a fit case for issue of a MISA warrant'; that he did not know the details of the allegations against this student but Shri Bhinder had told him that they had sufficient material for his detention and that the fact that Shri Bhinder had received the information from the PM's house had certainly influenced him. Shri Krishan Chand maintained that Shri Sushil Kumar had not brought the fact of mistaken identity to his notice and said that 'Mr. Bhinder was insisting again and again that we have got the right person'.

11.142 It is difficult to believe that Shri Krishan Chand was not informed by Shri Sushil Kumar that it was a case of mistaken identity. Shri Krishan Chand has admitted that he thought that whatever Shri Bhinder said must be accepted. Shri Krishan Chand obviously relied more on what Shri Bhinder said in this matter and ignored the information given by Shri Sushil Kumar on the basis of what Shri Ghosh had told him.

11.143 It is clear from the statements of Shri Prabir Purkayastha, Shakti Kak and Indrani Majumdar, the students, and Shri T.R. Anand and Shri Rajendra Mohan, the police officials, that Shri Bhinder had arrested Prabir Purkayastha in the mistaken belief that he was Shri D.P. Tripathi and finding it too late to retrace his steps, he insisted on the detention of Shri Prabir Purkayastha under MISA, and successfully persuaded the Lt. Governor to direct the District Magistrate to arrange for the issue of MISA warrant against Purkayastha.

11.144 Shri Prabir Purkayastha has stated that his request for grant of parole to enable him to take the viva voce examination for his ME thesis was refused and only after the Delhi High Court gave directions, he was sent to Naini Jail in handcuffs for taking his examination. Shri Prabir Purkayastha was transferred to Agra Jail after the jail break in Tihar Jail in March 1976 and was put in solitary confinement for about 25 days in Agra Jail as orders to this effect were issued to the Superintendent, Agra Jail, by IG (Prisons), U.P.

11.145 Shri Samar Mukherjee, Member of Parliament, wrote to Shri Om Mehta on October 31, 1975, giving an account of the circumstances of arrest of Shri Prabir Purkayastha and expressed the resentment it had caused amongst the students and the staff members of JNU. A report was called from the IB and it confirmed that Shri Prabir Purkayastha was not an active member of the Students Federation of India and had not come to notice for taking an active part in organising a students' strike in JNU on September 24, 1975.

11.146 The Ministry of Home Affairs wrote to the Delhi Administration on 14-4-1976, giving them the gist of the IB's report, and advised them to re-examine the case for revocation of orders. The Delhi Administration promised to consider the matter in the next four-monthly review due in May 1976 but the continued detention of Shri Purkayastha was again confirmed in this review on May 18, 1976.

11.147 Shri Krishan Chand has stated that when the report from the Ministry was placed before him, he consulted Shri

Bhinder who was also a member of the Screening Committee and Shri Bhinder reiterated the earlier stand that Shri Purkayastha was not wrongly detained. The case was again examined at the level of the Home Minister, and the Ministry of Home Affairs wrote to the Delhi Administration on July 9, 1976, to revoke the orders in respect of Shri Prabir Purkayastha. The Lt. Governor did not agree. According to the note in the file of the Delhi Administration, the Lt. Governor discussed the matter with Shri Om Mehta, MMHA, and it was decided to review the case in due course. The detention order was revoked ultimately on September 25, 1976. Shri Krishan Chand has admitted that he did not agree to the release of Shri Purkayastha even after receiving the letter dated July 9, 1976, from the Ministry of Home Affairs, because he was told by Shri Bhinder and other police authorities that Purkayastha's release at that stage 'might adversely affect the normal functioning of the University'.

11.148 Notices under Rule 5(2)(a) of the Commissions of Inquiry Rules and summons under section 8B of the Commissions of Inquiry Act were issued to Shri Krishan Chand and Shri P.S. Bhinder in this case. Shri Bhinder pleaded his inability to respond to the Commission's summons on the ground of his preoccupation with a murder case in which he happens to be an accused. The Commission even posted this case for a Saturday to suit the convenience of Shri Bhinder. Shri Bhinder was present but tendered no statement of his version contending that he could not get the legal assistance that he claimed was due to him, and on that account, he requested for adjournment of the case. The Commission, however, did not think it a justifiable request and proceeded with the case. The Commission has already had the benefit of Shri Blunder's assistance in the first stage of the hearing of the case when he had given a detailed account of his version of the case. Shri Krishan Chand responded to the summons and gave his version of the case which has been referred to earlier in this report.

From the Shah Commission Report

11.149 There is no denying the fact that Shri Krishan Chand did not at all exercise his independent judgment and went entirely by the version given to him by Shri Bhinder. In the process he misused his powers and abused his authority. Shri Bhinder, it is clear from all accounts, kidnapped Prabir Purkayastha believing him to be Shri D.P. Tripathi. That it was a clear case of mistaken identity is evident on the record. The manner in which Shri Bhinder went about the job discloses his callous attitude.

Because he received directions from the Prime Minister's house, he arrested the first male student he came across and even after he was repeatedly told that the student was not D.P. Tripathi against whom a warrant was issued he insisted upon obtaining an order of detention under MISA and ultimately set up a false story to justify his action. This was a gross abuse of authority. Even when informed that he had arrested the wrong person against whom the police had no evidence of prejudicial activity, he persuaded the authorities to detain and continue to keep Purkayastha in detention seriously aggravating his misconduct. The story of the arrest of Purkayastha by Shri Bhinder, the manner in which the Magistrate issued the detention orders, and the part played by the Lt. Governor illustrate the complete breakdown of the rule of law. The attitude of callous disregard of the rights of an innocent citizen exhibited by Shri Bhinder in arresting Purkayastha and ensuring that he be kept in custody for more than one year, during which Purkayastha was subjected to various forms of ill-treatment, merely with a view to please someone in the Prime Minister's house, is a sad commentary on the state of affairs which prevailed when power was exercised by functionaries who believed that they were not responsible for explaining their actions. The arrogance of untrammelled power, coupled with the spineless attitude disclosed by public servants who were responsible for the administration of the law, contributed to the happening of events which must remain a serious blot on the fair name of any administration.

Annexure 2
MISA Detentions During Emergency:
Prabir Purkayastha

Shri Pravir Purkayastha, a Ph.D. student of Jawaharlal Nehru University, was detained under MISA on 25.9.75 under the orders of Shri P. Ghosh, the then ADM (South) on the following grounds:

"Shri Pravir Purkayastha is an active S.F.I. (CPM) worker and belongs to its extremist group. He was an active organiser of the students strike started by the SFI w.e.f. 24.9.75 against JNU Administration and the Government. The strike was aimed at disrupting the academic activities of the JNU students. He took a prominent part in bringing out and distributing pamphlets giving call for the strike wherein the JNU Vice Chancellor and the Government were bitterly criticised for alleged anti-students activities and for not permitting the election to the Students Union this year."

Enquiries made with the Special Branch of Delhi Police to collect full facts about the alleged political character of Shri Pravir Purkayastha have revealed the following:-

"He is a staunch SFI worker, who has got good influence in the SFI Unit of JNU. Though he took admission only in the year 1975, yet had attracted Miss Ashok Lata Jain due to his political image.

In a meeting (45/50) on Aug. 26 he alongwith D.P. Tripathi criticised the VC for suspending Miss Ashok Lata Jain and supported the call of fighting against the alleged repressive policies of the University authorities.

In the two meetings (40/50) on Sept. 22, it was decided to continue with the old students union office bearers.

He was noticed stopping the students from attending classes

MISA Detentions During the Emergency

on Sept. 24, in order to support the SFI call for strike in the JNU. He was arrested under MISA by South Distt. on Sept. 25, 1975."

It is seen from the grounds of detention and the report of the Special Branch that no material appears to have been available with the Special Branch or with the detaining authorities to support the contention that he was a staunch SFI worker. The main ground of detention seems to be his alleged active participation in the students strike of Sept., 1975. However, it is not indicated what action under the normal law, if any, was taken in this connection.

Shri Pravir Purkayastha has, in his statement, tried to emphasise his non-political character by stating that 'I had joined the State Bank of Bikaner and Jaipur after detailed police verification as a Probationery officer from 31st March, 1974.' He has stated that he had resigned the job of Probationary Officer in August 1974 to continue his studies and had come to Delhi where he joined Ph.D. classes in early September, 1975. He admits to have participated in the boycott of classes as a form of protest on 25th Sept., 1975 against the expulsion of Ashok Lata Jain, who was an elected member of the Students Union. He has stated that:

"I was a participant in the boycott. Since the boycott was total, I, with three other students, Sarswathi Menon, Shakti Kak and Indrani Majumdar, were sitting on the lawns outside the school of Languages. At about 10 a.m. a black ambassador car came, stopped nearby and four persons walked to the place where I was sitting, and one of them asked me whether I was Devi Prasad Tripathi, the President of the Students Union, and I said I was not. In spite of my protests, I was physically dragged inside the car after a couple of minutes of scuffling, and the car drove off. Shakti Kak and Indrani Majumdar who tried to stop the car, were dragged some distance along with the car.

"That I was taken to R. K. Puram, Sector 4, Police Post where the person driving the car ordered the policemen to take me away. The SHO of the Police Station informed me that the person driving the car was Bhinder, DIG. I was held there throughout the day, and

I was given the MISa warrant at about 11.00 p.m. at night."

Miss Shakti Kak, a Ph.D. student of Jawaharlal Nehru University has stated that:-

"On 25th Sept., 1975 at about 10 o'clock in the morning I was sitting on the lawn in front of the school of Languages with the petitioner and three other students.

"That at that time the black Ambassador Car No. DLE-5747 with four people inside stopped near us and one man came down from the back side of the car and came to the petitioner and held him by the shoulder and asked him whether he was Devi Prasad Tripathi, he denied it and I also said that he was not the person. Yet he pulled him and took him near the car. By that time, three more persons got out of the car and tried to push him in the back seat. I along with other students, thinking that they were Gondas trying to abduct the petitioner went near the car to rescue him (petitioner). We succeeded in pulling the petitioner from the car. At that time two more persons came from the other side and pushed him into the car, they also got inside with him. He was caught by the waist while his arms and legs were out of the open car doors. The person who was driving the car immediately started it and the car sped away with doors swinging open. The persons who abducted the petitioner were rough with the students who were trying to rescue the petitioner.

"In the scuffle, the students did not realise that the person who first came and talked to the petitioner was left behind. As he quietly started walking away, one of the students recognised him and shouted to stop him. The students chased him and he was stopped near the gate of the University. By then sizeable crowd of the students had gathered there. The students were asking him questions about his identity and where they have taken the petitioner. He, however, did not answer any question. At that time some Police officers came up with the drawn revolvers and started rescuing him. At that time the students started telling the public that he was a part of the gang who had abducted the petitioner. The

Police told the students that they would take care of it. At that time Chief Proctor of the University Dr. K. P. Mishra and Coordinator of the Academic Affairs Shri P.N. Sharma, came to the scene and asked students to hand him over the Police. At that time I along with other students said that we had a right to know as to who this man was and "we want his explanation right now about the happening in the campus and where the petitioner had been taken." I also told the police that I had been present right through the incident and I could tell them what exactly had happened but they did not listen to me nor did they make any attempt afterwards to contact me. They took the person away who was left behind."

Miss Indrani Mazumdar and Shri Manoj Kumar Joshi, students of the JNU have stated that they had witnessed the incident narrated by Shri Pravir Purkayastha and Miss Shakti Kak and corroborated the statement given by Miss Shakti Kak.

Shri T. R. Anand, Dy. SP appears to be the police official who was referred to have been left behind in the JNU after Shri Pravir Purkayastha was taken away by the police party. Shri T. R. Anand has stated in this connection that:-

"I was present outside JNU in plainclothes along with Shri Rajinder Mohan SP/South and other police officers. DIG (Range) Shri P. S. Bhinder came there and made brief enquiries about the situation. He told the SP that Shri D. P. Tripathi was to be arrested since he was obstructing the students from attending classes and a MISA warrant for his arrest was pending execution. He decided to go into the campus and make arrest. He wanted me to accompany him in the car. I told him that I did not know Tripathi and hence could not identify him. On his insistence, I accompanied the DIG. When the car went into the campus and stopped near School of Languages, I got out of the car. In the meantime I saw the DIG and two constables (in plainclothes) picking up a student and driving away. I was left behind. The name of the arrested person was later disclosed as Shri Pravir Purkayastha and was arrested due to mistaken identity."

Shri Rajindra Mohan, the then SP (South Distt.) has also corroborated the above story by stating that:

"I was present outside JNU along with SDPO/H. Khas, Shri T.R. Anand and other police officers. DIG/Range Shri Bhinder came and made brief enquiries about the situation. He told me that D.P. Tripathi was to be arrested since he was the main leader of the agitators. He decided to go into the campus and make arrest. He along with SDPO/H. Khas Shri T. R. Anand his Lower Subordinates (Constables) went in and arrested another person whose name was disclosed as Pravir Purkayastha. He took him to R. K. Puram and asked me to book him under MISA. He told me that he was raising slogans and was one of the main agitators. Accordingly, a request was made to ADM/South who promptly issued a MISA warrant and Shri Purkayastha was arrested."

Shri P. Ghosh, the then ADM (South) who issued detention orders has stated in this connection that:

"On 25.9.75 (morning) I received a wireless message from SP/South requesting me to come to the police station, Hauz Khas urgently. On arrival at police station Hauz Khas, I was informed by Shri T.R. Anand and Shri Harpal Singh, DSPs that a scuffle had taken place involving police officials and JNU students. Thereafter the Dean of students and Registrar of JNU were requested to come to the police station Hauz Khas to discuss the matter. These University officers, however, stated that some police officials had entered the Campus and had kidnapped a student by name Pravir Purkayastha and they requested information about his whereabouts. They also protested against unauthorised entry of the police in the Campus and demanded to know the reasons for the arrest of Shri Pravir Purkayastha. Since the police had not mentioned anything about the arrest, I confronted SP (South), who had by then arrived at the police station, with the version of the University officers. Shri Rajinder Mohan confirmed that a student was arrested but was unable to give his name or other particulars. He, however, requested for issue of a MISA warrant against the person arrested and said that

MISA Detentions During the Emergency

he would furnish the name and other particulars after ascertaining the same from him. When I asked him the reason for the police action, he stated that Smt. Menka Gandhi had complained to Shri Sanjay Gandhi about the anti-government students activities in the University campus and Shri Sanjay Gandhi had summoned Shri P. S. Bhinder, DIG(R) and asked him to take drastic action. Shri Rajinder Mohan, SP (South) disclosed that the intention was to arrest Shri D. P. Tripathi against whom a MISA order was already pending un-executed, and that the person had been taken into custody in the belief that he was Shri D. P. Tripathi.

Since the version of the University officers was credible and had been more or less confirmed by SP (South) I proceeded to inform the District Magistrate of the incident. The Distt. Magistrate was also informed that in the circumstances the proper thing would be to release Shri Pravir Purkayastha. The Distt. Magistrate said that he would discuss the matter with the Lt. Governor and give further instructions to me. He, however, felt that in view of the fact that the provocation for police action came from Shri Sanjay Gandhi, there was likely to be no option but that a MISA order against the arrested person might have to be issued, and accordingly directed me to prepare MISA orders, but not to issue the same until he gave me further directions. At the time of my discussion with the Distt. Magistrate I gained impression that DIG(R) had already spoken to him about the matter.

"Late at night the Distt. Magistrate telephoned me at my residence and stated that he had discussed the matter with the LG and that the LG had ordered that the MISA orders against Shri Pravir Purkayastha be issued. MISA orders which had earlier been prepared on the instructions of the Distt. Magistrate Delhi were despatched to SP (South) who served the same on Shri Purkayastha late at night on 25.9.75. SP (South) sent the pre-dated grounds of detention after several days.

"Subsequently with a view to moving Delhi Admn. for review of the case I had written to SP (CID) SB to intimate whether there was any record of prejudicial activities on the part of Shri Pravir Purkayastha. SP/CID (SB) replied in writing in the negative. At a review meeting conducted by Distt. Magistrate the letter of SP/CID (SB) was produced before him. SP/CID (SB), however, maintained that since the detention of Shri Pravir Purkayastha was at the instance of Prime Minister's house, there was no question of recommending his release. Neither my latter to SP/CID (SB) nor his reply is presently available on the detention file."

Shri Sushil Kumar, the then DM has confirmed that Shri P. Ghosh had brought all the facts relating to the incident to his notice. He has stated in this connection that:-

"In the case of Shri Pravir Purkayastha I remember that ADM (South) had mentioned to me the circumstances of his arrest and the request of SP (South) for issue of MISA warrants against him. I discussed the case with the LG and brought to his notice all the facts that had been mentioned by ADM (South), but he ordered that ADM be asked to comply with the request of SP (South)."

The L.G., Delhi confirmed the detention of Shri Pravir Purkayastha on 8.10.75. Shri Purkayastha filed a writ petition in the Delhi High Court against his detention in December, 75 presenting it as a case of mistaken identity. The petition was, however, dismissed (in July, 1976) after the Supreme Court gave its ruling in the case of ADM Jabalpur vs. Shiv Kant Shukla on 28.4.76.

Shri Samar Mukherjee, MP wrote to Shri Om Mehta the then MMHA on 31st October, 1975 giving an account of the circumstances of arrest of Shri Pravir Purkayastha saying that:

"This caused great anger and resentment amongst the whole university community. The university teachers held a meeting and passed a resolution condemning the incident. Even the Deans' Committee issued a statement expressing concern over the incident in the absence of the Vice-Chancellor. Two days later the DIG informed the University that they had arrested Purkayastha under MISA after initially denying the event. Shri Purkayastha is

MISA Detentions During the Emergency

now lodged in Tihar Jail. It is evident that the police mistakenly took him away and then to cover up had to hold him under MISA. This is clear from the fact that Shri Purkayastha is a new student of the University having joined in July and had not been participating in any of the student activities on the campus."

It is seen from the MHA's file that the Delhi Admn. was asked to send a report and after the receipt of the reply which only reiterated that Shri Pravir Purkayastha was detained under MISA on account of his extremist connections and that it was not a case of mistaken identity, the IB was asked to look into the matter and send the report. The report of Shri S. Subramanian, Jt. Dy. Director quoted below is very significant in this connection:

"According to information available with us, Prabir Purkayastha, student of JNU is not an active worker of the Students's Federation of India. He had not come to notice for taking an active part in organising students' strike in JNU on Sept. 24, 1975.

Sd/- S. Subramanian

Jt. Dy. Director

11.12.75"

Shri S. C. Vaish, Director (IS) MHA wrote to Smt. S. Chandra, Special Secy. (Home) Delhi Admn. on 14.4.76 saying that:-

"according to our information Shri Purkayastha is not an active worker of the Students's Federation of India and that he did not take an active part in organising students' strike in JNU on 24.9.75. In view of this, the Delhi Admn. may like to re-examine this case for revocation of the orders of detention."

The Delhi Admn. wrote back to MHA on 6.5.76 that:

"the case was last reviewed by the Administrator under sub-section 4 of section 16-A of the MISA, 1971 on 20.1.76 and as a result the continued detention of Shri Purkayastha was considered necessary. The case is likely to be again reviewed sometime in May, 1976. Pending this review no action is proposed to be taken by this Admn. for the revocation of the detention orders in respect of the said individual."

However, continued detention of Shri Pravir Purkayastha was again confirmed in the next four-monthly review held on 18.5.76. When the Delhi Admn. was again reminded on 14.6.76 to send their report regarding the consideration of the case by the Screening Committee as promised in their letter of 6.5.76. Shri T. R. Kalia, Dy. Secy. (Home) replied that, the case could not be considered by the Screening Committee till then and moreover, the continued detention was considered necessary at the time of the four-monthly review held on 18.5.76. Shri R. L. Mishra, Joint Secretary, MHA wrote a d.o. letter to Smt. S. Chandra on 9.7.76 saying that:

"The case of Shri Pravir Purkayastha has been considered in detail in the Ministry and it is felt that even if the information available to the Delhi Admn. is presumed to be correct, the role of Shri Pravir Purkayastha in organising the strike was very peripheral and for that he has already been punished by detention for nearly 9 months. It does not seem necessary to continue this detention any longer for effectively dealing with the emergency. I am, therefore, desired to request that the order of detention in respect of Shri Pravir Purkayastha may be revoked under intimation to this Ministry.

This bears the approval of the Home Minister."

After the receipt of this clear direction from the MHA bearing the approval of the Home Minister, the papers were put up on 10.7.76 to the LG proposing the release of Shri Purkayastha. The LG recorded the following note and sent the file to the MMHA:

"Shri R. L. Mishra, Joint Secretary, Ministry of Home Affairs, has asked the Special Secy. (Home) Delhi Administration, vide his letter dated the 9th July, 1976 (P.131/C), that the order of detention in respect of Shri Pravir Purkayastha may be revoked. Shri Pravir Purkayastha was detained for his pre-judicial activities which were designed to disrupt the functioning of the Jawaharlal Nehru University.

2. The JNU is going to open shortly and I respectfully submit

that the release of Shri Pravir Purkayastha at this stage is likely to effect adversely the normal functioning of the JNU and will otherwise also be a menace to the public order as his release is likely to lead to agitational activity amongst the students in the JNU.

3. I would, therefore, respectfully submit that the Ministry may kindly reconsider its decision. I am not in favour of his release at this stage.

Sd/- Krishan Chand
13.7.76."

It is seen from the file that Shri Om Mehta had called the LG for discussion. The matter was discussed and Shri Om Mehta agreed to the suggestion of Shri Krishan Chand not to release Shri Purkayastha immediately but to review the case in due course. The detention order was revoked on 25.9.76.

PRABIR PURKAYASTHA is an engineer and a science activist in the power, telecom and software sectors. He is a founding member of the Delhi Science Forum. He is the author of *Knowledge as Commons: Towards Inclusive Science and Technology* (LeftWord 2023) and co-author, along with Vijay Prashad, of *Enron Blowout: Corporate Capitalism and Theft of the Global Commons* (LeftWord 2002), and along with Ninan Koshy, M.K. Bhadrakumar, of *Uncle Sam's Nuclear Cabin* (LeftWord 2007). He is co-editor with Indranil and Richa Chintan of *Political Journeys in Health: Essays by and for Amit Sengupta* (LeftWord 2021). He is the founder of Newsclick.in.

Prabir Purkayastha being taken into custody under the Unlawful Activities (Prevention) Act (UAPA) by Delhi Police on October 3, 2023 in New Delhi.

www.ingramcontent.com/pod-product-compliance
Lightning Source LLC
Chambersburg PA
CBHW031148020426
42333CB00013B/558